T0340209

European Port Cities and Urban Regeneration

Culture- and event-led regeneration have been catalysts for the transformation of redundant urban port areas and for the reframing of the image of many port cities, which notably feature among mega-event bidding and host cities. However, there is little understanding of the impacts of these processes on port-city relationships, as well as of how port city cultures shape mega events and the related regeneration strategies. The book examines the underexplored mutual links between, on the one hand, urban and socio-economic regeneration driven by cultural and sporting mega events and, on the other hand, the spatial, political and symbolic ties between cities and their ports.

By adopting a cross-national, comparative perspective, with in-depth case studies (Hull, Rotterdam, Genoa and Valencia) and examples from other port cities across the world where mega events were held, the book engages with issues such as the tension between port and cultural uses, reactions and opposition to mega events in port cities, clashing urban imaginaries drawing on port activity and culture, the role of port authorities and companies in the city's cultural life, the spectacularisation and commodification of local maritime culture and heritage, processes of cultural demaritimisation and remaritimisation of port cities.

The book is therefore a contribution towards the bridging of port city and mega-event studies, and it provides insights for port city policy makers and mega-event promoters, drawing from a range of international experiences. The book also shows how societal and political change in the current 'ontologically insecure' times may undermine the very paradigm of culture- and event-led regeneration in the years to come.

Enrico Tommarchi is Lecturer in Town Planning at London South Bank University. He took part in the JPICH-funded project HOMEE (Heritage Opportunities/threats within Mega-Events in Europe) and in the evaluation of Hull UK City of Culture 2017, undertaken by the Culture, Place and Policy Institute (CPPI) of the University of Hull, where he completed his PhD. His research focuses on culture- and event-led regeneration and port-city relationships. He is a spatial planner by training (IUAV University of Venice) and he is interested in the geographies of port and coastal cities, the socio-spatial and symbolic outcomes of mega events, culture-led urban regeneration.

Routledge Advances in Regional Economics, Science and Policy

For more information about this series, please visit: www.routledge.com/series/RAIRESP

European Port Cities and Urban Regeneration

Exploring Cultural and Sporting Mega Events at the Water's Edge

Enrico Tommarchi

Routledge
Taylor & Francis Group

LONDON AND NEW YORK

First published 2023
by Routledge
4 Park Square, Milton Park, Abingdon, Oxon OX14 4RN

and by Routledge
605 Third Avenue, New York, NY 10158

Routledge is an imprint of the Taylor & Francis Group, an informa business

© 2023 Enrico Tommarchi

British Library Cataloguing-in-Publication Data
A catalogue record for this book is available from the British Library

Library of Congress Cataloging-in-Publication Data
Names: Tommarchi, Enrico, author.
Title: European port cities and urban regeneration: exploring cultural and
    sporting mega events at the water's edge/Enrico Tommarchi.
Description: Milton Park, Abingdon, Oxon ; New York, NY : Routledge,
    2023. | Series: Routledge advances in regional economics, science and
    policy | Includes bibliographical references and index.
Identifiers: LCCN 2022005001 (print) | LCCN 2022005002 (ebook) |
    ISBN 9780367761769 (hardback) | ISBN 9780367761752 (paperback) |
    ISBN 9781003165811 (ebook)
Subjects: LCSH: Urban renewal—Europe. | Port cities—Europe. |
    Hosting of sporting event—Europe.
Classification: LCC HT178.E8 T66 2023 (print) | LCC HT178.E8 (ebook) |
    DDC 307.3/416094—dc23/eng/20220202
LC record available at https://lccn.loc.gov/2022005001
LC ebook record available at https://lccn.loc.gov/2022005002

ISBN: 978-0-367-76176-9 (hbk)
ISBN: 978-0-367-76175-2 (pbk)
ISBN: 978-1-003-16581-1 (ebk)

DOI: 10.4324/9781003165811

Typeset in Bembo
by Apex CoVantage, LLC

For Cristina and Luca

Contents

Figures

Tables

Acknowledgements

This book is the outcome of a doctoral research project that would not have been possible without the financial support of the University of Hull. My indebtedness and heartfelt gratitude go to Professor Franco Bianchini and Professor Andrew Jonas, who guided me through the research process with their knowledge and advice, and to Professor Vassos Argyrou and Dr Martin Wilcox for their support during my doctoral studies.

I am grateful to the academic community that surrounds the Culture, Place and Policy Institute of the University of Hull, where I enjoyed an exciting research environment and could benefit from the expertise and passion of many bright researchers and PhD students. I thank Dr Barbara Grabher, Jill Howitt and Dr Michael Howcroft for their insightful comments on the first draft of the book.

I sincerely thank the many policy makers, civil servants, city planners, experts and academics across Europe who took the time to participate in my research. Thank you for your invaluable contribution to the study behind the book.

Finally, I thank the Routledge team, particularly Christiana Mandizha, Kristina Abbotts, Natalie Tomlinson and Terry Clague, for their support throughout the publication process.

Abbreviations

ABP	Associated British Ports
APV	Autoridad Portuaria de Valencia (Valencia Port Authority/Valenciaport)
BP	British Petroleum
CoC	City/Capital of Culture
ECoC	European City/Capital of Culture
F1	Formula One/Formula 1
M4H	Merwe-Vierhaven
PAI	Programa de Actuación Integrada (Integrated Action Programme – planning tool)
PP	Partido Popular (People's Party)
RDM	Rotterdamsche Droogdok Maatschappij (Rotterdam Drydock Corporation)
UKCoC	UK City of Culture
ZAL	Zona de Actividades Logisticas (logistics area, port of Valencia)

1 Introduction

Exploring port cities of culture and events

The 1992 Olympic Games in Barcelona are widely considered to have been a game changer for the city (e.g. Jauhiainen, 1995; Marshall, 2004). The event was an integral part of an ambitious programme of urban regeneration and contributed to repositioning Barcelona as a global tourist destination. The 'Manchester of the Mediterranean', or the 'Catalan Manchester', with its industrial waterfront stretching between the rivers Besòs and Llobregat, is now a distant memory. The Olympic Games provided the political rationale, and the resources, to reconvert the historic inner harbour Port Vell and to develop Port Olímpic, a marina surrounded by the artificial sandy beaches and waterfront promenades that are now much appreciated by residents and tourists. Nevertheless, even if local imaginaries of the industrial port city have been replaced by those of a cosmopolitan, global metropolis by the sea, Barcelona is still one of the most important ports on the Mediterranean, albeit the ties among the city, its port and the sea have changed in the last decades. As in many other port cities across Europe, Barcelona's commercial port moved to the outskirts of the city, while the local population gradually lost track of maritime practices, which became difficult to observe and appreciate.

Twenty-five years later, fireworks and spectacular light show displays opened the UK City of Culture in Kingston-upon-Hull, in Northern England, celebrating the city's past as Britain's third most important port in the early 20th century (see e.g. East, 1931). This parallel between a medium-sized port city hosting a national cultural festival and an Olympic host city such as Barcelona might sound excessively audacious. However, in both localities, policy makers made use of large-scale events in the attempt to generate momentum around economic and urban regeneration. The transformative force of these events acted on the ties between the port and the city. In relative, context-specific terms, one could argue that very different events in rather different contexts were being perceived as unique opportunities for achieving long-lasting change. For instance, Hull, as the city is broadly referred to, had long been stigmatised due to socio-economic decline resulting from the reduction of maritime activities, particularly fishing (Tommarchi & Bianchini, 2022). As it will be discussed in the next chapters, Hull UK City of Culture 2017 was then framed by local policy makers as a 'once in a lifetime opportunity' to

DOI: 10.4324/9781003165811-1

achieve economic regeneration in the city, which would be coupled with the development of its port as a renewable energy hub in the country.

The much-heralded case of Barcelona and the more recent experience of Hull set well the background to present the book and show how the idea of using large-scale cultural, sporting or commercial events (e.g. the Olympics, FIFA World Cup, expos and national and international cultural festivals such as the European Capital of Culture, see Chapter 2) to achieve regeneration has spread across cities of any scale. The book embarks on a journey across maritime port cities where these events have been celebrated as milestones within long-term processes of urban regeneration. The key aim of the book is to explore the mutual influence between port-city relationships and event-led regeneration in maritime port cities, which is arguably overlooked in both port city studies and the literature on culture and regeneration. The key argument is that, on the one hand, regeneration processes driven by large-scale events do impact – directly or contingently – on the spatial, political and symbolic ties between ports and cities, while on the other hand, the maritime nature of port cities contributes to shaping these transformation processes. The book presents detailed accounts of event-led regeneration in four European port cities that whilst sharing common experiences in this regard, nevertheless differ in population size, economy and national political settings: Hull (UK), Rotterdam (the Netherlands), Genoa (Italy) and Valencia (Spain). These accounts are enriched with examples from other port cities across the world where large-scale and mega events have been held, such as Cape Town, Rio de Janeiro and Shanghai. In this introduction, firstly, the rationale for and the purpose of the book are presented. Secondly, preliminary definitions of some of the key concepts used are provided. These concepts are discussed more in detail in Chapter 2. Thirdly, the key themes of the book that guide the discussion in Chapters 4–7 are listed. Finally, the structure of the book is outlined.

Why exploring port cities of culture and events

This monograph[1] examines how event-led regeneration (understood as a form of culture-led regeneration driven by large-scale cultural, sporting or commercial events, see Chapter 2) contributes to shaping contemporary port-city relationships – intended as the set of spatial, socio-economic, cultural-symbolic and political relationships between the port and the city – and to what extent local maritime cultures and port-city relationships influence these processes of regeneration. Mega events – as these events are broadly referred to in the book – are interpreted as pivotal moments along longer-term trajectories of urban regeneration driven by cultural activity (as in Evans, 2011). Therefore, albeit with a focus on these events, this volume examines mutual connections between event-led regeneration and port-city relationships on a longer timeframe.

The rationale for this work, with its specific focus on port cities, is threefold. Firstly, mega events often take place at the water's edge. Januchta-Szostak and Biedermann (2014, p. 72) calculated that, from the second half of the 19th to the beginning of the 21st century, areas in proximity to water have hosted

66.7% of world and international exhibitions, 100% of gardening exhibitions, 88.9% of Summer Olympics, 72.7% of Winter Olympics and 70.5% of European City/Capital of Culture schemes. Despite this clear pattern, event studies seldom engage with the mutual influence between event-led regeneration and the relationships between cities and water, let alone with aspects of maritime history and heritage in the case of port cities. Secondly, the rhetoric of culture-led regeneration praises the reconversion of former areas of production – in this case, former port areas in proximity to city centres – into areas of consumption. This has been achieved especially between the 1980s and early 2010s in many deindustrialising European port cities such as Antwerp, Barcelona, Genoa, Glasgow, Hamburg, Marseille, Newcastle and Rotterdam, where culture- or event-led regeneration (including regeneration processes related to unsuccessful event bids) has also operated as a symbolic process shaping the image of these cities (see e.g. Bailey et al., 2004; García, 2004; Richards & Wilson, 2004; Andres, 2011; Gastaldi, 2012). Nevertheless, academic and policy research has devoted little attention to how these processes shape and are shaped by local maritime cultures and the relationships between cities and ports. Thirdly, notwithstanding an increasing number of cities – and port cities in particular – pursuing event-led regeneration for economic and, more recently, social goals, evaluation studies and academic research appear to focus mostly on the short-term economic impacts of these processes. These studies tend to overlook the broader and longer-term socio-cultural and political outcomes of these processes and fail to unravel their backward, forward and parallel linkages with other policy areas or processes (as noted in the 1990s by Hiller, 1998). All this suggests the need for further research addressing the broader spatial, socio-economic, political and cultural impacts of event-led regeneration in port cities. In addition, the study of event-led regeneration offers new ways of looking at port-city relationships, which itself is an emerging research topic in urban studies, such as the blend of maritime and urban functions on the waterfront, the emergence of innovative forms of urban living at the water's edge, the symbolic aspects of these relationships and the role of maritime culture in the everyday lives of port city dwellers.

In this monograph, both event-led regeneration and port-city relationships are interpreted as dynamic processes, in continuous evolution, which contribute to physically shaping the urban fabric and symbolically framing the imaginaries of port cities. Therefore, the overarching question behind the book is: how do event-led regeneration and port-city relationships influence and interact with each other, particularly in terms of the socio-spatial, political and symbolic aspects of these relationships? The originality of the book lies both in its call to consider event-led regeneration as a factor in the evolution of port-city relationships and in its exploration of these processes in relation to the maritime character of cities. On the one hand, port-city relationships are explored through the lens of mega events, providing an innovative perspective on their geographical and symbolic dimensions. On the other hand, event-led regeneration is approached considering the specific issues arising from the spatial, socio-economic, political and cultural relationships between cities and ports.

The book differs from the available studies on urban regeneration and waterfront redevelopment for its focus is on the port-city interface as a geographical space, its connection with the evolution of port-city relationships and the links with broader societal and symbolic aspects. For these reasons and for its interpretation of large-scale cultural, sporting and commercial events as special moments along longer-term trajectories of urban development and regeneration, the book differs from most studies on mega events as well. By bringing together insights from urban studies, urban planning, human geography, marine and maritime sociology and anthropology, cultural policy and planning, the book situates itself within the emerging field of port city studies and offers a critical framework for interpreting event-led regeneration in the context of port-city relationships and to deliver policy recommendations that can help policy makers and event promoters in port cities.

Port cities, culture and regeneration: key concepts

The discussion in the following chapters makes use of a number of concepts, which are explored more in detail in Chapter 2, such as port-city relationships, waterfront redevelopment, port-city interface, culture- and event-led regeneration and mega events. The *port* remains a real, yet unidentified object, generally understood as a transportation node where land and water meet (Ducruet, 2007). In this volume, a definition of 'port' is not outlined. Rather, this work encourages to think more broadly about commercial and industrial ports. The port is in this case conceptualised by stretching its meaning from the assemblage of working industrial and commercial areas where maritime activities take place to a broader socio-spatial entity encompassing aspects of material culture related to ports and local maritime cultures. This helps detect similar assets across port cities – for example inner harbours, redeveloped docks and quays – that constitute 'port cityscapes' (as defined by Hein, 2011) and outline a porous, 'ecotonal' transition from the port to the city as socio-spatial entities.

Port-city relationships are commonly understood in the literature as the spatial and functional ties between ports (intended as transport and industrial infrastructures) and cities (Hoyle & Pinder, 1992; Wiegmans & Louw, 2011; Daamen & Louw, 2016). Some of the port geography literature has also connected port-city spatial and functional ties with socio-cultural, symbolic links between ports and their cities. These contributions highlight for example the impact of the restructuring of ports and maritime practices on the lives of port city dwellers and on the imaginary, or the 'myth', of the port city (Van Hooydonk, 2007; Kokot, 2008; Bianchini & Bloomfield, 2012; Mah, 2014; Kowalewski, 2018).

This volume elaborates in particular on the model of port-city relationships outlined by Hoyle (1988, 1989, 2000). The model (see Chapter 2) portrays how, in the second half of the 20th century, deindustrialisation and port restructuring have exacerbated the separation, in spatial and functional terms, between ports and cities. This process produced derelict former port areas in virtually every port city across Europe and North America and provided the rationale for widespread redevelopment schemes. As a result, by the end of the 1980s, waterfront redevelopment became a global phenomenon (Breen & Rigby, 1996; Brownhill, 2013), despite its many controversial aspects (e.g. Jauhiainen, 1995; Ward, 2011). The *port-city interface* (Hayuth, 1982) is conceptualised as the geographical liminal space between ports and cities, where port migration and waterfront redevelopment have produced the most visible outcomes and where current port-city conflicts unfold.

Many redevelopment schemes on waterfronts and in urban port areas have made use of cultural activity as the catalyst for regeneration. In the book, *culture-led regeneration* is understood, along with Evans and Shaw (2004, p. 5), as an approach to urban regeneration where 'cultural activity is seen as the catalyst and engine of regeneration' and where '[t]he activity is likely to have a high-public profile and frequently to be cited as the sign of regeneration'. The discourse of urban regeneration, intended as a process to improve an area's 'economic, physical, social and environmental condition' (Roberts, 2017 [1999], p. 18), gained momentum in the 1980s, in particular under neoliberal conservative governments of the time, such as in the UK. In this period, cultural activity began to be part of urban regeneration schemes, as the focus of urban cultural policies shifted from social to economic and urban development goals (Bianchini, 1993, p. 2). Culture-led regeneration began to be understood as a means to counteract socio-economic decline and rising unemployment (Bianchini, 1993, p. 2; Miles, 2005, p. 893), in particular in industrial cities. Nevertheless, many of these schemes have been criticised for their controversial nature as urban spectacles (Gotham, 2005), shaped by middle-class values (Zukin, 2006 [1995]; Evans, 2005, p. 8), and for their connection with forms of state-driven gentrification and revanchist urbanism (MacLeod, 2002; Atkinson, 2003; Kallin & Slater, 2014; Paton, 2018).

Event-led regeneration is consequently understood as an approach to urban regeneration where flagship events are the catalyst for transformation. These events are interpreted in this monograph as 'large scale cultural (including commercial and sporting) events which have a dramatic character, mass popular appeal and international significance' (Roche, 2000, p. 1). As discussed in Chapter 2, in contrast with some of the literature, the book adheres to Roche's definition and considers large-scale cultural and sporting events as *mega events*. It also advocates an understanding of the 'mega' character of events in relative terms, rather than based solely on quantitative budgetary and visitor thresholds. The size of these events should be pondered by taking into account their magnitude against the demographic, geographical and socio-economic context of host cities. Along with recent scholarship (Di Vita & Wilson, 2020; Jones, 2020) and on the basis of the research behind the book, it is acknowledged that the largest of these schemes, such as the Olympic Games or the FIFA World Cup, are being disregarded by policy makers in many cities, while smaller-scale – albeit arguably large – events such as City/Capital of Culture (CoC) schemes are becoming increasingly popular among local policy makers in towns and cities across Europe.

The book engages in particular with four case studies: Hull, Rotterdam, Genoa and Valencia. These cases were selected through a scoping review of event-led regeneration across port cities on the Mediterranean, the North Sea, the Baltic Sea and the Atlantic Ocean. Shortlisting took into account factors such as demographics, role and characteristics of ports, socio-economic baseline issues (e.g. economic decline due to port restructuring), type of events held and approach to event programming, timeframe, with the aim of allowing diversity while seeking commensurability among instances. The role of cities in the European urban network (centrality) and the position of their ports within transnational maritime networks (intermediacy) were also considered, using Ducruet and Lee's (2006) matrix of port-city relations. The four case-study cities of the book appear in a more recent version of the aforementioned model (Ducruet, 2011; see Figure 1.1), where Hull is identified as urban port (low

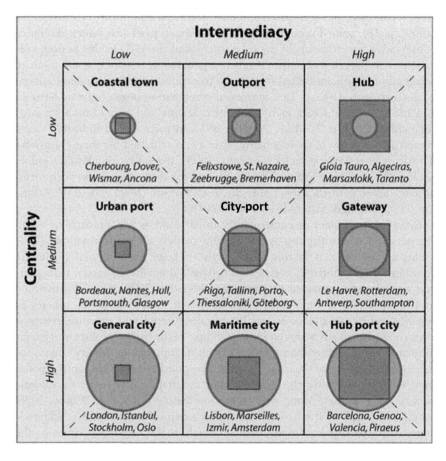

Figure 1.1 Matrix of port-city relationships.

Source: Ducruet (2011), published for the first time in Ducruet, C. (2011) The port city in multidisciplinary analysis, in Alemany, J., and Bruttomesso, R. (eds) *The port city in the XXIst century: New challenges in the relationship between port and city.* Venice: RETE, pp. 32–48.

Table 1.1 Case studies: key features.

City	Port	Port specialisation	Baseline	Mega event(s)
Hull 260,000 small city	Important port in the UK/North Sea	Ferry, food, renewables, timber	Deindustrialisation, socio-economic decline, negative image (2010s)	UK City of Culture 2017
Genoa 500,000 6th largest city in the country	Leading Mediterranean port	Container handling, cruise, ferry, food, petrochemicals, shipbuilding	Deindustrialisation, socio-economic decline (1980s)	• FIFA World Cup 1990 • Columbus Expo 1992 • G8 summit 2001 • European Capital of Culture 2004
Rotterdam 600,000 2nd largest city in the country	Europe's largest port – North Sea	Chemicals, container handling, cruise, ferry.	Young low-skilled population, negative image (1990s)	• Euro 2000 Football Cup • European Capital of Culture 2001 • event policy 2001-2015
Valencia 800,000 3rd largest city in the country	Leading Mediterranean port	Cruise, containers, ferry	Port-city separation (1990s)	• America's Cup 2007/2010 • F1 European Grand Prix 2008-2012

intermediacy and medium centrality), Rotterdam as gateway (high intermediacy and medium centrality) and Genoa and Valencia as hub port cities (high intermediacy and high centrality).

As shown by Ducruet and Lee's matrix, the selected case studies provide a broader perspective on port-city relationships by encompassing different profiles, yet they never sit at the extremes of the matrix, as would for example the pairs Gioia Tauro-London or Dover-Barcelona. Despite their context specificity, the selected cases do display similar characteristics and baseline issues, while at the same time provide diverse perspectives about the analysed processes (Table 1.1). They help explore the impact of mega events on port-city relationships on different timeframes and periods in relation to structural phenomena such as the 2008 financial and economic crisis.

The case-study analysis made use of primary and secondary data, and involved semi-structured interviews with policy makers (e.g. top officials from city councils and port authorities), city planners, event promoters, academics and other experts. It also involved a small number of street surveys with residents and visitors in redeveloped port areas and waterfronts, with the aim of gathering their views to identify aspects that were further discussed with the aforementioned informants, along with non-participant observations. Fieldwork in the four case-study cities was undertaken in 2018. A review of policy documents examined event bids and programmes (where available), relevant planning documents and local cultural strategies. The scale of analysis was limited to the transition space between urban port areas and the city centre or maritime urban districts. The focus is on central city locations. In order to demarcate the port-city interface, ports are considered – from a spatial perspective – as areas where maritime-related activities are prevalent. These spaces are also characterised by a certain restriction to access. The port-city interface is then understood as a set of 'waterfront zones in which the geography of the port and its city meet each other' (Daamen & Vries, 2013, p. 4), for example former docks, harbours, berths, port ring roads, but also urban areas that are or were shaped and influenced by maritime practices, but where urban uses are dominant.

Port cities, culture and regeneration: emerging themes

The study of the mutual influence between culture- and event-led regeneration processes and the socio-spatial, political and cultural-symbolic ties between ports and cities displays recurrent emerging themes across the case studies analysed. These themes, which are briefly presented later and discussed in detail in Chapters 4–7, include the acceptance or contestation of mega events and event-led regeneration, the spatiality of event-led regeneration within port-city relationships, the politics of these processes of transformation and their mutual connections with the cultural, symbolic and psychological ties among cities, ports and the sea.

Acceptance vs. contestation of mega events and event-led regeneration

Mega events have generated negative reactions and protests in many cities due to the considerable public spending associated with them, their debatable impacts in terms of economic development and employment, and their role in fostering gentrification, deprivation and the displacement of local populations (e.g. Cornelissen, 2012; Giulianotti et al., 2015). In port cities, these processes take place in specific socio-economic and spatial contexts, which may be characterised by a distinctive urban fabric, rich maritime heritage and cultures, multicultural populations and variegated social milieus. This 'exceptionalism' of port cities – in demographic, social and cultural terms (Lee, 1998; Belchem, 2000, 2006; Bianchini & Bloomfield, 2012; Hein et al., 2021) – and the myth of their independent and rebellious character (Van Hooydonk, 2007; Mah, 2014) raise questions as to how event-led regeneration is perceived. Event-led urban conflicts, or the acceptance of these events across local populations, must be examined in the light of the economic, yet also political and social, crisis that has been unfolding worldwide after the 2007–8 financial shock.

The geography of port-city relationships and event-led regeneration

Culture- and event-led urban regeneration add a further dimension to the study of spatial port-city relationships. Cultural activity is one among the many urban functions that populate the port-city interface. Waterfronts and the port-city interface may be understood as deterritorialised spaces, shaped by the interaction of processes operating at different scales (Desfor & Laidley, 2011). On the one hand, ports are shaped by broader, structural processes that extend well beyond the local scale, and therefore strategic decisions may be taken by global actors elsewhere in the world. Even where ports are managed by public actors, decisions may be taken by central governments, based hundreds of kilometres away. On the other hand, local values, meanings, stakes and forces interact with broader processes in the shaping of waterfront areas.

Land ownership regimes at the port-city interface

By definition, the port-city interface is a liminal space between these two entities. This means that the land in these parts of the city may be owned by different subjects, also depending on the nature of port authorities, which in turn may differ from a country to another. Many of the allegedly successful experiences of event-led regeneration involved the transformation of large areas of the city that were already owned by local councils. However, port areas may display rather different ownership regimes. This may result in the need for more complex negotiations between the city and the port to host mega events and achieve regeneration, which may ultimately impact on the accessibility of regenerated waterfronts and port areas, as physical and immaterial borders are retained.

The cultural role of port authorities

As part of their policies to gain public support (Van Hooydonk, 2007) and guarantee their 'licence to operate', port authorities display a growing role in local cultural policies. Typically, they fund or directly deliver cultural activity and events with the aim of communicating their own role and the economic role of ports. In most cases, mega events in port cities directly involve port authorities, who operate in partnership with other local institutions and event promoters. This 'cultural' role of port authorities is explored as a component of political port-city relationships, as well as a factor contributing to shaping the city's cultural offer and imaginaries.

The imaginaries of the 'port city' and the 'city of culture'

Port competitiveness is the motor of economic prosperity and wealth in port cities. Understandably, local political discourses and planning concepts may praise the imaginary of the 'port city', as a maritime adaptation of the capitalist ideal of the industrious city that never sleeps. The last decades have nonetheless heralded the emergence of the urban imaginary of the 'city of culture' – or of the 'host city' in the case of large-scale sporting or commercial events – as a sign of renaissance and strategic repositioning in times of economic restructuring. Although the presence of an attractive city *per se* is increasingly acknowledged as a prerequisite for the competitiveness of ports, these two imaginaries may be overlapping or conflicting, particularly as a result of tense political relationships between port and city actors.

Authenticity, commodification and port city cultures

As any other process of urban transformation, event-led regeneration influences – and in turn is influenced by – the context in which it takes place and the array of local values and meanings. In the case of port cities, there is a mutual influence between processes of event-led regeneration and local maritime cultures, values and meanings, as well as the existing socio-cultural and symbolic ties between ports and cities. Considering the homogenising (Evans, 2003) and commodifying (Hall, 2006) tendency of these schemes and their replication across cities (Richards & Wilson, 2006, p. 1932), these initiatives generally raise concerns in relation to authenticity. In port cities, this homogenising tendency may contribute – as either an unintended outcome or a deliberate goal of urban policy – to the erosion of maritime cultures or their reframing around different conditions.

How to approach the book

The book is organised in eight chapters, including this introduction. Chapter 2 looks more in detail into port-city relationships, culture-led urban regeneration and mega events, examining the key literature and the current academic debate on these topics. Culture-led urban regeneration is linked with models of the evolution of port-city relationships in relation to structural phenomena of port migration and waterfront redevelopment.

Chapter 3 introduces the four case studies and makes use of the experience of these cities to reflect on the rationale for bidding to host mega events as catalyst for urban transformation and to diversify the local economy. Case studies are not presented and discussed individually. Rather, this volume adopts a comparative perspective and provides examples from the case studies, as well as from other cities, in relation to the key themes identified.

In Chapter 4, the role and nature of mega events in the post-crisis world is examined, together with the reactions to event-led regeneration. The chapter builds on the idea that we are living in times of great economic, political and social uncertainty and turmoil, in which the public's ontological security is undermined. The current socio-economic and political context, which differs strikingly from that of economic restructuring and growth in which the rhetoric of mega events and urban regeneration emerged, is shaping mega events and their legacy and is exacerbating opposition and contestation. Even where mega events do not generate immediate substantial opposition, the longer-term trajectory and the legacy of event-led regeneration processes may play a role in structural processes of gentrification and touristification – for example contributing to the growth of cruise tourism – which may be strongly opposed by residents, in particular in times of economic recession, rising unemployment and reckless dismantling of the welfare state and of basic societal and democratic values.

The spatiality of port-city relationships and event-led regeneration is examined in Chapter 5, by connecting urban regeneration on the waterfront with port development trajectories. The chapter problematises the assumption that event-led regeneration processes are enabled by the public ownership of port areas (e.g. as in the case of many continental European countries in comparison with the UK, where port areas are generally privately owned). It also shows that, although the transitory character of mega events means that they do not necessarily entail prolonged disruption of port activity, event-led regeneration may encourage a permanent presence and development of cultural activities in former port areas, which may generate port-city conflicts in the light of a renewed interest in these areas from port authorities and companies.

Chapter 6 explores the politics of event-led regeneration in port cities, looking at aspects such as the role of port authorities in cultural activity or the emerging imaginaries of 'port' and 'cultural' cities. Despite the fact that port authorities and companies may feel they have to engage with mega events, they also engage with culture more broadly, either as a means to gain public support for their activity or as a sign of retightening relationships with urban actors. Narratives of 'port' and 'cultural' cities may generate clashing urban imaginaries, despite the greater economic relevance of port activities over cultural consumption. In some cases, these competing imaginaries may lead to port–city conflicts or to the willingness of policy makers to reframe, overlook or get rid of elements of the city's maritime identity.

The socio-cultural and symbolic aspects of port–city relationships and event-led regeneration are explored in Chapter 7. These include, for example, processes of commodification or erosion of maritime cultures and the relationships between the framing of port city cultures within event-led regeneration and actually existing port-city links. The chapter makes use of the concepts of cultural demaritimisation and remaritimisation of port cities (Tommarchi, 2021) to show how event-led regeneration can operate to the detriment of local maritime identities or can be deployed to restore or create – whether or not authentic – port city cultures. The link between proximity to water and city branding is explored, to unpack the rhetoric behind the branding or port cities and examine whether port city culture is mobilised or overlooked in favour of an image based merely on water as a saleable element of urban design. The emergence of maritime cultural quarters, which differ from past experiences of waterfront redevelopment due to a stronger connection with local maritime heritage, is explored as an aspect of the legacy of mega events or of more mature cultural urban policies. The chapter also looks at mega events and their legacy considering the *actually existing* symbolic ties between ports and cities and the values and meanings attributed locally to the port and to port city culture. It shows how mega events and event-led regeneration may have unpredictable outcomes or may be in part ineffective or damaging depending on how they relate to these existing ties.

Finally, Chapter 8 outlines a heuristic model to approach trajectories of culture- and event-led regeneration in maritime port cities. It reflects upon the wider implications of the book, in relation to the study of port–city relationships, the changing meaning of waterfronts and waterfront redevelopment, the politics of local economic development and regeneration and place making. It provides recommendations for urban policy and planning in relation to mega events, concerning structural socio-economic challenges, the role of maritime identity and activity, the value of existing port-city symbolic and psychological links, the blending of urban and maritime functions and the legacy of mega events at the port-city interface. Finally, the chapter raises some wider issues for further research, such as global trends in mega events in times of global capitalism and austerity, the spatial focus of culture-led regeneration and port city studies, the future of waterfronts, socio-spatial inequalities in port cities of culture and events, sustainability (in its different dimension) and the potential impacts of the transition to a post-oil society.

Note

1 The book is the result of a doctoral research project on event-led regeneration and port-city relationships in Europe, undertaken by the author in 2016–2020 and funded by the University of Hull through a scholarship on 'Culture-led regeneration'. The author also benefitted from his involvement in the evaluation of Hull UK City of Culture 2017, conducted by the Culture, Place and Policy Institute (CPPI) of the University of Hull and in the JPICH-funded project Heritage Opportunities/threats within Mega-Events in Europe (HOMEE), which was undertaken in 2018–2021 by an international team involving researchers from the Polytechnic of Milan (Italy), the University of Hull, the Neapolis University Pafos (Cyprus) and the International Cultural Centre (Poland).

Bibliography

Andres, L. (2011) Marseille 2013 or the final round of a long and complex regeneration strategy? *Town Planning Review*, 82(1), 61–76.

Atkinson, R. (2003) Domestication by cappuccino or a revenge on urban space? Control and empowerment in the management of public spaces. *Urban Studies*, 40(9), 1829–1843.

Bailey, C., Miles, S., & Stark, P. (2004) Culture-led urban regeneration and the revitalisation of identities in Newcastle, Gateshead and the North East of England. *International Journal of Cultural Policy*, 10(1), 47–65.

Belchem, J. (2000) *Merseypride: Essays in Liverpool Exceptionalism*. Liverpool: Liverpool University Press.

Belchem, J. (ed.) (2006) *Liverpool 800: Culture, Character and History*. Liverpool: Liverpool University Press.

Bianchini, F. (1993) Culture, conflict and cities: Issues and prospects for the 1990s. In Bianchini, F., & Parkinson, M. (eds.) *Cultural Policy and Urban Regeneration: The West European Experience*. Manchester: Manchester Press, 199–213.

Bianchini, F., & Bloomfield, J. (2012) Porous cities: On four European cities. *Eurozine*, 3rd July. Available at: www.eurozine.com/porous-cities/ [Accessed 22/11/2018].

Breen, A., & Rigby, D. (1996) *The New Waterfront: A Worldwide Urban Success Story*. New York: McGraw-Hill.

Brownhill, S. (2013) Just add water: Waterfront regeneration as a global phenomenon. In Leary, M. E., & McCarthy, J. (eds.) *The Routledge Companion to Urban Regeneration*. London: Routledge, 45–55.

Cornelissen, S. (2012) 'Our struggles are bigger than the World Cup': Civic activism, state-society relations and the socio-political legacies of the 2010 FIFA World Cup. *The British Journal of Sociology*, 63(2), 328–348.

Daamen, T. A., & Louw, E. (2016) The challenge of the Dutch port-city interface. *Tijdschrift Voor Economische En Sociale Geografie*, 107(5), 642–651.

Daamen, T. A., & Vries, I. (2013) Governing the European port-city interface: Institutional impacts on spatial projects between city and port. *Journal of Transport Geography*, 27, 4–13.

Desfor, G., & Laidley, J. (2011) Introduction: Fixity and flow of urban waterfront change. In Desfor, G., Laidley, J., Stevens, Q., & Schubert, D. (eds.) *Transforming Urban Waterfronts: Fixity and Flow*. London and New York: Routledge, 1–13.

Di Vita, S., & Wilson, M. (eds.) (2020) *Planning and Managing Smaller Events: Downsizing the Urban Spectacle*. London and New York: Routledge.

Ducruet, D. (2007) A metageography of port-city relationships. In Wang, J., Olivier, D., Notteboom, T., & Slack, B. (eds.) *Ports, Cities, and Global Supply Chains*. Aldershot: Ashgate, 157–172.

Ducruet, C. (2011) The port city in multidisciplinary analysis. In Alemany, J., & Bruttomesso, R. (eds.) *The Port City in the XXIst Century: New Challenges in the Relationship between Port and City*. Venice: RETE, 32–48.

Ducruet, C., & Lee, S. W. (2006) Frontline soldiers of globalisation: Port-city evolution and regional competition. *GeoJournal*, 67(2), 107–122.

East, W. G. (1931) The Port of Kingston-upon-Hull during the industrial revolution. *Economica*, 32, 190–212.

Evans, G. (2003) Hard-branding the Cultural City: From Prado to Prada. *International Journal of Urban and Regional Research*, 27(2), 417–440.

Evans, G. (2005) Measure for measure: Evaluating the evidence of culture's contribution to regeneration. *Urban Studies*, 42(5–6), 959–983.

Evans, G. (2011) Cities of culture and the regeneration game. *London Journal of Tourism, Sport and Creative Industries*, 5(6), 5–18.

Evans, G., & Shaw, P. (2004) *The Contribution of Culture to Regeneration in the UK: A Review of Evidence*. London: LondonMet.

García, B. (2004) Cultural policy and urban regeneration in western European cities: Lessons from experience, prospects for the future. *Local Economy*, 19(4), 312–326.

Gastaldi, F. (2012) Grandi eventi e rigenerazione urbana negli anni della grande trasformazione di Genova: 1992–2004. *Territorio Della Ricerca Su Insediamenti e Ambiente*, 9, 23–35.

Giulianotti, R., Armstrong, G., Hales, G., & Hobbs, D. (2015) Sport mega-events and public opposition: A sociological study of the London 2012 Olympics. *Journal of Sport and Social Issues*, 39(2), 99–119.

Gotham, K. F. (2005) Theorizing urban spectacles. *City*, 9(2), 225–246.

Hall, M. C. (2006) Urban entrepreneurship, corporate interests and sports mega-events: The thin policies of competitiveness within the hard outcomes of neoliberalism. *The Sociological Review*, 54(s2), 59–70.

Hayuth, Y. (1982) The port-urban interface: An area in transition. *Area*, 14(3), 219–224.

Hein, C. (2011) Port cityscapes: A networked analysis of the built environment. In Hein, C. (ed.) *Port Cities: Dynamic Landscapes and Global Networks*. London and New York: Routledge, 1–23.

Hein, C., Luning, S., & van de Laar, P. (2021) Port city cultures, values, and maritime mindsets: Defining what makes port cities special. *European Journal of Creative Practices in Cities and Landscapes*, 4(1), 7–20.

Hiller, H. H. (1998) Assessing the impact of mega-events: A linkage model. *Current Issues in Tourism*, 1(1), 47–57.

Hoyle, B. S. (1988) Development dynamics at the port-city interface. In Hoyle, B. S., Pinder, D. A., & Husain, M. S. (eds.) *Revitalising the Waterfront: International Dimensions of Dockland Redevelopment*. London: Belhaven Press, 3–19.

Hoyle, B. S. (1989) The port-city interface: Trends, problems and examples. *Geoforum*, 20(4), 429–435.

Hoyle, B. S. (2000) Global and local change on the port-city waterfront. *The Geographical Review*, 90(3), 395–417.

Hoyle, B. S., & Pinder, D. A. (eds.) (1992) *European Port Cities in Transition*. London: Belhaven Press.

Januchta-Szostak, A. B., & Biedermann, A. M. (2014) The impact of great cultural projects on the transformation of urban water-side spaces. *Czasopismo Techniczne*, 1A(1), 69–87.

Jauhiainen, J. S. (1995) Waterfront redevelopment and urban policy: The case of Barcelona, Cardiff and Genoa. *European Planning Studies*, 3(1), 3–23.

Jones, Z. M. (2020) *Cultural Mega-Events: Opportunities and Risks for Heritage Cities*. London: Routledge.

Kallin, H., & Slater, T. (2014) Activating territorial stigma: Gentrifying marginality on Edinburgh's periphery. *Environment and Planning A*, 46, 1351–1368.

Kokot, W. (2008) Port cities as areas of transition: Comparative ethnographic research. In Kokot, W., Wildner, K., & Wonneberger, A. (eds.) *Port Cities as Areas of Transition: Ethnographic Perspectives*. Bielefeld: Transcript Verlag, 7–24.

Kowalewski, M. (2018) Images and spaces of port cities in transition. *Space and Culture*, 24(1), 53–65.

Lee, R. (1998) The socio-economic and demographic characteristics of port cities: A typology for comparative analysis? *Urban History*, 25(2), 147–172.

MacLeod, G. (2002) From urban entrepreneurialism to a 'revanchist city'? On the spatial injustices of Glasgow's Renaissance. *Antipode*, 34(3), 602–624.

Mah, A. (2014) *Port Cities and Global Legacies: Urban Identity, Waterfront Work, and Radicalism*. Basingstoke: Palgrave MacMillan.

Marshall, T. (ed.) (2004) *Transforming Barcelona*. London: Routledge.

Miles, M. (2005) Interruptions: Testing the rhetoric of culturally led urban development. *Urban Studies*, 42(5–6), 889–911.

Paton, K. (2018) Beyond legacy: Backstage stigmatisation and 'trickle-up' politics of urban regeneration. *The Sociological Review Monographs*, 66(4), 919–934.

Richards, G., & Wilson, J. (2004) The impact of cultural events on city image: Rotterdam, cultural capital of Europe 2001. *Urban Studies*, 41(10), 1931–1951.

Richards, G., & Wilson, J. (2006) Developing creativity in tourist experiences: A solution to the serial reproduction of culture? *Tourism Management*, 27, 1209–1223.

Roberts, P. (2017 [1999]) The evolution, definition and purpose of urban regeneration. In Roberts, P., Sykes, H., & Granger, R. (eds.) *Urban Regeneration*. 2nd edition. London: Sage, 9–43.

Roche, M. (2000) *Mega-Events and Modernity: Olympics and Expos in the Growth of Global Culture*. London: Routledge.

Tommarchi, E. (2021) (Re-)generating symbolic port-city links: Urban regeneration and the cultural demaritimisation and remaritimisation of European port cities. *European Journal of Creative Practices in Cities and Landscapes*, 4(1), 59–75.

Tommarchi, E., & Bianchini, F. (2022) A heritage-inspired cultural mega event in a stigmatised city: Hull UK City of Culture 2017. *European Planning Studies*, 30(3), 478–498.

Van Hooydonk, E. (2007) *Soft Values of Seaports: A Strategy for the Restoration of Public Support of Seaports*. Antwerp: Garant.

Ward, S. (2011) Port cities and the global exchange of planning ideas. In Hein, C. (ed.) *Port Cities: Dynamic Landscapes and Global Networks*. London and New York: Routledge, 70–85.

Wiegmans, B. W., & Louw, E. (2011) Changing port-city relations at Amsterdam: A new phase at the interface? *Journal of Transport Geography*, 19, 575–583.

Zukin, S. (2006 [1995]) *The Cultures of Cities*. Cambridge and Oxford: Blackwell.

2 Bridging port–city relationships, urban regeneration and mega events

Port restructuring and changing maritime trade patterns in the second half of the 20th century have caused socio-economic decline and urban decay across many maritime port cities, in particular in Europe. In some cases, local policy makers have deployed cultural urban policy and events as a means to trigger economic and urban regeneration, to the extent that port cities are well represented among those cities where culture-led urban regeneration schemes have been implemented. Yet, studies on port–city relationships, waterfront redevelopment, culture-led regeneration and mega events have seldom engaged with the mutual influence between culture-led redevelopment processes and the maritime exceptionalism of port cities.

The book contributes to filling this gap and to bridging these different areas of knowledge, which are explored in this chapter. Firstly, the literature on port-city relationships is presented to discuss the conditions that led to the widespread redevelopment of former urban port areas, how waterfront redevelopment practices have emerged and have been spreading throughout the world and what the current trajectories of port-city relationships are. Secondly, the concepts of culture- and event-led regeneration are introduced, with a particular focus on large-scale events and their regenerative potential. Finally, the link between the nature of port cities and urban regeneration is commented upon.

Ports *and* cities in transition

The 1992 edited book *European Port Cities in Transition* (Hoyle & Pinder, 1992) became a seminal contribution to the study of port-city relationships in the 1990s and early 21st century. It illustrated how technological improvements and changing maritime world trade patterns led to the restructuring of ports and impacted on port cities, and how waterfront redevelopment consequently emerged. Twenty-eight years later, *European Port Cities in Transition. Moving Towards More Sustainable Sea Transport Hubs* (Carpenter & Lozano, 2020) focused the discussion on the complexity of port-city relationships in the 21st century, in particular in relation to issues of sustainability.

The book situates itself within this narrative of transition of port cities, by exploring how both ports *and* cities have been changing since the late 20th

DOI: 10.4324/9781003165811-2

century, and how this has been shaping the socio-spatial, political and symbolic ties between ports and cities. Culture- and event-led regeneration have been deployed primarily as a means to compensate for the negative impacts of port restructuring, for example to act as a catalyst for waterfront redevelopment, and to diversify local economies. Nevertheless, as these schemes act on the attractiveness of port cities, for instance by promoting them as cultural poles or tourist destinations, they contribute to producing broader socio-economic and symbolic impacts. On the one hand, a regained urban attractiveness has been welcomed as a factor enabling port competitiveness. Increasingly automatised and smart ports require more and more highly-skilled professionals in a range of areas, including logistics, renewable energy, business operations, communication and marketing. These highly-educated professionals are more inclined to appreciate and take into account a broader range of aspects in their location choices, including the provision of urban amenities and local cultural scenes. Therefore, a port city that is attractive as a place to live – and not only to work – may be a plus for highly-skilled workers to look for port-related jobs in the area and may have a competitive advantage in terms of human capital over other port cities. On the other hand, an increased attractiveness of the city also acts on its complex ties with the port. In particular in the long term, this may generate unintended and undesirable outcomes, such as the loss of maritime heritage and distinctiveness and the disengagement of port city dwellers with local maritime cultures. As this latter aspect is particularly underexplored in the study of port-city relationships and of cultural policy and planning, the book is a contribution to the exploration and understanding of the longer-term, broader impacts of culture- and event-led regeneration schemes in port cities.

Since the 1960s, the literature about the relationships between ports and cities has been growing substantially. Paradoxically, as observed by Ducruet (2011, p. 32), this growing interest emerged when many port cities began losing part of their maritime-related activities and identity. Much of the literature reflects the disciplinary boundaries between port and urban studies (as commented by Ducruet & Lee, 2006, p. 107) and among urban planning, port and transport economics or economic geography (Wiese & Thierstein, 2014). Port-city relationships have been investigated in particular from a geographical perspective, since Bird (1963) proposed the Anyport model, which describes the development of a hypothetical port, providing a framework that can be used to compare the development patterns of ports across the world (Table 2.1).

While Bird's Anyport model focuses on the development of the port infrastructure, Hoyle (1988, 1989, 2000) envisioned a model of the evolution of port-city relationships until the beginning of the 21st century. Both the Anyport and Hoyle's models have profoundly influenced the literature in the following decades. Both models suggest that the development of modern commercial and industrial ports has triggered a growing port-city spatial and functional separation, in contrast with the traditional tight relationships

Table 2.1 Stages of Bird's Anyport model.

Phases	Characteristics
I. 'Primitive era'	• original 'port nucleus' • road(s) from the waterfront to the hinterland • storage space for transiting goods • quay development (within the boundaries of the nucleus)
II. 'Marginal quay extension'	• linear quay development (outstripping urban development) • emergence of a 'separate port district' • physical limits to linear expansion
III. 'Marginal quays elaboration'	• docks on the river bank or jetties
IV. 'Dock elaboration'	• emergence of the 'first commercial dock', e.g. replacing an obsolete section of the nucleus
V. 'Simple lineal quayage'	• possible final phase if cargo is mainly 'packaged goods' or 'goods in small lots'
VI. 'Specialised quayage'	• development of port facilities along the waterfront outside the nucleus

Source: Table compiled by the author, summarising Bird (1963, pp. 27–33)

based on physical proximity and functional and symbolic interconnection between the port and the heart of the city. It is worth noting that in Bird's Anyport model – and this is understandable considering the context in which the model was conceived – port migration is acknowledged as an inevitable consequence of increased specialisation. However, as later shown by Hoyle (2000), this interpretation needs to be problematised in the light of an increasing interrelation between contemporary ports and their cities, not least from a spatial perspective.

It is important to note that, despite the fact that Hoyle's model can effectively represent the evolution of port–city relationships in many European and North American cases, maritime port cities across the world are the result of different generative processes and have been following different paths. Geographical and historical settings have a primary influence on current patterns of port-city relationships across the world as well. As noted by Ducruet (2006), coastal cities in Europe tend to suffer from their peripheral location, which in turn impacts on their economic specialisation. Conversely, for example, settlement patterns in Asia tend to be mostly coastal due to the impacts of the colonial model, to the extent that most primate cities in Asia tend to be port cities. Arguably, their location patterns are among the reasons why many European port cities experienced socio–economic decline when they were hit by deindustrialisation and port restructuring.

The remainder of this section explores more deeper into the evolution of port-city relationships in Europe. Firstly, the development of the modern industrial port and the separation between ports and cities are briefly discussed, highlighting the impact of port migration and deindustrialisation on European port cities. Secondly, the emergence and spread of waterfront redevelopment schemes across Europe is commented. Finally, the recent evolution of port-city relationships is briefly explored.

The rise and fall of European industrial port cities

From their initial setting on coastal areas, natural harbours or riverbanks, most European port cities have historically been characterised by tight port-city relationships, as ports were embedded into or in close proximity to city centres. As suggested by Schubert (2008, p. 28), historic town plans show that harbours were 'an integral part of the city, being closely integrated into the urban fabric'. Dwellings, commercial premises, warehouses and offices were located on the waterfront to help goods handling (Schubert, 2011a). This resulted in the tight relationship between ports and cities that in some cases is still visible. Different spatial relationships with the sea distinguish Northern European port cities, which were generally established more inland (see e.g. Meyer, 1999) on riverbanks, to ensure protection from the rage of the North Sea or the Atlantic Ocean. Alongside their openness to the sea, ports also depended on their hinterlands for a range of resources and for overland communication. As suggested by Braudel (1995 [1966], pp. 317–318), '[a]ll ports, by definition, stand where land and water meet. Every one stands at the end of a road or inland waterway . . . all ports face both ways [to the sea and to their hinterlands]'.

The industrial revolution, and the rapid development of modern industrial ports, caused 'a before and an after in the port-city relationship' (Andrade Marques, 2014, p. 31, author's translation). As shown in the Anyport model (phase III) and in Hoyle's model of port-city relationships (stage II), the development of ports triggered by industrialisation posed physical limits to port expansion around the original nucleus. In the 19th century, as industrialisation progressed and world trade grew and steam vessels began to be deployed, inner harbours and urban quays soon became inadequate. The need for wider dock and storage space, together with the development of rail networks, triggered an unprecedented development of large docks and quays in proximity to inner harbours, while urban waterfronts increasingly hosted dock offices and merchant companies' warehouses. Steam liners also contributed to the development of mass passenger transport, consolidating the role of port cities as gateways to the outside world. In this context, 'port cities became the shimmering theatre of the modern world' (Meyer, 1999, p. 32). Large port cities displayed in this stage a marked cosmopolitan character, and were able to attract the interest of the bourgeoisie (ibid., p. 30). Waterfronts were the point of arrival for passengers travelling on steam liners and were thus the skylines of European port cities. As observed by Hein (2011, pp. 11–12), their 'maritime façade' including non-local architectural styles reflects and showcases the global interconnection of these cities and contributes to building the 'global urban mindscape of port cities'.

European port cities also display cultural exceptionalism (see e.g. Belchem, 2000, 2006; Hein et al., 2021), as a result of their 'porosity' (Hein, 2021). Many of these cities share those features that, as observed by Benjamin and Lacis (1924 [1978]), made Naples a 'porous city'. They display a 'distinctive social structure . . . defined by face-to-face contact, direct communication, neighbourly relations and close social bonds' that have been retained in some forms despite the socio-economic restructuring that these cities went through in the late 20th century (Bianchini & Bloomfield, 2012, n.p.). In many cases, they retained the 'self-confidence' that emerged as the result of their past prosperity (Warsewa, 2017, p. 157) and their free and independent spirit. Port cities have historically been 'breeding ground for human intelligence' and have always inspired political innovation and originality (Van Hooydonk, 2007, pp. 71–72). Their role as knowledge hubs was prominent in this phase, before the reduction of reliance on the sea through the development of new modes of transportation and communication (Ward, 2011, p. 70).

The literature stresses that port cities have been perceived as both attractive and repulsive, as they used to convey both fantasies of freedom and distant places (Kokot, 2008, p. 10) and moral condemnation of the lifestyle of their dwellers (Meyer, 1999, p. 32). This was particularly the case of 19th- and early 20th-century sailortowns, which were considered dangerous and amoral (see e.g. Bell, 2016), and places apart from their cities or nations (Fox, 1932, in Beaven, 2016). At the same time, sailortowns across the world provided a 'sense of a global or "worldly" belonging' (Cuming, 2019, p. 464): a global 'dockworkers' (sub-)culture' emerged and is to some extent still visible nowadays (Schubert, 2011a, p. 56).

Traditional port-city relationships were profoundly impacted by the development of the industrial modern port in the 19th and 20th centuries and, subsequently, by port restructuring driven by deindustrialisation and technological developments in the late 20th century. As noted by Schubert (2008, p. 29): 'The close connection of port, work and living was gradually dissolved with industrialisation'. In this stage, the transition from coal to oil required in many ports the provision of additional space and facilities to accommodate oil refining and shipping, which were developed in dedicated areas along coastlines and riverbanks outside the boundaries of existing ports. This migration of port functions was the result of both physical limits to port expansion within urban contexts and the need of wider spaces due to changes in maritime practices and technological improvements. On the one hand, containerisation – which was later followed by other radical changes such as computerisation and the automatisation of handling operations – substantially reduced cargo handling times and costs (Chilcote, 1988). On the other hand, oil and container shipping, together with the reorganisation of cargo handling practices, led to an increase in vessel size (Hayuth & Hilling, 1992, pp. 42–43). Due to increasing port productivity and ship size, the necessary amount of storage space grew substantially (Hayuth, 1988, p. 55). These processes raised the need for deeper water, wider space and greater accessibility by road and rail (Hayuth & Hilling, 1992, pp. 44–45), fuelling the gradual migration of ports outside their traditional urban location. As cargo handling was now far less labour-intensive, ports no longer needed as many workers as they used to employ. Stage IV of Hoyle's model, the 'retreat from the waterfront', portrays how ports – particularly in Europe and North America – have left their traditional harbours and quays especially between the 1960s and the 1980s, leading to the wide-spread phenomenon of waterfront redevelopment.

Studies on port-city relationships between the 1980s and 2000s (e.g. Hoyle & Pinder, 1992; Meyer, 1999; Norcliffe et al., 1996) emphasised, in line with the migration process described by Bird's Anyport model, a growing physical-functional separation between the port and the city, which weakened tradi-tional port-city relationships. Nevertheless, port migration also contributed to strengthening the ties between ports and their hinterland (Merckx et al., 2004, p. 5), as the former now depended from the latter in terms of accessibility and labour. In the context of globalisation, port cities of any size face specific risks arising from the evolution of maritime transportation and world trade. Ports have become interconnected to transnational transportation networks, showing little blending with urban functions (Meyer, 1999, p. 26) and are less depen-dent from local labour markets (Hoyle & Pinder, 1992; Ducruet et al., 2010, in Hall & Jacobs, 2012). The destiny of ports is increasingly determined by external factors – beyond their control (Hayuth & Hilling, 1992, p. 40) – and by the strategic decisions of global companies that operate in ports (Olivier & Slack, 2006; Hesse, 2013) and yet are based in other parts of the world. This is connected with the idea of the deterritorialisation and 'dehumanisation' of ports (Van Hooydonk, 2007), of which the following chapters make use. In the last two decades, some studies have adopted a governance approach to explore the political dimension of port-city relationships (Notteboom & Winkelmans, 2001) and tend to interpret the port-city interface as 'a place with a pluralis-tic community of actors' (Daamen & Vries, 2013, p. 6), focusing on how the interactions among these actors contribute to shaping the port-city relationship (Notteboom et al., 2013).

As a result of the combination of factors including geographical and socio-economic contexts, port specialisation, typology of port-city relationships, European port cities have followed different restructuring trajectories in the late 20th century (Wiese & Thierstein, 2014, pp. 95–96). Some of them retained their strategic role or successfully diversified their maritime economy (e.g. Rotterdam or Hamburg). In other port cities, the loss of traditional mari-time functions led to socio-economic decline, especially where port industry was the core economic activity (Warsewa, 2006, p. 12). In the latter case, one could point to the experiences of 'structurally disadvantaged' maritime port cities – that is maritime port cities that are disadvantaged in the urban com-petition due to changing trade patterns or other factors such as geographic marginalisation, structural socio-economic problems and negative external perceptions – as for instance Hull, in the UK, or Bremerhaven in Germany (Jonas et al., 2017). The migration and restructuring of ports produced, in virtually every port city, unused quays and warehouses, generating vast derelict areas that characterised the appearance of many port cities (Schubert, 2008). As observed by Warsewa (2017), this was also coupled with the erosion of established institutional arrangements enabling maritime activities, such as the role of port authorities, harbour police and customs offices.

In addition, these processes altered the symbolic relationships between ports and cities, the representation of port cities and their living and working conditions (Kokot, 2008, p. 7). As pointed out by Kowalewski (2018, p. 2), modernisation produced a disenchantment with the myth of the port city, as ports have become inaccessible and lost their romantic appeal over rationalisation, while globalisation has contributed to the disintegration of the port city as a whole and the increasing association of waterfronts with leisure. Nevertheless, European port cities retained their distinctive and fascinating character, for both positive and negative aspects. They can be interpreted as being both 'blue' – in relation to their connection to the sea – and 'black' (Mah, 2014, pp. 27–29), which is associated with poverty, crime, but also derelict and polluted urban areas (Van Hooydonk, 2007) and dirty waters. The abandonment of historic harbours and quays also meant that port cities retained many maritime heritage assets, which, together with these areas' proximity to water, contributed to an increased attractiveness of waterfronts for leisure and tourism (Tunbridge & Ashworth, 1992; Kostopoulou, 2013).

Urban transformation at the water's edge: waterfront redevelopment as a structural process

Waterfront redevelopment became a major research strand in urban studies, in particular between the 1980s and early 2000s. As pointed out by Dovey (2005, p. 9), urban environments at the water's edge have been sites of experimentation in architecture, urban planning and governance. Waterfront redevelopment schemes have multiplied across the world, particularly since the 1980s, and have reached port towns and cities of any scale. As commented by Vallega (1993, p. 24), several meanings have been attributed to the term 'waterfront', which has increasingly been associated with leisure, tourism and city branding. The meaning of waterfronts changed from areas of production commonly associated with industrial or maritime activities, to areas of consumption and pleasant environments for a range of leisure activities. As a result, the symbolic connections between cities and water changed as well. Rivers and the sea, which used to be conceived more as transport or industrial infrastructure, became increasingly associated with leisure and framed as assets for the physical and psychological wellbeing of riverside and coastal communities.

Several authors have proposed attempts of periodisation of waterfront redevelopment. Although the proposed phases differ slightly, the first stage is widely connected with project-led approaches driving pioneering experiences in US cities, such as Baltimore or San Francisco, since the 1960s, where the impacts of port migration had been evident since the 1950s (Schubert, 2008, 2011b). These schemes were implemented within a deregulated planning framework and produced a certain 'likeness' of waterfronts (Schubert, 2008, p. 34). The second stage is generally understood as dominated by larger-scale schemes involving mixed uses, which were implemented in the 1980s by applying emerging neoliberal ideas and values. Waterfront redevelopment between the 1980s and 1990s has been considered by some authors (e.g. Hall, 1993; Jauhiainen, 1995) as one if not *the* most important event in urban planning agendas in that period and has been portrayed as a global phenomenon (see e.g. Breen & Rigby, 1996; Brownhill, 2013). Pioneering experiences in the US inspired a range of waterfront schemes in the 1980s and 1990s in other parts of the world – for example in Buenos Aires (Puerto Madero) or Cape Town (Victoria and Alfred Waterfront) – and in many European port cities (including both large and smaller waterfronts, Shaw, 2001, pp. 168–169) such as Bilbao, Cardiff (Cardiff Bay), Hamburg (HafenCity), Hull, Liverpool (Royal Albert Dock), London (Docklands), Newcastle-Gateshead (Quayside) and Rotterdam (e.g. Kop van Zuid). These schemes generally introduced tertiary functions on waterfronts, together with housing and cultural, leisure and retail facilities. Thirdly, in particular in the late 1980s and 1990s, mega events played a major role in attracting resources and generating momentum for the reconversion of large former port areas in European cities such as Barcelona (Port Vell, Port Olímpic) and Genoa (Porto Antico). Andrade and Costa (2020, pp. 192–193) describe this phase as a shift from the tertiary waterfront – that is, the result of American-inspired redevelopment schemes focusing on commercial and tertiary functions – to the 'mega-tertiary waterfront', shaped by mega-event facilities and spaces. More recent examples include Olympic host cities such as Rio de Janeiro (Porto Maravilha) or other sporting mega event host cities such as Cape Town (2010 FIFA World Cup facilities). Finally, in the last twenty years, waterfront redevelopment schemes have generally been relying even more on public-private partnerships (Schubert, 2008, p. 36, 2011b, p. 76), due to the chronic lack of public resources. Also, these projects have been displaying growing efforts to blend urban and maritime activities (e.g. Rotterdam's Makers District), as well as increased awareness and concerns around the different dimensions of sustainability (see e.g. Fusco Girard et al., 2014; Andrade & Costa, 2020, p. 193).

Due to the migration and relocation of port activities outside their traditional urban location, waterfronts display a considerable real estate potential (Ward, 2011, p. 71) as they provide 'space where space is scarce' (Kokot, 2008, p. 13), namely in proximity to city centres and water. Other driving forces behind this phenomenon have been the historic preservation movement, increasing environmental awareness and pressures for improving the quality of water in cities, pressures for the regeneration of inner cities, public initiatives of urban renewal projects (Merckx et al., 2004, pp. 9–10; Sairinen & Kumpulainen, 2006, p. 121). In particular, the aforementioned change in public attitudes towards waterfronts resulted in the fact that port functions began to compete with other (commercial, residential and leisure) functions for the use of these areas (Hayuth, 1988, p. 62).

Schubert (2008) proposes a model of a general cycle of transformation at the port-city interface to describe this phenomenon. Port migration produces derelict former port areas close to city centres. These areas remain underused or unused for a certain amount of time, during which urban regeneration visions and plans are developed. These plans are implemented, establishing new land uses, such as office space, recreation and housing, contributing to improving the attractiveness of these areas (Figure 2.1).

Although redeveloped waterfronts are in general mixed-use spaces, some authors have proposed a typology based on the predominant functions visible in these spaces. Breen and Rigby (1996) identify six types of waterfront redevelopments, in relation to their main function: 'commercial', 'cultural educational and environmental', 'historic', 'recreational', 'residential' and 'working' waterfronts. Similarly, Norcliffe et al. (1996) have identified five groups of activities on waterfronts: employment, housing (promoting distinctiveness and the displacement of the working class), recreation (addressed to the middle class), hospitality, culture and heritage (displaying a mixture of maritime heritage and cultural infrastructures). Waterfront redevelopment

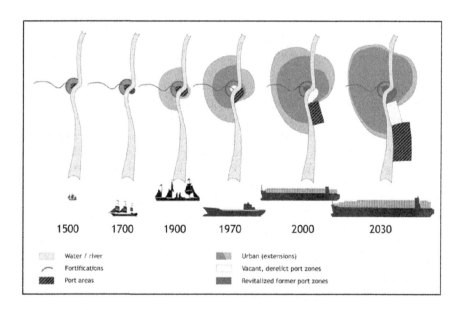

Figure 2.1 General cycle of transformation at the port-city interface.

Source: Schubert, D., Transformation Processes on Waterfronts in Seaport Cities – Causes and Trends between Divergence and Convergence, in Kokot, W., Wildner, K., Wonneberger, A., Port Cities as Areas of Transition, 2008, 25–46, DOI: 10.14361/9783839409497–002, reprinted by the permission of Transcript Verlag.

schemes have also been shaped by their macrogeographic context. Schubert (2017, p. 191) argues that North-western European schemes have more in common among them in comparison with projects in other areas of Europe. A rapid overview of the schemes implemented in North-western European cities would suggest that tertiary functions tend to be more common in these cases. Conversely, in Mediterranean port cities, tourist-historic variations of waterfront redevelopment were favoured by the physical environment (Tunbridge & Ashworth, 1992).

Despite its relevance in urban agendas, waterfront redevelopment is not widely interpreted as a success story. Schemes implemented in the 1980s and 1990s have been considered by policy makers as a kind of 'urban panacea' (Marshall, 2001, p. 6) and a means to re-launch the whole city by redeveloping a single area (Bruttomesso, 2001, p. 47). In addition, Jauhiainen (1995, p. 20) observed that even though waterfront redevelopment has produced remarkable physical transformation, 'when it comes to the social aspects the matter becomes much more complicated'. Critical studies undertaken in the 1990s and early 2000s interpret these projects as expressions of forces of capital (Malone, 1996), and as a means to affirm post-modern social values such as individualism and consumption – providing for instance luxury housing, cultural and leisure amenities and sport facilities – (Norcliffe et al., 1996) and post-industrial city-making (Marshall, 2001; Merckx et al., 2004). Criticisms about the social and economic impacts of waterfront redevelopment continued in relation to 21st-century projects. As noted by Ward (2017, p. 96), the shift from working port areas (of production) to post-industrial spaces (of consumption), based on retail, finance and tourism, 'was often socially painful and politically contentious'.

Other authors reflect on the impact of waterfront redevelopment on port-city relationships. Merckx et al. (2004, pp. 3 and 9) point out that this phenomenon has been playing a role in the recovery of port–city relationships after the separation generated by port migration and that, in some cases, these projects can be used as a form of compensation in order to get public support around port expansion schemes. However, as noted by Porfyriou and Sepe (2017, p. 3, italics in original), waterfront redevelopment '*affirmed a distinction between the waterfront and the city, which had never previously existed*': ports and their cities ceased to be perceived as a whole, while waterfront spaces began to be detached from their geographical context.

In commenting the wave of waterfront redevelopment schemes in the 1980s, Charlier (1992) questioned that redundant and derelict port areas would necessarily need to be reconverted to host urban uses, suggesting that new port uses could be introduced. More recently, in a similar vein, Andrade Marques (2014, p. 7) suggested that waterfront redevelopment practices may transform port-city relationships in a way that port cities are reduced to mere coastal cities, spoiled of their maritime attitude. Nevertheless, as mentioned earlier, since the 2000s, some of these projects have been displaying attempts to retain port functions, thus blending more maritime activities with urban and cultural uses (Andrade Marques, 2018, p. 7).

Another element of criticism is the homogenising character of waterfront redevelopment. Redeveloped waterfronts are designed to seek distinctiveness and 'to create memorable sensory experiences' for their users (Porfyriou & Sepe, 2017, pp. 8–9). The success of these spaces is perceived in relation to the presence of a tangible link with their past as sailortowns or former port areas (Merckx et al., 2004, p. 8). However, Bruttomesso warned about the danger of narrowing the potential diversity of such projects down to 'a few canons' (2001, p. 11). Ward (2017, p. 95) acknowledges that many similar urban environments have been created at the water's edge through these schemes. On the one hand, this is simply related to the interconnection of port cities across the world behind the production of port cityscapes (Hein, 2011). On the other hand, these schemes have been shaped through processes of mobile urbanism (McCann & Ward, 2011), consisting of mutual learning and knowledge transfer, but also of 'a more culturally and ideologically conditioned process of imagining, reflecting the images and stereotypes of the "source" country or city' (Ward, 2011, p. 72). This led to the 'sameness' (Norcliffe et al., 1996, p. 130) of redeveloped waterfronts across the world, sometimes cynically referred to as 'MacWaterfronts' (as reported by Daamen & van Gils, 2006, p. 2). In addition, the same designers and developers have been behind some of these schemes; for example, Enterprise Development Company, whose founder was involved in Baltimore's waterfront redevelopment, took part in the regeneration of Barcelona's Port Vell (and in the construction of the Maremagnum complex), as well as of Rotterdam's Kop van Zuid (Ward, 2017, p. 97). As a result of the global spread of these practices, a 'post-modern waterfront imaginary' emerged, shaped by informal social expectations about waterfront areas (Pagés Sánchez & Daamen, 2020, p. 131).

The issue of standardisation is also connected with the commodification of waterfronts, which aims at increasing the attractiveness of these environments and their cities, and thus encouraging inward investment. This argument builds on the aforementioned early criticisms from Malone (1996) and Norcliffe et al. (1996). As noted by Porfyriou and Sepe (2017, p. 7) 'waterfront regenerations – whether property led (as in the 1960s), housing led (as in the 1980s), or environmentally and culturally led . . . – remain, above all, market-led regenerations'. Zukin (2009, p. 544) suggests that the imposition of a hegemonic global urbanism increases property values to the detriment of distinctive local characters. Many of these schemes attempt 'a wholesale reconstruction of the urban image with spectacles of artistic, social and economic dynamism' (Dovey, 2005, p. 10).

Finally, as pointed out by Brownhill (2013), recent studies emphasise the juxtaposition of global and local forces and deploy innovative theoretical constructs such as the concept of urban assemblages, considering for instance the fixities of places and the flows of capital, information and knowledge (Desfor & Laidley, 2011). Waterfronts are perceived as deterritorialised spaces, shaped by both local forces, such as land use patterns, local contexts and stakes and global processes that stretch far beyond the city's boundaries. In the book, the concept of deterritorialisation is deployed in two ways: firstly, it is used to describe waterfronts as geographical spaces shaped by socio-economic processes transcending their physical dimension. This is driven by the presence of transnational companies, whose decisions take into account far broader and structural dynamics, or by highly centralised institutional arrangements (e.g. state-run port authorities). Secondly, deterritorialisation is understood in line with Tomlinson (1999) as a place-culture disconnection in times of globalisation. In particular, deterritorialisation and reterritorialisation are elaborated from a cultural-maritime perspective to highlight the loss of local maritime cultures or the introduction of new port-city cultural links (see Chapter 7).

A refashioning of port-city relationships

As noted by Ducruet (2011), the task of predicting the next step in the evolution of port-city relationships beyond Hoyle's model is generating opposition between scholars predicting further separation (Lee et al., 2008; Van Hooydonk, 2009) and those pointing at a retightening of these relationships (e.g. Wiegmans & Louw, 2011). The contemporary port-city relationship appears to be understood as a set of more complex interrelations (Wiese & Thierstein, 2014; Daamen & Louw, 2016). European port cities appear strongly exposed to the risks and threats arising from globalisation (Ducruet & Lee, 2006), growing complexity, competition among cities and climate change (Hanson et al., 2011) that are reshaping cities and urban societies. Network building, flows of information and organisational patterns are perceived as more prominent factors than infrastructure and accessibility in shaping port-city relationships (Hesse, 2013, p. 37). Works on spatial and political dynamics at the port-city interface appear to raise questions as to whether a new phase of port development is reshaping this space and the relationships between these two entities. Ports are still 'urban', although for different reasons (Hall & Jacobs, 2012), and yet the spatial driving force is no longer the port but the city, while local forces – such as sustainability paradigms – are stronger (Wiegmans & Louw, 2011, p. 582). The 'urban takeover' of either derelict or still active port areas is indeed producing spatial and political tensions (Daamen & Vries, 2013). Frictions of this kind about land-use change are among the current port-city conflicts identified by Bartłomiejski (2016) which encompass conservation of biodiversity, coastal defence, port-generated hazards and access.

The present reshaping, under different conditions, of port-city relationships shows the limits of established models. As pointed out by Merckx et al. (2004, p. 5), Hoyle's model does not take into account the changing land value of waterfronts. The authors propose an evolutionary model describing how pressure on city borders and on port renovation schemes leads to increased port-city tension. If there is enough space for port activities to expand, waterfront redevelopment schemes are likely to include functions that are not necessarily port-related. However, if there is not enough space for port expansion, tension on the waterfront is likely to emerge between port activities and urban functions. In either case, as noted by Vries (2014, pp. 110–111), urban governments are likely to continue putting pressure on port areas, aiming at their redevelopment, while port authorities will be less inclined to give away their areas.

Such spatial competition appears coupled with some extent of political separation. Ports are perceived as being administered separately from their cities. Port authorities and operators are considered to be more open to dialogue with other ports rather than with urban governments, as a result of the embeddedness of ports within transnational trade networks. Port authorities are indeed under pressure from increasingly powerful private players (Hesse, 2013, p. 36; Van Hooydonk, 2007, p. 32), governments that are less interested in the strategic role of ports and societal interest groups concerned with the negative externalities of port activity (Verhoeven, 2010, pp. 251–252). The ownership regime of ports and port authorities needs to be mentioned. In Europe, 87% of seaports are either owned by the state or by city councils, while 7% are run by public-private organisations (in particular in the UK), with some ports currently transitioning towards private-like management models (Pape, 2016, p. 3). Daamen and Vries (2013, p. 12) disagree that the corporatisation of ports has led to more distant relationships between urban and port institutions, considering the presence of supervisory boards and political committees that facilitate – or impose – such relationships. However, these trends impacted the relationships between the city's economic and port elites that Daamen and Louw (2016, p. 643) describe as 'a business affiliation gone cold'. Changes in institutional arrangements, port governance and world trade patterns are behind the increasing interdependence of port actors (Notteboom & Winkelmans, 2001; Vries, 2014) and of path dependency in port planning (Dooms et al., 2013; Hein, 2018). Local dependence (Cox, 1993) also shapes the activity of port authorities, who seek greater independence from local governments (Notteboom, 2006, in Daamen, 2010, p. 57).

Environmental and sustainability concerns are yet another factor contributing to the reshaping of port-city relationships (see e.g. Carpenter & Lozano, 2020). Van Hooydonk (2009, p. 18) argues that the recent tendency of relocation of port terminals is of a new nature, in contrast with Bird's Anyport model. According to Van Hooydonk, ports are capitulating to societal pressures against the environmental impact of maritime activities, through abrupt patterns of relocation which would produce a 'Banished-Port type' (ibid., p. 19). Rising environmental concerns, together with the tendency of port cities to diversify their local economy emulating non-port cities, are behind the idea of a 'general port city', which Lee et al. (2008) add to Hoyle's model as the next step in the evolution of Western port-city relationships. In their view, ports and port activities will be contracting due to environmental and economic pressures and port cities will become more similar to non-port cities.

Further uncertainty in the future evolution of port-city relationships arises from the transition to a post-oil economy. In North-western Europe, as predicted by Van den Bergh et al. (2016, p. 15), this may produce 'a refining legacy of unprecedented proportion'. Hein (2018, p. 921) also notes that '[c]hanges in the refining business will affect ports, cities, and transportation infrastructure. . . . As refineries and storage areas around the world disappear, they will require extensive and speciali[s]ed cleanup'. More broadly, this transition will impact what Hein calls the '*global palimpsestic petroleumscape*' (ibid., p. 888 italics in original), consisting of the physical, represented and everyday practices related to the production and consumption of oil and its refined products.

Although many studies have been focusing on a broader interpretation of the port-city relationship and have questioned the traditional view of an increasingly weaker tie between ports and cities, the available research still fails to address the implications of the geographical, economic, institutional and social implications of this changing relationship (Ng et al., 2014, p. 88), as well as its complexity in the light of its broader social, cultural and political dimensions. Exploring new developments in port-city relationships is an urgent issue for port and urban studies, which calls for multidisciplinary and integrated approaches that take into account spatial trajectories, socio-economic forces, cultural attitudes and governance landscapes at the port-city interface. The study of culture- and event-led regeneration exercises in port cities offers a chance to approach these issues from a broader socio-cultural and governance perspective, in contexts of rapid redevelopment.

Culture, mega events and urban regeneration

Many of the aforementioned redevelopment schemes of former port areas and waterfronts across European port cities have made use of culture-led regeneration, where flagship cultural facilities, activities or events were used as catalysts for urban regeneration, diversification of the local economy and strategic repositioning. This section explores the nexus between culture and regeneration and focuses on mega events as devices to trigger or boost urban regeneration. Firstly, the concept of culture-led regeneration is defined and the literature on urban regeneration through cultural activity is explored. Secondly, the concept of mega events is introduced and discussed. Finally, the link between mega events and urban regeneration is explored.

Culture and regeneration

Urban regeneration is commonly understood as a 'comprehensive vision and action which seeks to resolve urban problems and bring about a lasting improvement in the economic, physical, social and environmental condition of an area' (Roberts, 2017 [1999], p. 18). Whether focusing on city centres or waterfronts, urban regeneration in European port cities has often relied on the regenerative effects associated with cultural activity. Culture-led regeneration is intended in the book as a peculiar approach to urban regeneration characterised by cultural activity as the catalyst for change. Evans and Shaw (2004, p. 5) identify three models of the contribution of culture to regeneration, as follows:

- culture-led regeneration, where 'cultural activity is seen as the catalyst and engine of regeneration', is the form explored in the book; these interventions usually involve high-profile cultural facilities that trigger the regeneration of an area;
- cultural regeneration, where cultural activity is embedded into a regeneration strategy encompassing other (e.g. social, environmental) policy areas;
- culture and regeneration, where cultural activity is not fully integrated with other policy areas (e.g. in the case of small-scale projects involving public art).

Similarly, Vickery (2007, p. 19) suggests four possible driving forces of culture-led regeneration, namely the provision of flagship cultural facilities, landmark sculptures or public art schemes, innovative structural engineering projects (e.g. Gateshead Millennium Bridge), unique performances, events and festivals. With the exception of small-scale landmark sculptures or public art, all these typologies are taken into account in the book.

The link between culture and urban development has been recognised as early as the 19th century (Bassett, 1993, pp. 1173–1174), even though it has been incidental in cultural policies until the 1960s. In the 1970s, urban cultural policies gained political relevance (Bianchini, 1993b, pp. 9–11) and focused on the connection between cultural and social goals. However, the 1980s marked a major turning point in the connection between culture and urbanism (Freestone & Gibson, 2006, p. 32), in particular in countries at that time led by right-wing governments, such as the UK. Seminal studies began to investigate the role and potential of arts and culture in local development and the revitalisation of city centres (e.g. Bianchini et al., 1988; Myerscough, 1988). In a context of rapid economic restructuring and rising interurban competition (Bassett, 1993, pp. 1779–1780), the attention shifted from social concerns to goals of economic development and urban regeneration (Bianchini, 1993b, p. 2) – prioritising flagship projects and city branding as aspects that built the dominant discourse of culture-led regeneration – to the extent that culture increasingly became 'the business of cities' (Zukin, 2006 [1995], p. 2). This informed the experience of many 'resurgent' cities in the 1990s, including European port cities such as Glasgow, Bilbao and Barcelona (García, 2004a). The interest in culture and regeneration focused in particular on declining industrial cities (Miles, 2005, p. 893), where policy makers perceived culture as a means for responding to the loss of jobs in traditional sectors (Bianchini, 1993b, p. 2). The experience of Glasgow in particular provided credibility to the rhetoric of culture-led regeneration (Vickery, 2007, p. 22) and encouraged policy makers in other European cities – and port cities – to explore the potential of cultural activity in urban regeneration. The work of Richard Florida on the creative class also contributed to the success of the creative city policy paradigm. Florida understands the 21st-century economy as a creative economy (Florida, 2004 [2002], p. 44), profoundly shaped by the creative class – consisting of individuals whose professions deal with creating and developing new ideas, technologies and contents – and claims that creative centres, that is places with a vibrant cultural atmosphere, represent a key factor for cities to attract the new class as well as inward investment. In a context of growing interurban competition, Florida's ideas have become increasingly popular among policy makers and practitioners, to the extent that development strategies inspired by his idea of the creative city have become a recurrent feature of urban policy and planning across many towns and cities.

Urban cultural policies in the 1980s, strongly focused on urban regeneration, fuelled an early wave of criticisms that are still valid today. Harvey (1989a, p. 21) criticised these initiatives for being a 'carnival mask' concealing deeper social problems. Zukin (2006 [1995]) explored the connection between culture-led regeneration and economic and political interests, albeit focusing on large US cities, wondering what kind of culture – and city – was being promoted through this approach. In addition, Bianchini (1993a, pp. 201–203) suggested that projects in the 1980s and early 1990s raised three sets of dilemmas, involving their spatial dimension (e.g. centre–periphery tensions), economic perspectives (concerning the opposition between consumption- and production-oriented strategies) and funding approaches considering the either permanent or ephemeral character of cultural events. Critics of 1990s and 21st-century schemes claim that culture-led regeneration is easier than any investigations into structural social issues (e.g. Miles, 2005, p. 895). They also point at the instrumental use of culture that these schemes often display, as economic priorities dominate cultural goals (García, 2004a, p. 315). This to the extent that some raise questions as to whether these strategies are actually 'culture-led', considering that culture seems to play a marginal role (Evans, 2001, p. 216). The very rhetoric of culture-led regeneration and the effectiveness of these schemes have been questioned. For example, Miles (2005, p. 889) argues that few successful cases have been used as evidence of the revitalising power of culture.

Other authors stress that, paradoxically, many culture-led regeneration projects tend to expel artists and cultural activists who contribute to them, in particular because of rising land values (e.g. Lorente, 2002, p. 100). This introduces the general critique related to gentrification of the rhetoric of the creative class and the creative city policy paradigm built on Florida's ideas (e.g. Peck, 2005; Mould, 2017), as well as of cultural approaches to planning and regeneration (Stevenson, 2004; Miles, 2005). Culture-led regeneration projects are perceived as providing amenities and activities addressed to professional or managerial social groups (as reported by Evans, 2005, p. 8), thus changing the urban environment in a way that fosters gentrification. The middle-class attitude of culture-led urban regeneration has also been linked with the affirmation in European cities of American-inspired forms of revanchist urbanism (e.g. MacLeod, 2002), based on increasing spatial injustice, social exclusion and a – more or less subtle – criminalisation of poverty. This is linked with the broader idea that urban regeneration and the commodification of space act as a means to control the behaviour of users in public spaces (e.g. Zukin, 2006 [1995]; Atkinson, 2003).

Other critics interpret culture-led regeneration as a threat to local distinctiveness and identity. Many of these schemes tend to display a tendency to homogenise culture and urban environments across cities (see e.g. Evans, 2003; Richards & Wilson, 2006; Smith, 2007; Ponzini, 2012; De Frantz, 2013; Doak, 2016). This homogenisation can be interpreted as the outcome of two phenomena, namely the pressure on cities to have distinctive yet generalist features – such as flagship cultural facilities and fashionable urban spaces and amenities (Harvey, 1989b; Bell & Jayne, 2004) – and the 'just add culture and stir' approaches behind many of these schemes (Gibson & Stevenson, 2004, p. 1). However, Bailey et al. (2004, pp. 48–49) argue that this homogenisation is not always a negative aspect, and it can create the conditions for traditional identities to thrive, as some of these schemes actually engage with pre-existing local identities. According to the authors, such revitalisation should be pursued as a 'counter-balance to broader processes of cultural globalisation' (ibid., p. 49).

Large-scale events and mega events

The research on high-profile cultural, sporting or commercial events (referred to as mega events in the book) has gained momentum in the last decades in relation to the economic impacts of these special occasions on host cities. However, the literature on these events is quite fragmented, in particular due to the fact that defining them is not an easy task. Different keywords and conceptualisation of 'large-scale' events have been developed, including hallmark events, mega-events (whether or not hyphenated), cultural mega-events, mega sporting events, whose boundaries are becoming increasingly hazy.

A widely acknowledged definition is provided by Roche (2000, p. 1), who understands these events as 'large scale cultural (including commercial and sporting) events which have a dramatic character, mass popular appeal and international significance'. Other scholars understand mega events as either regular or one-off major festivals, expositions, cultural and sporting events (Hall, 1992, p. 1) or occasions characterised by a large number of visitors, national or international media coverage, large costs and impacts on cities and communities (Müller, 2015, p. 634). Both Hall and Roche's definitions appear in contrast with the separation between cultural and sporting events that is often visible in the literature. The concept of cultural mega-events has recently been deployed to distinguish cultural events and festivals (e.g. the European Capital of Culture) from larger mega events such as the Expo, the Olympic Games or the FIFA World Cup (see for instance Jones & Ponzini, 2018; Jones, 2020).

This approach is helpful to emphasise the artistic and cultural component of large-scale cultural festivals and to isolate these particular events from highly exceptional international mega events characterised by a predominantly sporting (or commercial in the case of Expos) nature, huge costs, greater disruptive effects on host cities and broader public and media visibility. The concept of cultural mega-events also allows us to distinguish a particular category of large-scale events that are increasingly popular among city policy makers (see Chapter 4). It is not the purpose of the book to engage with this debate and with the discussions on the scale of events. In the book, both cultural mega-events (as in Jones, 2020) such as the European Capital of Culture and sporting events such as the America's Cup and Formula One races are considered 'mega events', in line with the definitions provided by Hall and Roche.

The literature on mega events draws on seminal contributions from the fields of event management and tourism development (Ritchie, 1984; Hall, 1992; Getz, 1997) and displays a focus on the largest international sporting events such as the Olympic Games (e.g. Chalkley & Essex, 1999; Hall, 2006; Hiller, 2006). Mega events have been harshly criticised for being driven by corporate interests and economic goals and for displaying a tendency to commodify culture and to foster uneven development (Hall, 2006; Smith, 2012) and to affirm forms of revanchist urbanism (Tufts, 2004). This is also related to the critique of mega events as a form of spectacle (e.g. Gotham, 2005; Tomlinson & Young, 2006; Gruneau & Horne, 2016). Mega events are therefore criticised for being distant from, or even concealing, actual urban and social challenges (Harvey, 1989a; Hiller, 2000). In a recent contribution, Roche (2017) outlines a number of current issues in mega-event studies. Firstly, such events are increasingly digital media events, as TV broadcasting and online contents and interactions have broadened access and participation in an unprecedented way. Secondly, the emerging environmental awareness and political discourse around sustainability are leading to a 'greening' of mega events themselves, which has been impacting on some of the events analysed in the book. Finally, the changing geography of mega-event locations suggests that these events are no longer a prerogative of the Western world as they used to be in the 19th and 20th centuries. All these aspects influence perceptions of mega events, and therefore the role of these events as socio-economic or political projects, their legitimation and their acceptance among local populations.

The case studies of the book focus on the European Capital of Culture (ECoC), the UK City of Culture (UKCoC) and the America's Cup and Formula One events. The European City of Culture (rebranded as European Capital of Culture in 2001) was proposed in 1983 by the then Greek Minister of Culture Melina Mercouri and launched in 1985. The programme, which at the beginning celebrated primarily fine arts through relatively short festivals in established international cultural centres such as Florence or Paris, has increasingly been committed to urban regeneration and development. Glasgow European City of Culture 1990 represented a watershed in the history of the initiative (Bianchini et al., 2013), as its unprecedented 12-month cultural programme adopted a much broader definition of culture and explicitly aimed at regenerating the city centre, as well as the periphery. Since the experience of Glasgow, the ECoC has become increasingly attractive to policy makers as a catalyst for urban regeneration. Several studies investigate the regenerative potential of the ECoC, sometimes considering – even though without a specific focus – port cities as case studies. For instance, Richards and Wilson (2004) examine the impact of Rotterdam European Capital of Culture 2001 on the image of the city. García (2005) undertakes an evaluation of the impacts of Glasgow European City of Culture 1990 in the long term, focusing particularly on media discourses. Boland (2010) and Cox and O'Brien (2012) offer a critical interpretation of Liverpool European Capital of Culture 2008, and the 'Liverpool model' (García et al., 2010). Bianchini et al. (2013) explore the different dimensions of urban regeneration driven by the event, while Gomes and Librero-Cano (2018) use a difference-in-difference approach to analyse the economic performance of awarded cities in comparison with cities that unsuccessfully bid for the title, assessing the economic growth generated by the event. Finally, Jones (2020) discusses the synergies between the European Capital of Culture and urban heritage in Genoa, Liverpool and Istanbul.

As a result of the perceived success of the European Capital of Culture, the UK City of Culture was launched in 2009 as the country's quadrennial cultural festival. The programme was established with the aim of allowing UK cities to harness the regenerative potential of large-scale cultural events that was witnessed in the case of Glasgow and Liverpool (DCMS, 2009). Derry-Londonderry was the first UK City of Culture to celebrate the title in 2013, followed by Hull in 2017 and Coventry in 2021. Despite the relative novelty of the programme, a number of studies have been published about Derry-Londonderry 2013, considering for instance place imaginaries and post-conflict reconciliation (Doak, 2014, 2020; McDermott et al., 2016; Boland et al., 2019), regeneration and legacy (Boland et al., 2018, 2019).

The America's Cup is an international sailing contest that was first celebrated in 1851. It is traditionally held in the country of the defender, that is the reigning champion. For this reason, after its first edition held on the Isle of Wight, the competition took place in the US until 1983, when the Royal Perth Yacht Club eventually won the trophy and briefly moved the event to Australia. At that point, the America's Cup became a global sporting event (Prichard, 2000). The contest was held in Australia, the US and New Zealand, until the Société Nautique de Genève won the 2003 edition. As the rules state that the competition must be held at sea, the Swiss defender needed to designate a venue for the following 2007 edition. The 32nd America's Cup in 2007 and the following edition in 2010 were held in Valencia (Spain). Finally, the last two contests in 2013 and 2017 were held in the US, while the 2021 edition was held in New Zealand. The socio-economic impacts of the America's Cup have been explored in several studies (Soutar & McLeod, 1993; Orams & Brons, 1999; Barker et al., 2001; Macbeth et al., 2012; Parra Camacho et al., 2016). Other studies focus on the America's Cup as an expression of globalising forces. For example, John and Jackson (2010) explore the concept of corporate nationalism in the case of the America's Cup 2003.

Formula One (also known as Formula 1 or F1), is considered the world's highest class of motor racing. The sport is regulated by the Fédération Internationale de l'Automobile (FIA), albeit the brand is property of a private organisation (Formula One Group, now controlled by American media company Liberty Media Corporation). The F1 world championship is held every year and consists of a number of races, which has varied from 7 in its maiden season (1950) to 23 in the 2020-2022 seasons.[1] Nowadays' Formula One races are 3–4-day events, which include ancillary events such as races valid for other categories and parades involving historic cars. F1 races require *ad hoc* permanent or temporary racetracks and related facilities (e.g. pitlane, bleachers, motorhomes, hospitalities, press areas, first aid services, etc.), either located in the outskirts or, in some cases, in the streets of host cities. Social science research on Formula One events has focused primarily on their – mainly economic – impacts (Burns et al., 1986; Henderson et al., 2010; Fairley et al., 2011; Kim et al., 2017) and more recently on their 'greenwashing' in the attempt to adapt to the emerging environmental awareness and activism (Miller, 2016). Other studies have focused on Formula One as an expression of capitalist development and a vehicle to promote post-modern values. For example, Parker (2003a) analyses Formula One as a carnival – a 'liminal, transient space based on a morality of excess, spectacle and success' (ibid., p. 3) – and as a product of the integration of corporate capitalism, consumption, image, sport and entertainment, whose advertising logic promotes the ideal of the 'contemporary business nomad' (ibid., p. 12). Nichols and Savage (2017) use Formula One as a case study to discuss elite formation and capital accumulation processes.

Mega events and regeneration

Policy makers in European port cities have been keen on exploring the regenerative potential of large-scale cultural, sporting or commercial events. These events are claimed to offer international visibility, to attract investments and additional funding and to foster major urban projects. This has led to a widespread festivalisation of culture, understood as the use of festivals and events by local policy makers to brand their cities (Hitters, 2007, p. 282), and to the perception of events as a '"quick fix" solution' to problems of negative external perceptions (Quinn, 2005, p. 932).

Event-led regeneration (see e.g. Sadd, 2009; Smith, 2012; Lauermann, 2016a) can be understood as a form of regeneration that attempts to harness the regenerative potential of large-scale events, by triggering, accelerating, or showcasing a variety of redevelopment plans. The link between these events and urban development is nonetheless far from being new, and arguably emerged in the 19th century, when Universal Expositions acted as catalysts for transformation and for affirming emerging modern values (Roche, 2000). Large-scale events were used to streamline reconstruction and modernisation efforts after the Second World War. As in the case of culture-led regeneration, mega events taking place since the 1970s displayed attempts to respond to the negative impacts of deindustrialisation, and increasingly focused on economic development and urban regeneration at the turn of the millennium. As noted by Smith (2012), mega events in the 21st century have been showing a growing attention to their softer outcomes and legacy. Some events have sought to promote socio-economic regeneration, for instance by supporting skills development through volunteering programmes (Smith & Fox, 2007, p. 1128), which have become a recurrent feature for example in City/Capital of Culture schemes.

Mega events promoters have been criticised for levering on the exceptionality of these occasions to introduce controversial, 'fast-tracked' (Smith & Fox, 2007; Scherer, 2011; Jones & Ponzini, 2018) planning practices, which would not be acceptable under ordinary circumstances (Smith, 2012, p. 257). In Europe, criticisms concern in particular gentrification and the commodification and corporatisation of public space (as underlined by Bianchini et al., 2013). As suggested by Hall (2006, p. 63), the emergence of coalitions of interests around certain mega events may be described using Molotch's (1976) idea of the city as a growth machine, where the quest for economic growth and capital accumulation drives the efforts of local political and economic elites.

Mega events with a strong cultural component are nonetheless perceived as underpinned by an instrumental view of culture. For instance, despite the recognition that arts programmes and cultural activities contribute to urban regeneration more broadly, arts programming displays a 'tokenistic role' in many large-scale cultural events (García, 2004b, p. 103), which tend to be dominated by economic and corporate logics. This also leads to a replication of similar events across host cities (Richards & Wilson, 2004, p. 1932; Quinn, 2005, p. 937). In line with the idea of cultural urban policies as a worst-case scenario (Zukin, 2006 [1995], p. 273), this strategy is similarly interpreted as a desperate attempt to 'compensate for the failure of more conventional urban policy' (Smith, 2012, p. 10). With regards to the European Capital of Culture, Evans (2003, p. 426) suggests that, in the 1990s and early 2000s, it has acted as a 'Trojan horse' – bypassing national and local preferences in funding allocation (Evans & Foord, 2000) – and it has fuelled a 'culture city competition'.

Critics of event-led regeneration understand it as a component of the Florida-inspired creative city 'policy package', thus as a strategy to strengthen cities' competitive advantage and to pursue neoliberal urban agendas. As early as the end of the 1980s, Harvey (1989b, p. 9, italics added) commented that 'the city *has to* appear as an innovative, exciting, creative and safe place to live or to visit, to play and consume in' – an idea that has profoundly shaped the rhetoric of many 'resurgent' cities across the last decades – and that the delivery of temporary and permanent urban spectacles is a key strategy of entrepreneurial approaches to governance. Eisinger (2000) focuses on event-related entertainment projects and sport facilities in US cities to explore the implications of building a 'city for visitors'. Policy makers in many European cities, inspired by the 'Barcelona model', have sometimes adopted aggressive branding strategies based on mega events, which exploit local identities as a marketing device (García, 2004a, p. 322). This is linked with criticisms of mega events as devices fostering social inequalities and targeting middle-class social groups. For example, Mooney (2004) shows how Workers City, a local activist group, contested Glasgow European City of Culture 1990 and the related process of urban regeneration for neglecting the city's working-class character. In critiquing the dominant discourse of city boosterism fuelled by interurban competition, mega events and related flagship projects are interpreted as examples of urban propaganda projects (Boyle, 1999), aimed at legitimising political projects that pursue the interest of local elites. Cavalcanti et al. (2016) understand these events as a force of creative destruction, as many of them entail demolition and displacement to create space for ad hoc infrastructure and facilities, which eventually become mega-event 'ruins'. Mega events in European cities raise criticisms about the displacement of certain social groups or local communities, with the aim of 'sanitising' the city as a clean and safe venue (e.g. Atkinson & Laurier, 1998), whose image can be 'sold' to tourist and investors.

As pointed out by Evans (2011), mega events should be interpreted as devices for the festivalisation of certain moments in cities' trajectories of culture and regeneration. As a matter of fact, the legacy of these events has become a key political discourse. However, only a few studies examine the relationship between mega events and planning (e.g. Roche, 1994; Bramwell, 1997; Monclús, 2006), suggesting that positive outcomes and long-term legacy are more likely when mega events are integrated into broader strategies of urban development. A few studies examine the potential of these events to encourage partnership building and empower local actors, focusing on the positive effects of unsuccessful bids (ICC, 2012; Lauermann, 2016b) and on the positive impacts of the anticipation of events (Anderson & Holden, 2008). However, much of the research tends to neglect backward and forward linkages between mega events and local communities, producing very partial analyses of their impacts (Hiller, 1998). The growing body of research on event-led regeneration also tends to display a spatial focus either on city centres/symbolic spaces or on events' target areas, and to be dominated by economic perspectives.

Port cities, culture and mega events

Few studies engage with the connection between cultural and sporting events and the maritime character of port cities. For example, Parker (2003b) analyses how the America's Cup contributed to shaping urban spaces for the elite on the waterfront in Auckland. Griffiths (2006) compares the bids of Liverpool, Bristol and Cardiff for the 2008 title, using discourse analysis to emphasise recurrent aspects and the perceived potential social and economic benefits of the programme, and mentions how maritime history and heritage featured in

Liverpool and Cardiff's bids. Tommarchi and Cavalleri (2020) examine the Hull UK City of Culture 2017 and Pafos European Capital of Culture 2017 to reflect on the role and impacts of these events in port and coastal towns and cities. Tommarchi and Bianchini (2022) show how maritime heritage was mobilised in the case of Hull to counter port-related stigmatisation.

These events have been perceived as a strategy to regain part of the geographical power of port cities (Evans, 2011), which was lost due to port restructuring in the late 20th century. In recent years, City/Capital of Culture schemes have been particularly popular among small and medium-sized European port cities, albeit focusing on socio-economic rather than physical regeneration. For instance, Aarhus and Pafos were the European Capitals of Culture 2017, while Valletta and Rijeka celebrated the title respectively in 2018 and 2020. Hull was designated as the UK City of Culture 2017 at the end of a competition that involved eight port towns and cities across the country.[2] This is not necessarily a European phenomenon. For example, Cape Town, where the World Cup 2010 was hosted, Rio de Janeiro, the host city of the World Cup 2014 and the 2016 Olympics, and Buenos Aires all competed for the 2004 Summer Olympics, which were eventually awarded to Athens. Shanghai, where the world's largest and busiest port is located, hosted the World Expo in 2010, while the 2023 edition will be held in Buenos Aires. This attitude of port cities in relation to mega events is not surprising: former port areas are excellent locations for cultural activities and large-scale events because of their good accessibility by road and rail, their robust dock environment, the availability of versatile and easily adaptable port buildings and not least for their spectacular location at the water's edge which features well on TV images and promotional materials.

However, culture- and event-led regeneration at the port-city interface since the 1990s has meant that cities were – and still are – in competition with ports. As commented by Andrade Marques (2018, p. 8, author's translation), this widespread effort to redevelop waterfronts and transform them into cultural quarters 'has taken its toll' in terms of port development and maritime activities. As mentioned earlier, the gradual 'urban takeover' of port areas fuels socio-spatial and political conflicts (Daamen & Vries, 2013), which – also due to issues of safety and security – foster some degree of 'port enclavism' from a spatial and political perspective. This appears to be part of a process of 'dehumanisation' of seaports (Van Hooydonk, 2007, p. 42), characterised by further technological developments, the displacement of local companies by transnational groups and – also as a consequence of the recent security policies – the fencing off of port areas. This spatial fragmentation implies that physical constraints to the permeability of waterfronts remain, despite the emergence of policy discourses mobilising maritime identity. In many port cities, former port facilities and spaces have been spoilt of their functions to accommodate new and clean uses, for example residential, commercial or leisure uses, under a logic of exploitation and commodification of maritime heritage and identity (Atkinson et al., 2002, p. 28; Shaw, 2009). The decline and loss of their distinctive way of life is indeed an emerging issue in the narrative of European port cities (Mah, 2014, p. 29).

The cultural exceptionalism of European port cities is often neglected in culture- and event-led regeneration. Such aggressive strategies, aimed at providing standardised urban environments and amenities to pursue property development, may be perceived as threatening by local communities. This happened for instance in Liverpool (Lorente, 2002, p. 95) and Hamburg (Desfor & Laidley, 2011, p. 2) where some historic port facilities and spaces were replaced by new 'global' functions (ibid., pp. 2–3). The much-heralded experience of Barcelona provides a striking example. Apart from the 1888 and 1929 Universal Expositions, the Catalan city hosted the 1992 Olympic Games and the 2004 Universal Forum of Cultures. If it is true that the redevelopment of Port Vell and the area of the Olympic Village and Port Olímpic in order to host the Games rapidly became new urban centralities and examples of 'best practice' in urban planning, waterfront redevelopment schemes linked to the 2004 Forum have been interpreted rather differently. For example, Muñoz (2015, p. 183) sees Diagonal Mar and Parc del Fórum as 'a kind of second-hand Florida, highly disconnected from the local urban landscape and culture, reproduced in a very short-time, and generating strong disagreements between local inhabitants'. There are nonetheless examples of schemes involving lesser extents of homogenisation, such as Newcastle-Gateshead Quayside (Bailey et al., 2004, p. 62; Middleton & Freestone, 2008, pp. 7–8; Yarker, 2018), where pre-existing elements of the area's identity have survived its transformation.

The juxtaposition of 'regenerated' and 'non-regenerated' – or 'sanitised' and 'unsanitised' – spaces plays a crucial role. On the one hand, this contrast appears a key feature of culture-led regeneration itself, considering the two opposing discourses of urban boosterism, which enhances the positive characteristics of the city and hides its 'shadows' (Short, 1999, pp. 40–41). On the other hand, this approach appears to emphasise the duality of European port cities described earlier. The port-city interface may consist of fragmented environments where cultural spaces and luxury housing for the newcomers from the creative class are developed next to working-class housing districts. This new population is a further factor influencing local socio-economic profiles, which are already unbalanced due to the juxtaposition of highly-educated professionals and low-skilled workers that characterises contemporary ports (Daamen & van Gils, 2006, p. 4).

If gentrification is considered a likely output of culture-led regeneration, further research appears necessary to understands its impacts and to explore issues of socio-spatial tensions in contexts that retain their original population, such as port cities. In addition, issues of safety need to be explored: Evans (2005, p. 17) suggests that flagship projects, especially on waterfronts, are often disconnected from local business and residential communities and tend to produce unused or unsafe urban environments.

To summarise, the literature on port-city relationships and on culture-led urban regeneration have seldom connected. Yet, urban regeneration in

European port cities has often made use of large-scale events and cultural activities. On the one hand, policy makers in European port cities have been keen on exploring the regenerative potential of culture to tackle the socio-economic and urban challenges emerging from port restructuring. On the other hand, former port areas and waterfronts have proved to be ideal event venues due to their strategic location, accessibility and adaptability. However, waterfront redevelopment and culture- and event-led regeneration in European port cities have raised a number of issues, including the social impacts of and reactions against these schemes in the socio-economic context of European port cities, the homogenisation of local cultures and urban environments on the waterfront, the competition between port and cultural activities. These aspects are explored from a comparative perspective in the next chapters.

Notes

1 The 23-race calendar of the 2020-2022 seasons has been impacted by cancellations and replacements as a result of the COVID-19 pandemic and of the war in Ukraine.
2 Eleven bidders competed for the title of UK City of Culture 2017: Aberdeen, Chester, Dundee, East Kent (Canterbury, Ashford, Folkestone, Dover and Thanet), Hastings and Bexhill-on-Sea, Hull, Leicester, Plymouth, Portsmouth and Southampton (joint bid), Southend-on-Sea, Swansea Bay (Swansea, Neath Port Talbot and Carmarthenshire). Eight port towns and cities – Aberdeen, Dover (East Kent), Hull, Plymouth, Portsmouth, Southampton, Swansea and Port Talbot (Swansea Bay) submitted a bid or were involved in joint bids.

Bibliography

Anderson, B., & Holden, A. (2008) Affective urbanism and the event of hope. *Space and Culture*, 11(2), 142–159.

Andrade, M. J., & Costa, P. J. (2020) Touristification of European port-cities: Impacts on local populations and cultural heritage. In Carpenter, A., & Lozano, R. (eds.) *European Port Cities in Transition: Moving towards More Sustainable Sea Transport Hubs*. Cham: Springer, 187–204.

Andrade Marques, M. J. (2014) Puertos: Paisajes de memoria, lugares de oportunidad. *EDaP*, 7, 28–37.

Andrade Marques, M. J. (2018) The port-city in the post-crisis context: Identity and humanisation in the process of touristification. *25th APDR Congress 'Circular Economy: Urban Metabolism and Regional Development'*, Lisbon, 5–8 July.

Atkinson, D., Cooke, S., & Spooner, D. J. (2002) Tales from the riverbank: Place-marketing and maritime heritages. *International Journal of Heritage Studies*, 8(1), 25–40.

Atkinson, D., & Laurier, E. (1998) A sanitised city? Social exclusion at Bristol's 1996 International Festival of the Sea. *Geoforum*, 29(2), 199–206.

Atkinson, R. (2003) Domestication by cappuccino or a revenge on urban space? Control and empowerment in the management of public spaces. *Urban Studies*, 40(9), 1829–1843.

Bailey, C., Miles, S., & Stark, P. (2004) Culture-led urban regeneration and the revitalisation of identities in Newcastle, Gateshead and the North East of England. *International Journal of Cultural Policy*, 10(1), 47–65.

Barker, M., Page, S. J., & Meyer, D. (2001) Evaluating the impact of the 2000 America's Cup on Auckland, New Zealand. *Event Management*, 7(2), 79–92.

Bartłomiejski, R. (2016) Environmental conflicts in port cities. *Opuscula Sociologica*, 18, 33–44.

Bassett, K. (1993) Urban cultural strategies and urban regeneration: A case study and critique. *Environment and Planning A*, 52, 1773–1788.

Beaven, B. (2016) The resilience of sailortown culture in English naval ports, c. 1820–1900. *Urban History*, 43(1), 72–95.

Belchem, J. (2000) *Merseypride: Essays in Liverpool Exceptionalism*. Liverpool: Liverpool University Press.

Belchem, J. (ed.) (2006) *Liverpool 800: Culture, Character and History*. Liverpool: Liverpool University Press.

Bell, D., & Jayne, M. (2004) Conceptualizing the City of Quarters. In Bell, D., & Jayne, M. (eds.) *City of Quarters: Urban Villages in the Contemporary City*. Aldershot: Ashgate, 1–12.

Bell, K. (2016) 'They are without Christ and without hope': 'Heathenism', popular religion, and supernatural belief in Portsmouth's maritime community, c. 1851–1901. In Beaven, B., Bell, K., & James, R. (eds.) *Port Towns and Urban Cultures: International Histories on the Waterfront, c.1700–2000*. Basingstoke: Palgrave Macmillan, 49–67.

Benjamin, W., & Lacis, A. (1924) Naples. In Benjamin, W. (ed.) *Reflections: Essays, Aphorisms, Autobiographical Writings*. New York and London: Harcourt Brace Jovanovich, 163–173.

Bianchini, F. (1993a) Culture, conflict and cities: Issues and prospects for the 1990s. In Bianchini, F., & Parkinson, M. (eds.) *Cultural Policy and Urban Regeneration: The West European Experience*. Manchester: Manchester Press, 199–213.

Bianchini, F. (1993b) Remaking European cities: The role of cultural policies. In Bianchini, F., & Parkinson, M. (eds.) *Cultural Policy and Urban Regeneration: The West European Experience*. Manchester: Manchester Press, 1–20.

Bianchini, F., Albano, R., & Bollo, A. (2013) The regenerative impacts of the European City/Capital of Culture events. In Leary, M. E., & McCarthy, J. (eds.) *The Routledge Companion to Urban Regeneration*. London: Routledge, 515–525.

Bianchini, F., & Bloomfield, J. (2012) Porous cities: On four European cities. *Eurozine*, 3rd July. Available at: www.eurozine.com/porous-cities/ [Accessed 22/11/2018].

Bianchini, F., Fisher, M., Montgomery, J., & Worpole, K. (1988) *City Centres, City Cultures: The Role of the Arts in the Revitalisation of Towns and Cities*. Manchester: Centre for Local Economic Development Strategies.

Bird, J. (1963) *The Major Seaports of the United Kingdom*. London: Hutchison of London.

Boland, P. (2010) 'Capital of Culture – You must be having a laugh!' Challenging the official rhetoric of Liverpool as the 2008 European cultural capital. *Social and Cultural Geography*, 11(7), 627–645.

Boland, P., Murtagh, B., & Shirlow, P. (2018) Neoliberal place competition and culturephilia: Explored through the lens of Derry-Londonderry. *Social and Cultural Geography*. https://doi.org/10.1080/14649365.2018.1514649.

Boland, P., Murtagh, B., & Shirlow, P. (2019) Fashioning a City of Culture: 'Life and place changing' or '12 month party'? *International Journal of Cultural Policy*, 25(2), 246–265.

Boyle, M. (1999) Growth machines and propaganda projects: A review of readings of the role of civic boosterism in the politics of local economic development. In Jonas, A. E. G., & Wilson, D. (eds.) *The Urban Growth Machine: Critical Perspectives Two Decades Later*. Albany: State University of New York Press, 55–70.

Bramwell, B. (1997) Strategic planning before and after a mega-event. *Tourism Management*, 18(3), 167–176.

Braudel, F. (1995 [1966]) *The Mediterranean and the Mediterranean World in the Age of Philip II: Vol. I.* Berkeley: University of California Press.

Breen, A., & Rigby, D. (1996) *The New Waterfront: A Worldwide Urban Success Story.* New York: McGraw-Hill.

Brownhill, S. (2013) Just add water: Waterfront regeneration as a global phenomenon. In Leary, M. E., & McCarthy, J. (eds.) *The Routledge Companion to Urban Regeneration.* London: Routledge, 45–55.

Bruttomesso, R. (2001) Complexity on the urban waterfront. In Marshall, R. (eds.) *Waterfronts in Post-Industrial Cities.* London: Spon Press, 39–49.

Burns, J., Hatch, J., & Mules, T. (eds.) (1986) *The Adelaide Grand Prix: The Impact of a Special Event.* Adelaide: The Centre for South Australian Economic Studies, University of Adelaide.

Carpenter, A., & Lozano, R. (eds.) (2020) *European Port Cities in Transition: Moving towards More Sustainable Sea Transport Hubs.* Cham: Springer.

Cavalcanti, M., O'Donnell, J., & Sampaio, L. (2016) Futures and ruins of an Olympic City. In Carvalho, B., Cavalcanti, M., & Rao, V. V. (eds.) *Occupy All Streets: Olympic Urbanism and Contested Futures in Rio de Janeiro.* New York: Terreform, 60–89.

Chalkley, B., & Essex, S. (1999) Urban development through hosting international events: A history of the Olympic Games. *Planning Perspectives,* 14(4), 369–394.

Charlier, J. (1992) The regeneration of old port areas for new port uses. In Hoyle, B. S., Pinder, D. A., & Husain, M. S. (eds.) *Revitalising the Waterfront: International Dimensions of Dockland Redevelopment.* London: Belhaven Press, 137–154.

Chilcote, P. W. (1988) The containerization story: Meeting the competition in trade. In Hershman, M. J. (ed.) *Urban Ports and Harbor Management: Responding to Change along U.S. Waterfronts.* New York: Routledge, 125–145.

Cox, K. R. (1993) The local and the global in the new urban politics: A critical view. *Environment and Planning D: Society and Space,* 11, 433–448.

Cox, T., & O'Brien, D. (2012) The 'scouse wedding' and other myths: Reflections on the evolution of a 'Liverpool model' for culture-led urban regeneration. *Cultural Trends,* 21(2), 93–101.

Cuming, E. (2019) At home in the world? The ornamental life of sailors in Victorian sailortown. *Victorian Literature and Culture,* 47(3), 463–485.

Daamen, T. A. (2010) *Strategy as Force: Towards Effective Strategies for Urban Development Projects: The Case of Rotterdam City Ports.* Amsterdam: IOS Press.

Daamen, T. A., & Louw, E. (2016) The challenge of the Dutch port-city interface. *Tijdschrift Voor Economische En Sociale Geografie,* 107(5), 642–651.

Daamen, T. A., & van Gils, M. (2006) Development challenges in the evolving port-city interface defining complex development problems in the European main seaport-city interface: Rotterdam and Hamburg. *10th International Conference Cities and Ports,* Sydney, 5–9 November.

Daamen, T. A., & Vries, I. (2013) Governing the European port-city interface: Institutional impacts on spatial projects between city and port. *Journal of Transport Geography,* 27, 4–13.

DCMS (2009) *City of Culture: Working Group Report: June 2009.* London: DCMS.

De Frantz, M. (2013) Culture-led urban regeneration: The discursive politics of institutional change. In Leary, M. E. & McCarthy, J. (eds.) *The Routledge Companion to Urban Regeneration.* London: Routledge, 526–535.

Desfor, G., & Laidley, J. (2011) Introduction: Fixity and flow of urban waterfront change. In Desfor, G., Laidley, J., Stevens, Q., & Schubert, D. (eds.) *Transforming Urban Waterfronts: Fixity and Flow.* London and New York: Routledge, 1–13.

Doak, P. (2014) Beyond Derry or Londonderry: Towards a framework for understanding the emerging spatial contradictions of Derry-Londonderry: UK City of Culture 2013. *City*, 18(4–5), 488–496.

Doak, P. (2016) Culture-led regeneration in Derry-Londonderry, UK City of Culture 2013. In Epinoux, E., & Healy, F. (eds.) *Post Celtic Tiger Ireland: Exploring New Cultural Spaces.* Newcastle upon Tyne: Cambridge Scholars Publishing, 86–104.

Doak, P. (2020) Cultural policy as conflict transformation? Problematising the peacebuilding potential of cultural policy in Derry-Londonderry: UK City of Culture 2013. *International Journal of Cultural Policy*, 26(1), 46–60.

Dooms, M., Verbeken, A., & Haezendonck, E. (2013) Stakeholder management and path dependence in large-scale transport infrastructure development: The port of Antwerp case (1960–2010). *Journal of Transport Geography*, 27, 14–25.

Dovey, K. (2005) *Fluid City: Transforming Melbourne's Urban Waterfront.* Sydney: University of New South Wales Press.

Ducruet, C. (2006) Port-city relationships in Europe and Asia. *Journal of International Logistics and Trade*, 4(2), 13–35.

Ducruet, C. (2011) The port city in multidisciplinary analysis. In Alemany, J., & Bruttomesso, R. (eds.) *The Port city in the XXIst Century: New Challenges in the Relationship between Port and City.* Venice: RETE, 32–48.

Ducruet, C., & Lee, S. W. (2006) Frontline soldiers of globalisation: Port-city evolution and regional competition. *GeoJournal*, 67(2), 107–122.

Eisinger, P. (2000) The politics of bread and circuses: Building the city for the visitor class. *Urban Affairs Review*, 35(3), 316–353.

Evans, G. (2001) *Cultural Planning: An Urban Renaissance?* London: Routledge.

Evans, G. (2003) Hard-branding the Cultural City: From Prado to Prada. *International Journal of Urban and Regional Research*, 27(2), 417–440.

Evans, G. (2005) Measure for measure: Evaluating the evidence of culture's contribution to regeneration. *Urban Studies*, 42(5–6), 959–983.

Evans, G. (2011) Cities of culture and the regeneration game. *London Journal of Tourism, Sport and Creative Industries*, 5(6), 5–18.

Evans, G., & Foord, J. (2000) European funding of culture: Promoting common culture or regional growth? *Cultural Trends*, 9(36), 53–87.

Evans, G., & Shaw, P. (2004) *The Contribution of Culture to Regeneration in the UK: A Review of Evidence.* London: LondonMet.

Fairley, S., Tyler, B. D., Kellett, P., & D'Elia, K. (2011) The Formula One Australian Grand Prix: Exploring the triple bottom line. *Sport Management Review*, 14, 141–152.

Florida, R. (2004 [2002]) *The Rise of the Creative Class: And How It's Transforming Work, Leisure, Community, and Everyday Life.* New York: Basic Books.

Freestone, R., & Gibson, C. (2006) The cultural dimension of urban strategic planning. In Monclús, J., & Guárdia, M. (eds.) *Culture, Urbanism and Planning.* Burlington: Ashgate, 22–41.

Fusco Girard, L., Kourtit, K., & Nijkamp, P. (2014) Waterfront areas as hotspots of sustainable and creative development of cities. *Sustainability*, 6, 4580–4586.

García, B. (2004a) Cultural policy and urban regeneration in western European cities: Lessons from experience, prospects for the future. *Local Economy*, 19(4), 312–326.

García, B. (2004b) Urban regeneration, arts programming and major events. *International Journal of Cultural Policy*, 10(1), 103–118.

García, B. (2005) Deconstructing the City of Culture: The long-term cultural legacies of Glasgow 1990. *Urban Studies*, 42(5–6), 841–868.

García, B., Melville, R., & Cox, T. (2010) *Creating an Impact: Liverpool's Experience as European Capital of Culture.* Liverpool: Impact 08, University of Liverpool and Liverpool John Moores University.

Getz, D. (1997) *Event Management and Event Tourism.* New York: Cognizant Communication Corporation.

Gibson, L., & Stevenson, D. (2004) Urban spaces and the uses of culture. *International Journal of Cultural Policy*, 10(1), 1–4.

Gomes, P., & Librero-Cano, A. (2018) Evaluating three decades of the European Capital of Culture programme: A difference-in-differences approach. *Journal of Cultural Economics*, 42, 57–73.

Gotham, K. F. (2005) Theorizing urban spectacles. *City*, 9(2), 225–246.

Griffiths, R. (2006) City/culture discourses: Evidence from the competition to select the European capital of culture 2008. *European Planning Studies*, 14(4), 415–430.

Gruneau, R., & Horne, J. (2016) Mega-events and globalization: A critical introduction. In Gruneau, R., & Horne, J. (eds.) *Mega-Events and Globalization: Capital and Spectacle in a Changing World Order.* London and New York: Routledge, 1–28.

Hall, M. C. (1992) *Hallmark Tourist Events.* London: Belhaven Press.

Hall, M. C. (2006) Urban entrepreneurship, corporate interests and sports mega-events: The thin policies of competitiveness within the hard outcomes of neoliberalism. *The Sociological Review*, 54(s2), 59–70.

Hall, P. (1993) Waterfronts: A new urban frontier. In Bruttomesso, R. (ed.) *Waterfronts: A New Frontier for Cities on Water.* Venice: Centro Internazionale Città d'Acqua, 12–20.

Hall, P. V., & Jacobs, W. (2012) Why are maritime ports (still) urban, and why should policymakers care? *Maritime Policy & Management*, 39(2), 189–206.

Hanson, S., Nicholls, R., Ranger, N., Hallegatte, S., Corfee-Morlot, J., Herweijer, C., & Chateau, J. (2011) A global ranking of port cities with high exposure to climate extremes. *Climatic Change*, 104, 89–111.

Harvey, D. (1989a) Down towns. *Marxism Today*, January, 21.

Harvey, D. (1989b) From managerialism to entrepreneurialism: The transformation in urban governance in late capitalism. *Geografiska Annaler*, 70(1), 3–17.

Hayuth, Y. (1988) Changes on the waterfront: A model-based approach. In Hoyle, B. S., Pinder, D. A., & Husain, M. S. (eds.) *Revitalising the Waterfront: International Dimensions of Dockland Redevelopment.* London: Belhaven Press, 52–64.

Hayuth, Y., & Hilling, D. (1992) Technological change and seaport development. In Hoyle, B. S., & Pinder, D. A. (eds.) *European Port Cities in Transition.* London: Belhaven Press, 40–58.

Hein, C. (2011) Port cityscapes: A networked analysis of the built environment. In Hein, C. (ed.) *Port Cities: Dynamic Landscapes and Global Networks.* London and New York: Routledge, 1–23.

Hein, C. (2018) Oil spaces: The global petroleumscape in the Rotterdam/The Hague area. *Journal of Urban History*, 44(5), 887–929.

Hein, C. (2021) Port city porosity: Boundaries, flows, and territories. *Urban Planning*, 6(3), 1–9.

Hein, C., Luning, S., & van de Laar, P. (2021) Port city cultures, values, and maritime mindsets: Defining what makes port cities special. *European Journal of Creative Practices in Cities and Landscapes*, 4(1), 7–20.

Henderson, J. C., Foo, K., Lim, H., & Yip, S. (2010) Sports events and tourism: The Singapore Formula One Grand Prix. *International Journal of Event and Festival Management*, 1(1), 60–73.

Hesse, M. (2013) Cities and flows: Re-asserting a relationship as fundamental as it is delicate. *Journal of Transport Geography*, 29, 33–42.

Hiller, H. H. (1998) Assessing the impact of mega-events: A linkage model. *Current Issues in Tourism*, 1(1), 47–57.

Hiller, H. H. (2000) Mega-events, urban boosterism and growth strategies: An analysis of the objectives and legitimations of the Cape Town 2004 Olympic bid. *International Journal of Urban and Regional Research*, 24(2), 436–458.

Hiller, H. H. (2006) Post-event outcomes and the post-modern turn: The Olympics and urban transformations. *European Sport Management Quarterly*, 6(4), 317–332.

Hitters, E. (2007) Porto and Rotterdam as European Capitals of Culture: Towards the festivalization of urban cultural policy. In Richards, G. (ed.) *Cultural Tourism: Global and Local Perspectives*. New York: Haworth Press, 281–301.

Hoyle, B. S. (1988) Development dynamics at the port-city interface. In Hoyle, B. S., Pinder, D. A., & Husain, M. S. (eds.) *Revitalising the Waterfront: International Dimensions of Dockland Redevelopment*. London: Belhaven Press, 3–19.

Hoyle, B. S. (1989) The port-city interface: Trends, problems and examples. *Geoforum*, 20(4), 429–435.

Hoyle, B. S. (2000) Global and local change on the port-city waterfront. *The Geographical Review*, 90(3), 395–417.

Hoyle, B. S., & Pinder, D. A. (eds.) (1992) *European Port Cities in Transition*. London: Belhaven Press.

ICC (2012) *It's Not Winning . . . Reconsidering the Cultural City*. A report on the Cultural City Research Network. Available at: http://culturalcitiesresearch.net/wpcontent/uploads/2012/07/Cultural-Cities-FINAL-report-July-2012.pdf [Accessed 23/12/2016].

Jauhiainen, J. S. (1995) Waterfront redevelopment and urban policy: The case of Barcelona, Cardiff and Genoa. *European Planning Studies*, 3(1), 3–23.

John, A., & Jackson, S. (2010) Call me loyal: Globalization, corporate nationalism and the America's Cup. *International Review for the Sociology of Sport*, 46(4), 399–417.

Jonas, A. E. G., Wurzel, R. K. W., Monaghan, E., & Osthorst, W. (2017) Climate change, the green economy and reimagining the city: The case of structurally disadvantaged European maritime port cities. *Die Erde*, 148(4), 197–211.

Jones, Z. M. (2020) *Cultural Mega-Events: Opportunities and Risks for Heritage Cities*. London: Routledge.

Jones, Z. M., & Ponzini, D. (2018) Mega-events and the preservation of urban heritage: Literature gaps, potential overlaps, and a call for further research. *Journal of Planning Literature*, 33(4), 433–450.

Kim, M. K., Kim, S.-K., Park, J.-A., Carroll, M., Yu, J.-G., & Na, K. (2017) Measuring the economic impacts of major sports events: The case of Formula One Grand Prix (F1). *Asia Pacific Journal of Tourism Research*, 22(1), 64–73.

Kokot, W. (2008) Port cities as areas of transition: Comparative ethnographic research. In Kokot, W., Wildner, K., & Wonneberger, A. (eds.) *Port Cities as Areas of Transition: Ethnographic Perspectives*. Bielefeld: Transcript Verlag, 7–24.

Kostopoulou, S. (2013) On the revitalized waterfront: Creative milieu for creative tourism. *Sustainability*, 5, 4578–4593.

Kowalewski, M. (2018) Images and spaces of port cities in transition. *Space and Culture*, 24(1), 53–65.

Lauermann (2016a) Boston's Olympic bid and the evolving urban politics of event-led development. *Urban Geography*, 37(2), 313–321.

Lauermann, J. (2016b) Temporary projects, durable outcomes: Urban development through failed Olympic bids? *Urban Studies*, 53(9), 1885–1901.

Lee, S. W., Song, D.-W., & Ducruet, C. (2008) A tale of Asia's world ports: The spatial evolution in global hub port cities. *Geoforum*, 39, 372–385.

Lorente, J. P. (2002) Urban cultural policy and urban regeneration: The special case of declining port cities: Liverpool, Marseilles, Bilbao. In Crane, D., Kawashima, N., & Kawasaki, K. (eds.) *Global Culture: Media, Arts, Policy and Globalization*. New York: Routledge, 93–104.

Macbeth, J., Selwood, J., & Veitch, S. (2012) Paradigm shift or a drop in the ocean? The America's Cup impact on Fremantle. *Tourism Geographies*, 14(1), 162–182.

MacLeod, G. (2002) From urban entrepreneurialism to a 'revanchist city'? On the spatial injustices of Glasgow's Renaissance. *Antipode*, 34(3), 602–624.

Mah, A. (2014) *Port Cities and Global Legacies: Urban Identity, Waterfront Work, and Radicalism*. Basingstoke: Palgrave MacMillan.

Malone, P. (ed.) (1996) *City, Capital and Water*. London: Routledge.

Marshall, R. (2001) Contemporary urban space-making at the water's edge. In Marshall, R. (ed.) *Waterfronts in Post-Industrial Cities*. London: Spon Press, 3–14.

McCann, E., & Ward, K. (eds.) (2011) *Mobile Urbanism: Cities and Policymaking in the Global Age*. Minneapolis: University of Minnesota Press.

McDermott, P., Máiréad, N. C., & Strani, K. (2016) Public space, collective memory and intercultural dialogue in a (UK) city of culture. *Identities: Global Studies in Culture and Power*, 23(5), 610–627.

Merckx, F., Notteboom, T. E., & Winkelmans, W. (2004) Spatial models of waterfront redevelopment: The tension between city and ports revisited. *IAME 2004 Conference*, Izmir, 30 June–2 July.

Meyer, H. (1999) *City and Port: Urban Planning as a Cultural Venture in London, Barcelona, New York, and Rotterdam: Changing Relation between Public Urban Space and Large-Scale Infrastructure*. Rotterdam: International Books.

Middleton, C., & Freestone, P. (2008) The impact of culture-led regeneration on regional identity in North East England. *Regional Studies Association International Conference 'The Dilemmas of Integration and Competition'*, Prague, 27–29 May.

Miles, M. (2005) Interruptions: Testing the rhetoric of culturally led urban development. *Urban Studies*, 42(5–6), 889–911.

Miller, T. (2016) Greenwashed sports and environmental activism: Formula 1 and FIFA. *Environmental Communication*, 10(6), 719–733.

Molotch, H. (1976) The city as a growth machine: Towards a political economy of place. *American Journal of Sociology*, 82(2), 309–332.

Monclús, J. F. (2006) International exhibitions and planning: Hosting large-scale events as place promotion and as catalysts of urban regeneration. In Monclús, J. F., & Guárdia, M. (eds.) *Culture, Urbanism and Planning*. Burlington: Ashgate, 215–239.

Mooney, G. (2004) Cultural policy as urban transformation? Critical reflections on Glasgow, European City of Culture 1990. *Local Economy*, 19(4), 327–340.

Mould, O. (2017) *Urban Subversion and the Creative City*. London: Routledge.

Müller, M. (2015) What makes an event a mega-event? Definitions and sizes. *Leisure Studies*, 34(6), 627–642.

Muñoz, F. (2015) Olympic urbanism and Olympic Villages: Planning strategies in Olympic host cities, London 1908 to London 2012. *The Sociological Review*, 54(2), 175–187.

Myerscough, J. (1988) *The Economic Importance of the Arts in Britain*. London: Policy Studies Institute.

Ng, A. K. Y., Ducruet, C., Jacobs, W., Monios, J., Notteboom, T., Rodrigue, J.-P., Slack, B., Tamg, K., & Wil, G. (2014) Port geography at the crossroads with human geography: Between flows and spaces. *Journal of Transport Geography*, 41, 84–96.

Nichols, G., & Savage, M. (2017) A social analysis of an elite constellation: The case of Formula 1. *Theory, Culture & Society*, 34(5–6), 201–225.

Norcliffe, G., Bassett, K., & Hoare, T. (1996) The emergence of postmodernism on the urban waterfront: Geographical perspectives on changing relationships. *Journal of Transport Geography*, 4(2), 123–134.

Notteboom, T. E., De Langen, P., & Jacobs, W. (2013) Institutional plasticity and path dependence in seaports: Interactions between institutions, port governance reforms and port authority routines. *Journal of Transport Geography*, 27, 26–35.

Notteboom, T. E., & Winkelmans, W. (2001) Structural changes in logistics: How will port authorities face the challenge? *Maritime Policy & Management*, 28(1), 71–89.

Olivier, D., & Slack, B. (2006) Rethinking the port. *Environment and Planning A*, 38, 1409–1427.

Orams, M. B., & Brons, A. (1999) Potential impacts of a major sport/tourism event: The America's Cup 2000, Auckland, New Zealand. *Visions in Leisure and Business*, 18(1), 14–28.

Pagés Sánchez, J., & Daamen, T. A. (2020) Governance and planning issues in European waterfront redevelopment 1999–2019. In Carpenter, A., & Lozano, R. (eds.) *European Port Cities in Transition: Moving towards More Sustainable Sea Transport Hubs*. Cham: Springer, 127–148.

Pape, M. (2016) EU port cities and port area regeneration. *European Union*. Available at: www.europarl.europa.eu/RegData/etudes/BRIE/2016/593500/EPRS_BRI(2016)593500_EN.pdf [Accessed 31/10/2019].

Parker, K. (2003a) The circus is in town: Exploring consumption, mobility, and corporate capitalism in the world of Formula 1 motor racing. *Social Change in the 21st Century Conference*, Brisbane, 21 November.

Parker, K. (2003b) Two visions of globalisation: An account of the America's Cup Harbour and South Auckland. *Creating Spaces Conference: Interdisciplinary Writings in the Social Science*, Canberra, July.

Parra Camacho, D., Añó Sanz, V., & Calabuig Moreno, F. (2016) Percepción de los residentes sobre el legado de la America's Cup. *Cuadernos de Psicología del Deporte*, 16(1), 325–338.

Peck, J. (2005) Struggling with the creative class. *International Journal of Urban and Regional Research*, 29(4), 740–770.

Ponzini, D. (2012) Competing cities and spectacularizing urban landscapes. In Anheier, H., & Yudhishthir, R. I. (eds.) *Cities, Cultural Policy and Governance*. London: Sage, 99–102.

Porfyriou, H., & Sepe, M. (2017) Introduction: Port cities and waterfront developments: From the re-actualization of history to a new city image. In Porfyriou, H., & Sepe, M. (eds.) *Waterfront Revisited: European Ports in a Historic and Global Perspective*. New York and London: Routledge, 1–16.

Prichard, C. (2000) Hailing a nation of TV sailors: A preliminary critical discourse analysis of the televisual practices of the America's Cup. *NSCA Conference 2000*, Lismore, 3–5 July.

Quinn, B. (2005) Arts festivals and the city. *Urban Studies*, 42(5–6), 927–943.

Richards, G., & Wilson, J. (2004) The impact of cultural events on city Image: Rotterdam, Cultural Capital of Europe 2001. *Urban Studies*, 41(10), 1931–1951.

Richards, G., & Wilson, J. (2006) Developing creativity in tourist experiences: A solution to the serial reproduction of culture? *Tourism Management*, 27, 1209–1223.

Ritchie, J. R. B. (1984) Assessing the impact of hallmark events: Conceptual and research issues. *Journal of Travel Research*, 22(1), 2–11.

Roberts, P. (2017 [1999]) The evolution, definition and purpose of urban regeneration. In Roberts, P., Sykes, H., & Granger, R. (eds.) *Urban Regeneration*. 2nd edition. London: Sage, 9–43.

Roche, M. (1994) Mega-events and urban policy. *Annals of Tourism Research*, 21, 1–19.

Roche, M. (2000) *Mega-Events and Modernity: Olympics and Expos in the Growth of Global Culture*. London: Routledge.

Roche, M. (2017) *Mega-Events and Social Change: Spectacle, Legacy and Public Culture*. Manchester: Manchester University Press.

Sadd, D. (2009) What is event-led regeneration? Are we confusing terminology or will London 2012 be the first games to truly benefit the local existing population? *Event Management*, 13, 265–275.

Sairinen, R., & Kumpulainen, S. (2006) Assessing social impacts in urban waterfront regeneration. *Environmental Impact Assessment Review*, 26, 120–135.

Scherer, J. (2011) Olympic Villages and large-scale urban development: Crises of capitalism, deficits of democracy? *Sociology*, 45(5), 782–797.

Schubert, D. (2008) Transformation processes on waterfronts in seaport cities: Causes and trends between divergence and convergence. In Kokot, W., Wildner, K., & Wonneberger, A. (eds.) *Port Cities as Areas of Transition: Ethnographic Perspectives*. Bielefeld: Transcript Verlag, 25–46.

Schubert, D. (2011a) Seaport cities: Phases of spatial restructuring and types and dimensions of redevelopment. In Hein, C. (ed.) *Port Cities: Dynamic Landscapes and Global Networks*. London and New York: Routledge, 54–69.

Schubert, D. (2011b) Waterfront revitalizations: From a local to a regional perspective in London, Barcelona, Rotterdam, and Hamburg. In Desfor, G., Laidley, J., Stevens, Q., & Schubert, D. (eds.) *Transforming Urban Waterfronts: Fixity and Flow*. London and New York: Routledge, 74–97.

Schubert, D. (2017) The transformation of north-western European urban waterfronts: Divergence and convergence of redevelopment strategies. In Porfyriou, H., & Sepe, M. (eds.) *Waterfronts Revisited: European Ports in a Historic and Global Perspective*. London and New York: Routledge, 191–206.

Shaw, B. (2009) Historic port cities: Issues of heritage, politics and identity. *Historic Environment*, 22(2), 6–11.

Shaw, B. (2001) History at the water's edge. In Marshall, R. (ed.) *Waterfronts in Post-Industrial Cities*. London: Spon Press, 160–172.

Short, J. R. (1999) Urban imagineers: Boosterism and the representation of cities. In Jonas, A. E. G., & Wilson, D. (eds.) *The Urban Growth Machine: Critical Perspectives Two Decades Later*. Albany: State University of New York Press, 37–54.

Smith, A. (2012) *Events and Urban Regeneration: The Strategic Use of Events to Revitalise Cities*. London and New York: Routledge.

Smith, A., & Fox, T. (2007) From 'event-led' to 'event-themed' regeneration: The 2002 Commonwealth Games Legacy Programme. *Urban Studies*, 4(5/6), 1125–1143.

Smith, M. (2007) Space, place and placelessness in the culturally regenerated city. In Richards, G. (ed.) *Cultural Tourism: Global and Local Perspectives*. New York: Hawthorn Press, 91–111.

Soutar, G. N., & McLeod, P. B. (1993) Residents' perception on impact of the America's Cup. *Annals of Tourism Research*, 20, 571–582.

Stevenson, D. (2004) Civic gold rush: Cultural planning and the politics of the third way. *International Journal of Cultural Policy*, 10(1), 119–131.

Tomlinson, A., & Young, C. (eds.) (2006) *National Identity and Global Sports Events: Culture, Politics and Spectacle in the Olympics and the Football World Cup*. Albany: State University of New York Press.

Tomlinson, J. (1999) *Globalization and Culture*. Chicago: University of Chicago Press.

Tommarchi, E., & Bianchini, F. (2022) A heritage-inspired cultural mega event in a stigmatised city: Hull UK City of Culture 2017. *European Planning Studies*, 30(3), 478–498.

Tommarchi, E., & Cavalleri, F. (2020) City/Capital of Culture schemes in European medium-sized coastal cities: The cases of Hull (UK) and Pafos (Cyprus). In Di Vita, S., & Wilson, M. (eds.) *Planning and Managing Smaller Events: Downsizing the Urban Spectacle*. London and New York: Routledge, 128–143.

Tufts, S. (2004) Building the 'competitive city': Labour and Toronto's bid to host the Olympic games. *Geoforum*, 35, 47–58.

Tunbridge, J., & Ashworth, G. (1992) Leisure resource development in city port revitalization: The tourist-historic dimension. In Hoyle, B. S., & Pinder, D. A. (eds.) *European Port Cities in Transition*. London: Belhaven Press, 177–199.

Vallega, A. (1993) Waterfront redevelopment: A central objective for coastal management. In Bruttomesso, R. (ed.) *Waterfronts: A New Frontier for Cities on Water*. Venice: Centro Internazionale Città d'Acqua, 24–31.

Van den Bergh, R., Nivard, M., & Kreijkes, M. (2016) *Long-Term Prospects for Northwest European Refining: Asymmetric Change: A Looming Government Dilemma*. The Hague: Clingendael International Energy Programme.

Van Hooydonk, E. (2007) *Soft Values of Seaports: A Strategy for the Restoration of Public Support of Seaports*. Antwerp: Garant.

Van Hooydonk, E. (2009) Port city identity and urban planning. *Portus*, 18, 16–23.

Verhoeven, P. (2010) A review of port authority functions: Towards a renaissance? *Maritime Policy & Management*, 37(3), 247–270.

Vickery, J. (2007) *The Emergence of Culture-Led Regeneration: A Policy Concept and Its Discontents*. Warwick: Centre for Cultural Policy Studies.

Vries, I. (2014) From shipyard to brainyard: The redevelopment of RDM as an example of a contemporary port-city relationship. In Alix, Y., Delsalle, B., & Comtois, C. (eds.) *Port-City Governance*. Paris: Editions EMS, 107–126.

Ward, S. (2011) Port cities and the global exchange of planning ideas. In Hein, C. (ed.) *Port Cities: Dynamic Landscapes and Global Networks*. London and New York: Routledge, 70–85.

Ward, S. V. (2017) Internationalizing port regeneration: Models and emulators. In Porfyriou, H., & Sepe, M. (eds.) *Waterfronts Revisited: European Ports in a Historic and Global Perspective*. New York and London: Routledge, 95–107.

Warsewa, G. (2006) The transformation of European port cities: Final report on the new EPOC port city audit. *IAW Forschungsbericht*, 11. Bremen: University of Bremen.

Warsewa, G. (2017) The transformation of port cities: Local culture and the post-industrial maritime city. *WIT Transactions on the Built Environment*, 170, 149–159.

Wiegmans, B. W., & Louw, E. (2011) Changing port-city relations at Amsterdam: A new phase at the interface? *Journal of Transport Geography*, 19, 575–583.

Wiese, A., & Thierstein, A. (2014) European port cities: Embodiments of interaction-knowledge and freight flows as catalyst of spatial development. In Coventz, S., Derudder,

B., Thierstein, A., & Witlox, F. (eds.) *Hub Cities in the Knowledge Economy*. London: Routledge, 95–119.

Yarker, S. (2018) Tangential attachments: Towards a more nuanced understanding of the impacts of cultural urban regeneration on local identities. *Urban Studies*, 55(15), 3421–3436.

Zukin, S. (2006 [1995]) *The Cultures of Cities*. Cambridge and Oxford: Blackwell.

Zukin, S. (2009) Changing landscapes of power: Opulence and the urge for authenticity. *International Journal of Urban and Regional Research*, 33(2), 543–553.

3 Waterfront redevelopment and the rationale for hosting mega events

This chapter looks more in depth into the rationale behind waterfront redevelopment and the transformation of former port areas in central city locations, as well as into how culture and mega events have been mobilised as catalysts to achieve physical and symbolic transformation in maritime port cities. The chapter explores how these aspects work on the ground by engaging with the experience of the four case-study cities of the book. Firstly, it provides background information about these cities. Secondly, it reconstructs the trajectories of port and urban development in these cities, shedding light on the rationale for hosting large-scale cultural or sporting events. Thirdly, it shows how these events have been deployed to achieve physical transformation on the waterfront or to reshape the image of these cities. This information supports the discussion of mega events within the spatial, political and symbolic relationships between ports and cities in the remainder of the book.

Introducing four European port cities

The book explores event-led regeneration in port cities focusing on four case-study cities, namely Hull (UK), Rotterdam (The Netherlands), Genoa (Italy) and Valencia (Spain). This section looks at the geographies, the socio-economic contexts and political settings of these cities. It then reconstructs their long-term trajectories of urban regeneration at the water's edge, with the aim of exploring how physical and symbolic processes of urban transformation in these cities led to the rationale for hosting mega events.

Hull

Kingston upon Hull, or Hull, is a port city in Northern England, at the junction between the River Hull and the Humber Estuary, at approximately 30 km from the North Sea coast. Although it is located at the end of the M62 corridor, which connects major cities such as Liverpool, Manchester and Leeds, Hull is characterised – as in the case of many European port and coastal cities – by a certain extent of geographical isolation.

DOI: 10.4324/9781003165811-3

Approximately 310,000 people live in Hull's urban area, which includes nearby towns such as Hessle, Anlaby and Cottingham. The city's overall catchment area is home to a population of approximately 500,000 inhabitants.[1] Hull's population grew steadily during the Industrial Revolution, peaking at about 300,000 inhabitants in the 1930s, and then gradually declined over the rest of the century. The recent increase to about 260,000 inhabitants is predominantly linked to immigration. Hull displays a relatively younger population in comparison with the national average.[2] Although for most of the 20th and early 21st centuries Hull's population has not been significantly diverse (Evans, 2017, p. 170), with ethnic minority groups accounting for a small proportion of the total population (Platts-Fowler & Robinson, 2015, p. 483), the last fifteen years have heralded a growing number of asylum seekers and refugees from the Balkans and the Middle East, as well as of workers from Eastern Europe. Hull's foreign-born population tends to concentrate in the city centre and the University area, as well as along Beverley Road. The local government has traditionally been led by the Labour Party, apart from a short Labour minority government in 2003–2006 and a Liberal Democratic leadership from 2007 to 2010. In the 2016 EU Referendum,[3] Leave vote in Hull accounted for 67% (Hull City Council, 2016, see Chapter 4).

Rotterdam

Rotterdam is the largest container port in Europe and the second largest city in the Netherlands. It is part of the urban region known as the Randstad (edge city), which also includes Amsterdam, The Hague and Utrecht. Rotterdam is located approximately 50 km inland, at the junction between the River Rotte and the Nieuwe Maas. As in the case of Hull, this is due to the fact that inland ports on rivers and estuaries are naturally protected from the North Sea. However, the working port of Rotterdam gradually moved towards the coast.

The population within the municipality of Rotterdam accounts for approximately 630,000 people. The city is nonetheless part of a metropolitan region including The Hague and Delft, with a population of 2.3 million.[4] The Randstad is the fourth largest urban area in Europe after London, Paris and Rhine-Ruhr, with a population of 8.1 million (Regio Randstad, 2017). Post-war demographic growth was curbed by the 1970s economic crisis and by the impact of the 1960s national overspill policy, aimed at encouraging people to move from the country's largest cities to satellites cities (Hajer, 1993, pp. 52–53). Rotterdam, where nearly half of residents are foreign-born (Entzinger & Godfried, 2014, p. 4) can be understood as a superdiverse city (Scholten et al., 2019). Immigrants from China and the Dutch former colonies concentrated in the city's working-class neighbourhoods, in particular in the south of the city. A geographical divide has historically distinguished the wealthier north bank of the river, where the city centre is located, from the poorer south bank, although this difference is being levelled. The City Council has traditionally implemented open integration policies. However, from 2002 to 2006, resentments towards immigrants encouraged a more assimilationist policy (Dekker et al., 2015, p. 643). Since 2006, immigration policies have been focusing on participation in local labour market and socio-economic activities (ibid., p. 644).

Although the port plays a crucial role in terms of employment in all the four localities, the port of Rotterdam stands out in terms of traffic and value added to the economy, which is estimated to be approximately 2.6–2.7% of the Dutch GDP (Erasmus Centre for Urban, Port and Transport Economics, 2018, p. 17).

Rotterdam City Council was led by the Dutch Labour Party from 1945 to 1998. Mayor Bram Peper, who led the Council from 1982 to 1998, was the promoter of the European Capital of Culture 2001. The 2002 General Elections were overshadowed by the assassination of Pim Fortuyn, leader of the populist movement Liveable Netherlands. In 2002, the local branch of the movement, Liveable Rotterdam, became the first party in the city with 37% of the votes. A coalition led by Liveable Rotterdam governed the Council from 2002 to 2006 and from 2014 to 2018. At the time of writing, the Council is led by a coalition consisting of Greens, Liberal-Democrats, D66 Social-Liberals and the Labour Party.

Genoa

Genoa is one of Italy's main ports and the sixth largest city in the country. It is located in Northwest Italy, between the hills and mountains of the Appennino Ligure and the Ligurian Sea. The city centre faces Porto Antico (the old harbour). Although Genoa is close to Milan, Turin and the Po Valley, the Appennino immediately at its periphery and a relatively weak transport network influence its connectivity with Northern Italy. Genoa can be considered as 'an outstanding and long lasting example of a City-Port, that is: (i) a representative type of a city whose morphology and economy are strictly connected to the presence of a port and the way it works; (ii) an exceptional one, as the city has maintained its basic function' (Bobbio, 2005, p. 1). Because of its location between the mountains and the Mediterranean Sea, the city, together with its the port, grew along the coast.

In Genoa, demographic growth mirrored Italy's economic boom in the 1950s and 1960s, when Genoa, Milan and Turin marked the Industrial Triangle, that is the core industrial region of Italy. The city's population peaked in the early 1970s at more than 800,000 inhabitants. However, since the 1970s, port restructuring within a broader context of deindustrialisation and decline of state-owned heavy and manufacturing industries fuelled a declining demographic trend (ibid., p. 2), which brought the population within the city's boundaries to 580,000 inhabitants. Genoa's population in the wider metropolitan area is about 850,000.[5] A relevant aspect to consider is a notable ageing process, as in the rest of the country. The city is home to a relatively large Ecuadorian community and to migrants from Eastern Europe, the Balkans, North Africa and East Asia, who tend to concentrate in the city centre.

A fragmented picture characterises the history of local government in Genoa, with shorter administrations led by the Christian Democratic Party, the Socialist Party and the Republican Party until 1997. The Council was then led by the Democratic Party until 2012. Mayor Giuseppe Pericu was in office until 2007 and then replaced by Mayor Marta Vincenzi. Although the political hue of the Council did not change in that period, the 2007 Local Elections marked a change of approach. Mayor Vincenzi announced that she would act in *discontinuity* with the approach that was behind the hosting of mega events (see e.g. Rizzini, 2008), by implementing a programme more oriented to sustainability, greater quality of life and balance of port-city relationships (Gastaldi, 2012, p. 34). At the time of writing, the Council is led by a right-wing coalition including the populist Northern League and independent parties, in office since 2017.

Valencia

Valencia is the third largest city in Spain and one of the busiest commercial ports on the Mediterranean. The city was established by the Romans on a fertile plain, the Horta,[6] approximately 5 km inland along the natural bed of the River Túria, which was diverted to the south of the city after the 1957 flood. The port of Valencia directly faces the Mediterranean Sea and is surrounded by a number of historic maritime villages, namely Cabanyal, Grau, Malvarrosa and Natzaret. These were annexed to the Municipality of Valencia at the end of the 19th century, forming the Poblats Marítims district, and were gradually connected to the city through urban development along Avenida Blasco Ibañez (Prytherch & Boira i Maiques, 2009, p. 105). This port-city physical separation is due to the fact that Spanish port cities were established directly on the coast where the presence of hills helped defend them from pirate attacks. This is the case for example of Barcelona (protected by Montjuïc), Alicante (Benacantil) and Málaga (Gibralfaro), while other port cities such as Valencia and Castellón de la Plana were established inland due to the lack of such natural defensive structures. In Valencia, more than 800,000 people live within the city's administrative boundaries, while the metropolitan area hosts a population of 1.5 million inhabitants.[7] A marked ageing process characterises Valencia's demographics, as in the case of Genoa (Figure 3.1).

After the end of Francoism, Valencia was governed by the Partido Socialista Obrero Español (Spanish Socialist Workers' Party – PSOE) until 1991. In 1982, a socialist electoral sweep known as 'el cambio' ('the change', ibid., p. 107) marked the beginning of a deep revision of the 1966 spatial plan. The vision for the future of Valencia, however, radically changed after 1991, when the leadership of the Council shifted to a right-wing coalition consisting of the conservative Partido Popular (People's Party, PP) and the nationalist Unión Valenciana. Rita Barberá Nolla was elected mayor. Her party governed Valencia until 2015 with a considerable majority throughout subsequent elections. The highest majority (56.67%) was reached in 2007, the year of the America's Cup and

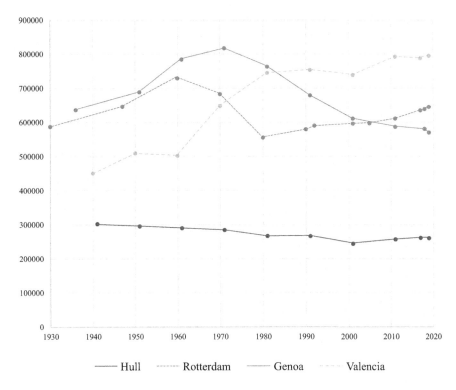

Figure 3.1 Population time series for the case-study cities. Figures consider local authorities only.

Sources: Hull – Office for National Statistics; Rotterdam – Centraal Bureau voor de Statistiek; Genoa – Censimento Generale della Popolazione e delle Abitazioni, ISTAT Istituto Nazionale di Statistica; Valencia – Censo de Población y Vivienda, Instituto Nacional de Estadística; Oficina de Estadística del Ayuntamiento de Valencia.

the agreement on the Formula One European Grand Prix. The conservative government pursued a vision of Valencia as a global tourist destination, which was founded on international events. In 2015, Joan Ribó became mayor and a left-wing coalition including Progressive Nationalists (Compromís), the Socialist Party (PSPV-PSOE) and Podemos has led the Council from 2015 to 2019. The 2019 Local elections confirmed Mayor Ribó and a coalition including Compromís and the Socialist Party.

Trajectories of port and urban development: the rationale for waterfront redevelopment and event-led regeneration

In the case-study cities, mega events represented significant moments along long-term trajectories of urban development and operated alongside the development of the port. This section looks at the key steps in port development in these cities and it briefly reconstructs the course of urban regeneration on the waterfront that anticipated the celebration of mega events.

Port development

Hull is a maritime gateway since the 12th century, with strong trade connections with many Hanseatic cities. Maritime trade has historically been the main economic activity. Whaling and shipbuilding thrived in particular since the 18th century along the River Hull.[8] The 18-fold increase in shipping tonnage from 1716 to 1793 (Kirby & Hinkkanen, 2000, p. 81), led to the development of the City Docks between the 1750s and the 1840s. Congestion remained a major issue, to the extent that some said that it used to take more time to enter the port of Hull rather than to sail to Hull from St. Petersburg (ibid., p. 81). This led to the construction of Victoria Dock, opened in 1850. Albert Dock and William Wright Dock were opened in 1880 to accommodate the needs of the fishing industry. Initially designed for coal trade, St. Andrew's Dock, completed in 1883, was used as a fishing dock (Figure 3.2).

The mid-19th century witnessed the decline of traditional whaling and the rise of fishing, to the extent that Hull and Grimsby became the main English ports for steam trawler traffic (Kerby et al., 2012, p. 624). With three million people transiting through them, Hull and Grimsby were also amongst the main

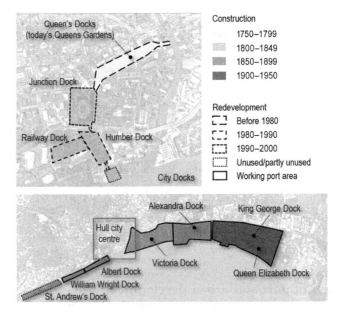

Figure 3.2 Evolution of the port of Hull.

Source: Background maps: Imagery ©2019 Google, Map data ©2019 Google.

UK ports for transmigration in the late 19th and early 20th centuries (Evans, 2001, p. 71). Prior to the Second World War, the port of Hull was considered the third most important one in the country (City of Hull Development Committee, 1937).

Hull's fishing industry entered a steady decline in the 1970s, due to a combination of factors including the oil crisis, overfishing, the UK-Iceland 'Cod Wars', competition from Eastern bloc fleets and the implementation of the European Common Fisheries Policy (Byrne, 2015, pp. 817–818). The contraction of the local fishing industry fuelled a steady economic decline, which nonetheless should be interpreted in the context of deindustrialisation and socio-economic decline in many UK coastal towns and cities. In the 1980s, port ownership and management in the UK changed due to privatisation and deregulation. Between 1981 and 1984, Associated British Ports (ABP) took control over 21 ports in the country, including Hull, and was privatised (Thomas, 1994, p. 142). Hull was also an exception in the general trend of decline of upstream urban ports as a result of containerisation (Baird, 1996, pp. 150–151).

In the 2010s, the port of Hull increasingly turned towards the renewable energy sector. In 2011, the UK government approved the Humber Renewable Energy Super Cluster and the Humber Green Port Corridor Enterprise Zones,[9] while the 2013 City Plan set the development of renewable energies as a strategic priority. In 2013, Hull City Council, East Riding of Yorkshire Council and Associated British Ports, along with partner organisations, issued the Green Port Hull vision, centred on the development of the port as a national hub for renewable energy. This created the conditions for German-based manufacturer Siemens to invest £310 million in a new wind turbine manufacturing plant at Alexandra Dock.

Rotterdam can be considered an exemplary case of mainport development against the structural changes facing port cities in the last decades (Hesse & McDonough, 2018, p. 361). Originally a fishing port, it grew as one of the Netherlands' colonial trading ports during the Dutch Golden Age. With the Industrial Revolution, both the city and the port grew rapidly. In the late 18th and early 19th centuries, port functions were moved to Waterstad, which subsequently included a blend of industrial and urban functions (Meyer, 1999, p. 293). In the 19th century, Rotterdam was in a strategic position to become a gateway to and from major industrial areas (ibid., p. 296), such as the Ruhr (Hesse & McDonough, 2018, p. 361). This led to the construction, initiated in 1864, of the Nieuwe Waterweg (New Waterway), which would provide a suitable connection to the North Sea. Port expansion concentrated in the Kop van Zuid on the opposite side of the river. Nonetheless, since the late 19th century, maritime functions began to migrate westwards, abandoning traditional urban port areas. Waalhaven and Merwehaven were completed in the first half of the 20th century. After the First World War, both the city and the port began to turn away from the Kop van Zuid (Meyer, 1999, p. 316). The massive bombing of Rotterdam occurred on 14th May 1940, known as the Rotterdam Blitz, caused extensive damage both to the city centre and the port estate. However, the reconstruction of the port was given priority over that of the city (McCarthy, 1999, p. 293), as the port was a key infrastructure for moving US military troops to West Germany at the beginning of the Cold War. The port developed towards the North Sea, as wider spaces and new facilities were required. Former port areas were abandoned, raising a range of issues including increasing crime levels.

In order to accommodate the needs of the growing petrochemical industry, which had made existing facilities inadequate, new port areas (Botlek and later Rotterdam Europoort) were developed. In the 1970s, the advent of containerisation led to a rapid restructuring and expansion of the port. Initially, port areas along the river, such as Waalhaven, were adapted for this purpose. However, the rapid growth of maritime traffic and in particular container traffic led in the 1980s to the development of Maasvlakte (Maas plain) on land reclaimed from the North Sea. Amsterdam Schiphol Airport and the port of Rotterdam were given priority in their development as the country's main transport infrastructures. This policy led to a major reclamation of land from the North Sea to develop Maasvlakte II, initiated in 2008 and in operation since 2013. This development, which is expected to be completed by 2030, made it possible for Rotterdam to host the largest container terminal in Europe, which is largely automatised (Figure 3.3).

Genoa is a good example to illustrate the traditionally tight port-city relationships at the foundations of the typical Mediterranean port city. Genoa was one of the city-states known as the Maritime Republics – together with Amalfi, Pisa and Venice, but also Ancona, Gaeta, Noli and Ragusa (today's Dubrovnik) – that ruled the Mediterranean in the Middle Age and Renaissance. As in the case of Venice, Genoa gradually declined as a maritime power – it was annexed to the Kingdom of Sardinia in the 19th century – due to the growing importance of transoceanic maritime trade routes via the Cape of Good Hope and to the Americas, which played to the detriment of the economic prosperity of many

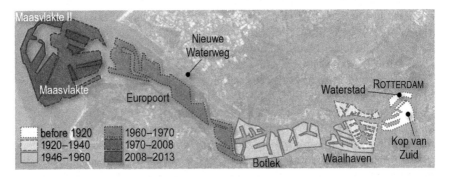

Figure 3.3 Evolution of the port of Rotterdam. Author's work, data from Port of Rotterdam.

Source: Background map: Imagery ©2019 Google, Data SIO, NOAA, US Navy, NGA, GEBCO, DigitalGlobe, Map data ©2019 Google.

Mediterranean port cities. However, Genoa's symbiotic relationship with the port and the sea through its history was the reason behind a very close physical, functional and cultural connection between the city and its port.

Until the 1920s, the port infrastructure was still located in Porto Antico (old harbour), in the very heart of the city. Prior to the Second World War, however, the port began to expand westwards with the construction of docks by the Lanterna (the historic lighthouse) and later at Sampierdarena. In 1930 the new passenger terminal (Stazione Marittima) was completed. Port facilities were heavily damaged during the Second World War, which led to a long period of reconstruction. In the 1950s and 1960s, the rise of state-owned petrochemical industry in Italy led to the development of the Multedo oil terminal. In the same period, the airport was built next to the oil terminal on land reclaimed from the sea, while in 1965 the Sopraelevata (flyover) was completed to improve the accessibility of the port. A waterfront area to the east of Porto Antico was transformed into the Fair complex, completed in 1960, to host commercial events. In the late 1960s, at the beginning of containerisation, the first container terminal was built at Sampierdarena.

A gradual decrease in traffic and a deep decline of the port itself followed between the mid-1970s and the early 1990s. This was fuelled by a number of factors including the collapse of state-owned heavy industry particularly since the 1980s and the growing struggle between port companies and *camalli* (how Genoese dock workers were referred to). As a response, new container terminals were developed, while the cruise and ferry terminals were renewed. This generated an increase in freight and passenger flows during the 1990s (Bobbio, 2005, p. 2). The port was further developed and restructured, also administratively, and was able to recover from the crisis (Bisio & Bobbio, 2003). Such restructuring had nonetheless a cost: heavy

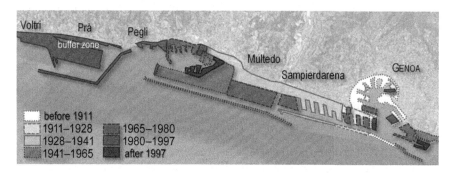

Figure 3.4 Evolution of the port of Genoa. Author's work, data from Autorità Portuale di Genova.

Source: Background map: Imagery ©2019 Google, Data SIO, NOAA, US Navy, NGA, GEBCO, TerraMetrics, Map data ©2019 Google.

industry, which used to provide 60% of local jobs in the 1970s, provided 20% of jobs in the 1990s (Bobbio, 2005, p. 6). The container terminal of Prà-Voltri was opened in 1992 and it currently marks the western edge of the port (Figure 3.4). This meant that Prà lost its seafront, generating a port-city conflict that was subsequently addressed through the construction of a public park and a canal for leisure purposes in the port buffer zone (called *fascia di rispetto portuale*) regulated by spatial planning laws. In 2001, the port plan that is still valid today was approved, replacing the 1964 plan. The port of Genoa is today part of the Western Ligurian Sea port system, which includes the ports of Savona and Vado Ligure.

In the case of Valencia, as mentioned, the lack of a natural harbour or of natural defensive structures was a major constraint to port development in ancient times. The port of Valencia was established in the late 15th century at Grau, with the construction of a pier called Pont de la Fusta. Valencia's traditional economy was based on agriculture and horticulture, while trade (including trade with the Americas), shipbuilding and fishing were its core maritime activities. Agricultural produces, in particular citrus, were exported via the port (Prytherch & Boira i Maiques, 2009, p. 105). The city grew towards the sea in parallel with the development of its port. A rapid process of industrialisation took place in the 20th century, in particular in relation to the production of rolling stock (see e.g. Del Álamo Andrés, 1999). The early 20th century heralded the construction of some of the iconic buildings that constitute the current port cityscape. For example, the passenger terminal now known as Edificio del Reloj was opened in 1916, the tinglados (sheds) were completed in the 1920s, and the Aduana Marítima (custom building) was opened in the 1930s. In these decades, shipyards were also developed within the historic harbour. The Gran Riada de Valencia (the Great Flood) in 1957 led to the so-called Solución Sur (South Solution) in 1958, consisting in the deviation of the River Túria to the south of the city and the provision of a new road access from the south. This spatial vision was included into the 1966 local plan, together with a proposal involving the construction of a bypass road on the dry bed of the Túria, whose natural mouth was also blocked by port expansion. In the 1970s, fishing and shipbuilding experienced a sharp contraction, which caused economic and demographic decline in Poblats Marítims (Del Romero Renau & Trudelle, 2011, p. 4).

Since the 1980s, the port has been developed for container traffic. The period between the late 1980s and early 2000s witnessed a considerable expansion of the port and the construction of a logistics area (Figure 3.5). From 1993 to 2006, maritime trade flows increased from 6.6 million tons to 40 million tons (Prytherch & Boira i Maiques, 2009, p. 110). The 2015 port plan aims at increasing container traffic up to 68 million tons, with the approval of the fourth container terminal announced in October 2018 (Valenciaport, 2018). This highly automatised terminal will be developed at the northern edge of the port, next to the exit channel of the leisure port and Malvarrosa beach.

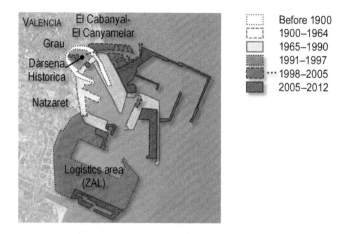

Figure 3.5 Evolution of the port of Valencia. Author's work, data from APV.

Source: Background map: Imagery ©2019 Google, DigitalGlobe, Map data ©2019 Google, Inst. Geogr. Nacional.

Before event-led regeneration: trajectories of urban regeneration in future port host cities

In Hull, many waterfront areas were transformed in the 1980s and early 1990s. Victoria Dock, closed in 1970, was purchased by the City Council from ABP in 1987 and redeveloped between 1988 and 2004 into Victoria Dock Village, a housing estate. Hull Marina opened in 1983 after the redevelopment of Humber and Railway Docks, while Junction Dock was redeveloped into Princes Quay Shopping Centre in 1991. Part of St. Andrew's Dock became a retail and leisure complex. The eastern part of the dock is a site of conflicting relationships between port and urban actors, where a proposal of redevelopment by Grosvenor Waterside has repeatedly been opposed by activist groups such as the St. Andrew's Dock Heritage Park Action Group (STAND) and by the City Council itself (Atkinson et al., 2002), who rejected a proposal including the demolition of the historic headquarters of the Lord Line trawler company in 2019.

The 1994 regeneration strategy (City Regeneration Strategy Group, 1994a, 1994b) aimed at addressing problems such as unemployment levels above the European, national and regional average, low educational aspirations and achievements, high levels of social deprivation, poverty and crime. Key elements were the regeneration of the city centre, in particular by strengthening its retail offer, but also the recognition of a developing port. Geographical Priority Areas for urban regeneration included the aforementioned eastern section of St. Andrew's Dock, still owned by ABP, and Sammy's Point, acquired by the City Council. The 2000 City Plan (Hull City Council, 2000) aimed at promoting the growth of the port and further regeneration on the waterfront, through a 'Docklands strategy'. Regeneration priority areas included King George, Queen Elizabeth and Alexandra Dock, Island Wharf – where the

Figure 3.6 The Deep aquarium in Hull.

World Trade Centre Hull & Humber opened in 2008 – and Sammy's Point, where the aquarium The Deep opened in 2002 (Figure 3.6).

Regenerating the city centre and strengthening its retail provisions were key objective in following sub-local planning documents, such as the 2003 City Centre Masterplan (Hull Citybuild, 2003) and the 2008 City Centre Area Action Plan (Hull City Council, 2008). The implementation of the latter was nonetheless halted in 2010 due to the impacts of the economic and financial crisis.

At the local scale, port development was encouraged. ABP was recognised as a key agency involved in the implementation of the 2000 City Plan itself. However, a first redevelopment of Alexandra Dock by ABP – a riverside container terminal referred to as Quay 2005 – encountered strong opposition from the community of Victoria Dock Village.[10] The 2013 City Plan (Hull City Council, n.d.) aims at making Hull an energy port city – a hub for renewable energies and maritime functions – and a leading destination for cultural tourism.

In Rotterdam, the 1946 Basisplan envisioned a completely different city centre (McCarthy, 1999, p. 295) shaped by the ideas of Dutch modernism, Le Corbusier and the CIAM movement (Hajer, 1993, p. 50). Although the restoration of the port was prioritised, the 1950s and 1960s witnessed a focus on the city centre due to housing shortages. Housing, particularly social housing, remained a priority in the following decade and was a pillar of the 1974 strategic plan (McCarthy, 1999, p. 298). The 1975 Discussienota

Herstructurering Oude Havengebieden (Working Paper on the Restructuring of Old Docklands) allocated new housing in Waterstad (Romein, 2005, p. 3).

By the end of the 20th century, social housing accounted for a substantial proportion of Rotterdam's housing stock,[11] contributing to high deprivation levels in the city centre. As a reaction to this and in line with similar trends in other European countries, the 1980s witnessed extensive regeneration of the city centre, driven by the idea that culture could be a means to promote the city as a place to live and invest (McCarthy, 1999, p. 299). The 1985 Binnestadsplan (Inner City Plan) was implemented around three core spatial concepts. Firstly, Waterstad was envisioned as an extension of the city centre and a maritime cultural quarter (Hajer, 1993, pp. 53–57), with the aim of reconnecting the city with the river (Romein, 2005, p. 4). Secondly, the Museum Triangle was intended as a cultural quarter around the art museum Boijmans van Beuningen. Thirdly, the plan included areas for high-rise developments, such as Wilhelminapier and Coolsingel (McCarthy, 1999, p. 300). Waterstad and Kop van Zuid were conceived as part of a Riverside City.

The implementation of the Binnestadsplan included the redevelopment of Kop van Zuid, a former port area that hosted Holland America Line's terminal of transoceanic liners. However, as the port migrated westwards in the 1960s and 1970s, maritime activities gradually abandoned the area. The redevelopment of Kop van Zuid was initially envisaged with the idea of prioritising social housing; however, this vision changed in the mid-1980s, as Kop van Zuid was understood as an asset to unite the north and south banks in physical, economic and social terms (Doucet, 2013, pp. 2039–2040). In 1986, the redevelopment scheme by Riek Bakker framed the new Kop van Zuid as a mixed-use area with a distinctive post-modern appearance created by high-rise buildings. Approved in 1991, the project was a 'collage city', seeking a tighter relationship between the city and the river (Meyer, 1999, pp. 361 and 371). A better connection with the city centre was ensured through the construction of the iconic Erasmusbrug (Erasmus Bridge) in 1995 (Figure 3.7).

In Genoa, the redevelopment of Porto Antico can be considered as a result of a series of actions, rather than a single large-scale transformation project (Gastaldi, 2012, p. 32). This involved the use of a variegated set of planning tools, ranging from statutory spatial planning to specific action programmes introduced in the national planning system in the 1990s, such as the national programme PRUSST (Programme for Urban Regeneration and Sustainable Regional Development) or the EU-funded scheme URBAN. In addition, other actions contributed to triggering and sustaining regeneration, such as the relocation of the Faculties of Economics and Architecture respectively in the Darsena and in the city centre. All these actions contributed to transforming Genoa from a 'City-Port' into a 'City on Water' (Bobbio, 2005, p. 2) and are arguably at the basis of recent discussions of waterfront redevelopment in the eastern area of the port. As in the other cases and in many European port cities, this regeneration process stemmed from port migration and restructuring. In the case of Genoa, as port-city relationships became more problematic, the city's waterfront was gradually rediscovered (ibid., p. 2). This process was

Figure 3.7 The Erasmus Bridge and the skyline of Kop van Zuid.

initiated in the mid–1980s, when Regione Liguria, Comune di Genova and Consorzio Autonomo del Porto (as the Port Authority was formerly known) signed an agreement about the displacement of port functions in Porto Antico and its redevelopment for leisure purposes. This transformation was triggered and driven by mega events and is therefore commented in the next section.

In Valencia, the transformation of the partly abandoned old harbour (Dársena Histórica) began in the 1980s. The discourse of waterfront redevelopment gained momentum in relation to the proposal of a linear park on the dry bed of the River Túria, which set the port and the seafront as points of reference (Llavador, 2010, p. 32). The linear park known as Jardín del Túria was built in stages from 1986. This intervention included flagship projects such as the Palau de la Música, a music venue built in 1987, the Palacio de Congresos, a congress hall designed by Norman Foster and built in 1998, and most notably Santiago Calatrava and Félix Candela's Ciutat de les Arts i les Ciències (City of Arts and Sciences), built at the south–eastern edge of the park between 1998 and 2002 (Figure 3.8).

This latter project, which costed approximately 1.28 billion Euros (Rius-Ulldemolins et al., 2019, p. 7), was envisioned by the city's Socialist government in 1989 as an attempt to trigger waterfront redevelopment on the basis of the experience of other European port cities (Carrasco & Pitarch-Garrido, 2017, p. 725).

Figure 3.8 Palau de la Música (top left) and Ciutat de les Arts i les Ciències.

The first convenio (agreement) between the city and the port in 1986 included the transformation of the Dársena into a leisure port – although constraints to permeability remained – and the Solución Sur, that is the southern access to the port and the city (Boira i Maiques, 2013). The 1988 spatial plan conveyed the willingness of connecting Valencia to the sea through the redevelopment of the Dársena (Boira i Maiques, 2013; Marrades, 2018, pp. 191–192). The plan focuses on the spatial concept of the 'T', which represented the implementation of Jardín del Túria and the redevelopment of the waterfront and Poblats Marítims (Sorribes i Monrabal, 2015, p. 238), particularly through the beach promenade now known as Paseo Marítimo and Paseo Neptuno.

The change in local government in 1991 marked a watershed in urban regeneration policies at the port-city interface, which began to focus on international visibility. The end of a short economic crisis in the country which took place between 1992 and 1995 – together with the impacts of the newly introduced 1994 Ley Urbanística (Town Planning Act) at the regional level, which simplified planning procedures – laid out the beginning of the 'reign' of Rita Barberá (ibid., p. 43), member of the People's Party and Mayor of Valencia from 1991 to 2015.

A second port-city convenio in 1997 examined the Balcón al Mar project, a proposal for a retail- and leisure-oriented redevelopment of the Dársena Histórica similar to that of Barcelona's Port Vell. This spatial vision, included in the 1988 spatial plan and the 1997 strategic plan, was subsequently reframed when Valencia was designated as the venue of the America's Cup 2007. A controversial pillar of the spatial vision of the Partido Popular (People's Party) was the idea, launched in 1998, of extending Avenida Blasco Ibañez towards the seafront, as in the case of Avinguda Diagonal in Barcelona.[12] This intervention would imply the demolition of approximately 1,600 buildings in El Cabanyal-El Canyamelar (Del Romero Renau & Trudelle, 2011, p. 4) and generated strong opposition, for example through the campaign Salvem el Cabanyal (Save Cabanyal).

Eventually, the local financial crisis that hit Valencia in the 2010s and the demise of the conservative local leadership prevented this project from being fully implemented and part of the traditional urban fabric was retained. As noted by Marrades (2018, p. 191, author's translation), the city's maritime districts 'survived a great fire, bombings during the Spanish Civil War, the [1957] flood and the predatory urbanism that severely damaged them'.

The rationale for hosting mega events

The appeal of mega events to policy makers and local actors relates to the pursuit of economic growth. In the case of events that are smaller in scale in comparison with the largest schemes, the driving forces behind the 'mega event race' to achieve growth appear more nuanced. In other words, one could observe different 'variegations' in the use of mega events in urban and economic regeneration which, depending on local specificities and settings, may prioritise aspects such as the creation of jobs locally, countering stigmatisation, economic diversification and capital accumulation through the real estate sector.

The case-study cities of the book display different baseline contexts and different rationales for hosting mega events as a means to pursue urban and economic development. Hull City Council bid twice for the UK City of Culture, first in 2010, when Derry-Londonderry was eventually awarded the title, and then successfully in 2013. The city displayed figures above the national average regarding unemployment, health issues and deprivation. The media impact and success among the general public of *The Idler Book of Crap Towns* (Jordison & Kieran, 2003), where Hull ranked as the worst place to live in the UK, contributed to deteriorating external perceptions of the city. External preconceptions and scepticisms arising since the shortlisting and peaking at the designation as the UKCoC 2017 – in 'a city unusually sensitive to its image' (Atkinson et al., 2002, p. 27) – may indeed have contributed to generate and sustain interest amongst the local community around the initiative. In the bid document, expressions such as 'once in a life time opportunity' were used to emphasise the potential benefits of the event for 'a city coming out of the shadows' (Hull UK City of Culture 2017, 2013, pp. 4 and 88) and to back the idea that the city *needed* such an opportunity (Tables 3.1 and 3.2).

Table 3.1 Hull's timeline.

t	*1980s*	*1990s*	*2000s*	*2010–2014*	*2015–2020*
CMEs				UKCoC 2013 bid UKCoC 2017 bid	UKCoC 2017 Legacy company
Urban policy	Waterfront regen. – Hull Marina, Victoria Dock, etc.	City Regen. Strategy	City Centre regen. plans	City Plan 2013 Public Realm Strategy 2014 Local Plan 2016	
Port development				Green Port Hull Siemens' plant	
Political changes			Economic crisis		EU referendum Erosion of Labour local majority Brexit

Table 3.2 Hull UK City of Culture 2017 at a glance.

Hull – UK City of Culture 2017	
Bid/designation	2013
Celebration	2017
Promoters	Hull City Council, Hull 2017 Ltd
Key actors involved	Arts Council England, BBC, British Council, Heritage Lottery Fund (HLF), Spirit of 2012, University of Hull, Visit Britain
Total working budget	• Cultural programme – £32.8 million • Capital investment – £100 million
Infrastructure	• Refurbishment of cultural facilities (Ferens Art Gallery, Hull New Theatre) • Public realm improvements
Key impacts	• 5.3 million attendees and 6.2 million visitors • £220 million investment partially or totally attributable to the event

Source: Author's work, data from Culture, Place and Policy Institute (2018).

In the case of Rotterdam, the interest of policy makers in cultural events and mega events may be understood in relation to the city's status as a European port metropolis. Rotterdam City Council aimed at retaining jobs for low-skilled workers and, at the same time, diversifying the local economy to generate job opportunities for high-skilled professionals (Vries, 2014, p. 116). The Council made use of mega events as a tool to improve the city's cultural offer and image, in order to attract middle-income households and professionals. Thus, Rotterdam's competitiveness as a port also depended on its attractiveness as a place to live, and culture was considered as a factor playing a part in this. Until the 1990s, Rotterdam was perceived as an industrial port city, populated by merchants and dockers, without a real cultural life and which tourists appeared to avoid (Chen, 2012, p. 31). The city used to live in the shadow of Amsterdam (Richards & Wilson, 2004, p. 1938), particularly in terms of cultural opportunities. Social-Democrat Mayor Peper was the first to put culture in the agenda in the 1980s. He believed that, since the port and the city had been rebuilt, the next step was to rebuild culture (interview, expert 4, February 2018). This was perceived by policy makers to go hand in hand with the aim of attracting higher-income households, thus culture became part of the same policy (interview, city planner 4, April 2018). As the city displayed a relatively poor offer in terms of cultural infrastructure (Richards & Wilson, 2004, p. 1938), the City Council invested heavily in this area, on a range of facilities including Rotterdamsche Schouwburg, the Kunsthal and the Museum Boijmans van Beuningen (Hitters, 2000, p. 189).

After pioneering experiences such as the festival *Rotterdam: de stad als podium* (Rotterdam: the city as podium) in 1988 (see e.g. Hajer, 1993, p. 54) and *Rotterdam 650*, events and festivals became a key element of the city's cultural policy and were perceived as a tool to connect culture with socio-economic development (Hitters, 2000, p. 190). Rotterdam Festivals was established as an independent company acting as a buffer between the City Council and cultural organisations (interview, event team member 3, May 2018). The City Council has implemented a cultural policy founded on major events, festivals and cultural events from the 1990s to the mid-2010s. In the 1990s, Rotterdam was not particularly associated with culture, despite its vibrant art scene. However, the new skyline of Kop van Zuid contributed to contrasting the port-dominated external image of the city (interview, city planner 3, April 2018). The European Capital of Culture 2001 was pursued in the light of its success in Antwerp in 1993 (Richards & Wilson, 2004, p. 1938). It was intended to be the apex of the process of rebuilding of the city's cultural infrastructure (Hitters, 2000, p. 185) and socio-cultural life, celebrating the previous 40 years of reconstruction. The event was celebrated the year after the EURO 2000 Football Cup, whose final match was played at Feyenoord Stadium (Tables 3.3 and 3.4).

In Genoa, the Council's mega-event policy from the late 1980s to the early 2000s needs to be explored considering the deep socio-economic decline caused by deindustrialisation and port restructuring. The hosting of mega events was backed by the willingness of presenting Genoa as a city of culture,

Table 3.3 Rotterdam's timeline.

	1990s	2000s	2010s	2020s
Event policy	• Social focus • Cultural engagement	• Rotterdam as a cultural/festival city • Mega event profile • Little connection with urban regeneration	• Focus on quality • Less events, in line with the DNA of the city (e.g. sport and music events)	• World Police and Fire Games 2021 • Youth Olympics 2022 • North Sea Jazz Festival • Architecture Biennale (IABR)
Cultural and sporting events	• Opzomeren programme	• EURO 2000 • ECoC 2001 • Thematic years – water (2003), sport (2005), architecture (2007), youth (2009) • Red Bull Air Race • North Sea Jazz Festival • Architecture Biennale (IABR)	• Start of Tour de France 2010 • Rotterdam viert de stad 2015 • Innovation Expo 2018 • North Sea Jazz Festival • Architecture Biennale (IABR)	
Urban policy/ port development	• Redevelopment of Kop van Zuid • Erasmus Bridge	• Stadshavens vision • Rotterdam Spatial Development Strategy 2030 • Redevelopment of Katendrecht • RDM Campus • Completion of Maasvlakte I	• Development of Maasvlakte II • Rotterdam Makers District • Rotterdam Maritime Capital of Europe	
Political change	• Cultural agenda promoted by Mayor Peper	• 2002–2006 local government led by Liveable Rotterdam	• Economic crisis • 2014–2018 local government led by Liveable Rotterdam • 2018- local government led by a left-wing coalition	

Table 3.4 Rotterdam European Capital of Culture 2001 at a glance.

Rotterdam – European Capital of Culture	
Bid/designation	1994
Celebration	2001
Promoters	Gemeente Rotterdam, Rotterdam 2001
Key actors involved	Central government, Port Authority, nearby municipalities
Total working budget	34.1 million Euros (source: Palmer-Rae Associates, 2004)
Infrastructure	• Refurbishment of Las Palmas building • Villa Zebra – art museum for children • The Parasite – temporary structure
Key impacts	• 2.25 million attendees • 17 million Euros visitor expenditure (source: Palmer-Rae Associates, 2004; Richards and Wilson, 2004)

rather than just a port city. Culture was perceived as an alternative not only in terms of economic development, but also to reframe the city's identity. As noted by two interviewees:

> [Genoa was] a city with a really strong industrial base. As soon as this base declined, [people] asked themselves 'What are we? Who are we? Where are we going?'. So, there was a process that actually was not that superficial. It was also a process of identity building.
>
> (interview, expert 9, May 2018, author's translation)

> I would say that this issue [of mega events] is embedded in a broader context, which is that of the 'factory city', a port and industrial city where, at some point, perhaps a bit late, [policy makers] sought to redefine their strategies and [the city's] economic base pursuing a more diversified model. Within this perspective, the theme of mega events emerged and has characterised the city for about fifteen years.
>
> (interview, expert 10, June 2018, author's translation)

Genoa was perceived by local policy makers as a city with remarkably rich cultural resources and heritage that needed to be presented to a broader public. Mega events were perceived as an opportunity to attract funding from the state (interview, expert 11, June 2018). Policy makers in Genoa made use of mega events to set deadlines and build consensus around major transformations, to invest in regeneration and cultural heritage and to build a long-lasting legacy, as in the case of the reconversion of Porto Antico. Mega events were arguably milestones of a long-term strategy initiated in the 1990s under Mayor Sansa (interview, expert 10, June 2018; Tables 3.5 and 3.6).

In the case of Valencia's mega-event policy, three key rationales emerge. Firstly, the Conservative local government aimed at making Valencia a global

Table 3.5 Genoa's timeline.

	1980s	1990s	2000s	2010s
CMEs		FIFA World Cup 1990 Expo 1992	ECoC 2004	Focus on smaller events (e.g. Regata Repubbliche Marinare)
Urban policy/ Port dev.	Protocollo di Intesa Porto Antico	Redevelopment of Porto Antico Strategic Conference Prà-Voltri terminal	Redevelopment of Darsena Comunale	
Political change		Mayor Sansa elected	Mayor Pericu elected	G8 2001 Mayor Vincenzi elected Economic crisis	Mayor Doria elected	Mayor Bucci elected (right wing)

Table 3.6 Genoa European Capital of Culture 2004 at a glance.

Genoa – European Capital of Culture	
Bid/designation	1998
Celebration	2004
Promoters	Genoa City Council, Genova 2004 Srl
Key actors involved	Liguria Regional Council, Genoa Provincial Council, University of Genoa, Chamber of Commerce, Port Authority
Total working budget	• Cultural programme – 33 million Euros (source: CONSAV, 2005) • Capital investment – 200 million Euros (source: Palmer-Rae Associates, 2004)
Infrastructure	• Musei della Darsena (including Galata Museo del Mare) • Public realm improvements (including Piazza Caricamento) • Refurbishment of cultural facilities and heritage buildings (e.g. Rolli palaces) in the city centre
Key impacts	• 2.8 million attendees • +15,82% visitors in 2004 (in comparison with 2003) • 220 Million Euros estimated economic impact • UNESCO World Heritage status for Strade Nuove and system of Palazzi dei Rolli (2006) (source: Genova srl, 2005)

city – a member of 'the club of VIP cities' (interview, policy maker 9, May 2018, author's translation) – and saw mega events as a means to achieve such a vision. Secondly, the America's Cup was seen as an opportunity to *unite* – and not *reunite* – the port and the city centre (interview, expert 15, May 2018).

Thirdly, mega events and megaprojects were also a means to contrast centralisation and 'a response to the way Central Government had left Valencia out in the cold when dishing out major events in the early 1990s' (Rius-Ulldemolins & Gisbert, 2019, p. 381). In terms of mega events, the year 1992 was an *annus mirabilis* for Spain, as the Olympic Games were held in Barcelona, the World Expo took place in Seville, and Madrid was the European City of Culture. In addition, in the 1990s, Bilbao became a benchmark for culture-led regeneration in Europe. Valencia – the third largest city in the country – was the only major Spanish city where nothing of this magnitude had been achieved. Local policy makers had long been complaining that the city and the Valencian Community (the autonomous region where the city is located) had received considerably less funding from the state in comparison with other large cities in the country (interview, policy maker 7, May 2018). This fuelled an inferiority complex towards Barcelona and Seville (Marrades, 2018, p. 192), which can be compared with that of Rotterdam towards Amsterdam.

The period 1996–2006 was marked by a 'globalist focus on the arts' (Hernández i Martí & Rius-Ulldemolins, 2016, p. 71), by the – unsuccessful – bid for the European City of Culture 2000 and by a series of Arts Biennials from 2001 to 2007. In 2006, the city hosted the V World Meeting of Families, with Pope Benedict XVI celebrating the event in the newly built Ciutat de les Arts i les Ciències. At that point, the America's Cup and later Formula One were seen as opportunities to host high-profile international events, as it appeared difficult to get other mega events that had already been celebrated across Spain. Unlike similar experiences in other cities, mega events in Valencia were promoted primarily by the Regional Council, rather than by the City Council (Tables 3.7, 3.8 and 3.9).

Mega events and event-led regeneration

After having examined the trajectories of urban regeneration in the case-study cities before mega events took place, it is worth focusing on the urban and economic transformation driven by these events. In Hull, the UKCoC 2017 arguably helped convey more resources and accelerate the pace of transformations that were already in the agenda or would have been implemented in any case, albeit over a longer timeframe. A £100 million investment by the City Council included a range of interventions, which contributed to transforming the city centre and some waterfront areas. The flagship project that the event contributed to marketing the most was the redevelopment of Fruit Market. The wholesale Fruit Market was moved to a dedicated space in the periphery of the city, while this area between the Old Town and the waterfront was redeveloped in a new urban village and creative hub (Figure 3.9). Alongside cultural facilities such as Humber Street Gallery, a new space for hi-tech start-ups, the Centre for Digital Innovation (C4DI), was developed, together with an outdoor amphitheatre on a dry dock on the River Hull known as the Stage@The Dock.

Table 3.7 Valencia's timeline.

	1980s	1990s	2000–2006	2007–2010	2010–2015	2015–
CMEs			America's Cup bid/ designation	America's Cup 2007 and 2010 F1 2008–2010	F1 2010– 2012	
Urban policy/ Port dev.	1988 spatial plan Implementation of Solución Sur Jardín del Túria Palau de la Musica	Ciutat de les Arts i les Ciències Proposal of extension of Av. Blasco Ibañez Strategic plan Port expansion and ZAL	Port America's Cup New port exit channel	Valencia Street Circuit		Proposal of 4th logistic terminal
Political changes		Mayor Barberá elected – conservative government		Conservative peak in electoral consensus Economic crisis		Mayor Ribó elected – left-wing government

Table 3.8 The America's Cup in Valencia at a glance.

Valencia – America's Cup	
Bid/designation	2003
Celebration	2007 and 2010
Promoters	Société Nautique de Genève Valencia's Yacht Club Generalitat Valenciana (Regional Council) America's Cup Management (ACM) Consorcio Valencia 2007
Key actors involved	Ayuntamiento de Valencia (Valencia City Council) Autoridad Portuaria de Valencia (APV, Port Authority)
Total estimated cost	486 million Euros (source: Rius-Ulldemolins & Gisbert, 2019)
Infrastructure	• Redevelopment of the old harbour • New port exit channel • Team bases • Exhibition space in the tinglados • Veles e Vents building (designed by David Chipperfield)

Key impacts	• 2007: 2,476,300 visitors in the marina during regattas (2007);
	  2010: 200,000 visitors
	• 2007: 5,748 million Euros in terms of production (+2.67%
	  GDP in the region); 73,859 new jobs (+3.29% employment in
	  the region)
	
	(source: IVIE, 2007; Del Romero Renau and Trudelle, 2011)

Table 3.9 The Formula One European Grand Prix in Valencia at a glance.

Valencia – Formula One European Grand Prix	
Bid/designation	2007
Celebration	Once a year from 2008–2012
Promoters	Generalitat Valenciana
Key actors involved	Formula One Management Valmor Sport Ayuntamiento de Valencia Autoridad Portuaria de Valencia (APV, Port Authority)
Total estimated cost	183 million Euros (source: Rius-Ulldemolins & Gisbert, 2019)
Infrastructure	• Valencia Street Circuit
Key impacts	Not available

Although studies on the economic impact of Formula 1 events were carried out by IVIE, no impact study reports were accessible.

A similar pattern is visible in the case of Rotterdam. Neither EURO 2000 nor the European Capital of Culture 2001 involved considerable spatial intervention. Feyenoord Stadium was refurbished for EURO 2000, albeit there was no substantial impact on urban development (Chen, 2012, p. 33). In relation

Figure 3.9 Humber Street in Hull's Fruit Market.

to the ECoC, the Las Palmas building (Figure 3.10), an abandoned industrial building on Wilhelminapier, was renovated and used to host exhibitions during the year. The building was closed for refurbishment in 2005 and hosts at the time of writing the Nederlands Fotomuseum, the headquarters of real estate developer OVG and a restaurant. Villa Zebra, a visual arts museum for children, was established for the event and then moved in 2005 to Kop van Zuid. During the event, the Parasite, a temporary structure designed to encourage reflections about the use of space in architecture, was installed on the top of the Las Palmas building and subsequently removed. In April 2001, the new Luxor Theater opened in the same area, albeit this project was not implemented as a result of the event taking place.

In the case of Rotterdam, it is worth mentioning a few regeneration programmes implemented after the events analysed took place. In 2002, the large-scale inner-city vision Stadshavens (CityPorts), encompassing 1,600 hectares of land and water in the heart of the city (Daamen, 2010; Aarts et al., 2012), was launched. Such waterfront redevelopment strategy was conceived with a dual purpose (Vries, 2014, p. 115): strengthening the local economy through an increased sustainability of its port and creating a more attractive city. However, it was soon clear that such a strategy would not be implemented as it had been outlined and needed to be reframed in 2007 (Aarts et al., 2012, p. 1).

Within this overall structural vision, three notable examples of regeneration of former port areas driven by creativity and culture can be mentioned. Firstly, the RDM campus (Vries, 2014) was developed in a former port area owned

Figure 3.10 Las Palmas building.

by the Rotterdamsche Droogdok Maatschappij (Rotterdam Drydock Corporation, RDM), a local shipbuilding company. The area was developed as a shipyard in the early 20th century, together with a nearby village for the company's workers, which would later become Heijplaat. By the early 2000s, port-related activities abandoned the area, while Heijplaat risked being demolished in the mid-2000s due to depopulation. The RDM Campus was developed in the derelict shipyard in 2009 to accommodate some of the technical activities of Hogeschool Rotterdam and Albeda College. The area functions as a hub for innovation and smart port technologies and hosts conferences, exhibitions and cultural events in a conference centre and in the Onderzeebootloods, a submarine wharf. Secondly, Katendrecht, a former 'sailortown' associated with negative perceptions in relation to crime and prostitution (interview, event team member 3, May 2018), has been undergoing culture-led regeneration since the early 21st century, which has been focusing on the use of cultural facilities and amenities as place-making devices. The scheme benefitted from the construction of Theater Walhalla, a number of bars locating on the waterfront, the acquisition of the SS Rotterdam – which was built at the RDM shipyard – and the construction of the Erasmus Bridge. Thirdly, it is worth mentioning that the RDM area is included, together with the Merwe-Vierhaven (M4H) area, in the ongoing regeneration programme known as Makers District. The programme was anticipated by plans elaborated in 2004 to gradually move food handling activities out of the area (Jansen et al., 2021). The transformation of this set of riverside areas is envisioned as combining innovative manufacturing and new forms of urban living on the waterfront, accessible by public transport on water. This is leading to an increasing concentration of creative jobs in architecture, graphic and industrial design, marketing (ibid.).

In Genoa, the 1992 Specialist Expo, the 2001 G8 summit and the ECoC 2004 contributed to radically transforming Porto Antico and the interface between the harbour and the city centre. Nevertheless, such events were milestones – or 'pulsar effects' (Bisio & Bobbio, 2003) – within a long-term process. The regeneration of the city centre and the waterfront was the main focus of urban policy in the 1990s and at the beginning of the 21st century (Gastaldi, 2012, p. 24). The concentration of resources and efforts in these pivotal areas was expected to generate spillovers across the city and to facilitate the transition to a more diversified economic base (Gastaldi, 2010). However, the idea of reconverting Porto Antico had already emerged, as urban functions within Porto Antico were first introduced in the 1980 spatial plan (ibid.). In 1984, the Genoese architect Renzo Piano was appointed for the redesign of part of the harbour, while the following year the City Council, the Regional Council and Consorzio Autonomo del Porto signed an agreement for the decommissioning of part of the harbour and its redevelopment for leisure purposes.

In 1986, the Bureau International des Expositions designated Genoa as the host city of a Specialist Expo to be held in 1992, alongside the World Expo in Seville. This led to the fast-tracking of planning procedures through *ad hoc* national laws, which were also issued for the 1990 FIFA World Cup. The master plan for Porto Antico was amended to remove custom barriers and reconvert some of the docks to accommodate urban functions (Gastaldi, 2017, p. 124). The 1992 Specialist Expo was unsuccessful in terms of visibility (interview, policy maker 5, June 2018; interview, event team member 4, June 2018; interview, event team member 5, June 2018; interview, expert 10, June 2018) and visitor numbers (Gastaldi, 2012, p. 28). The overestimation of visitor numbers also led to financial issues (Jauhiainen, 1995, p. 19). Delays in construction works meant that only some of the planned facilities were used in 1992, while criticisms about the project were raised (ibid., p. 19). In addition, the reuse of facilities after the event was initially problematic (Bisio & Bobbio, 2003; Gastaldi, 2012, p. 23). However, the event can be considered a success in terms of regeneration, as it led to the reconversion of part of the harbour, the construction of the Aquarium and the restoration of Magazzini del Cotone (cotton warehouses). A crane-inspired building called Bigo was designed for the event by Renzo Piano and was equipped with a panoramic lift. The Genoese architect also designed a roofing for the existing Piazza delle Feste (Figure 3.11).

The G8 summit held in Genoa in 2001 – which is not explored in the book – represented an opportunity to get additional funding from central government

Figure 3.11 Bigo, Piazza delle Feste and Biosfera in Genoa's Porto Antico.

and to pursue further regeneration in the city centre and Porto Antico. The national funding for mega events was considered by Genoese policy makers as a 'compensation' (interview, expert 10, June 2018) for having been 'left behind' in the past. The G8 summit was an opportunity to showcase Genoa and its refurbished spaces. The much-opposed event had a positive impact on the regeneration of Porto Antico, with further pedestrianisation, the refurbishment of the Stazione Marittima (cruise and ferry terminal) and the construction of a public footpath to the Lanterna lighthouse. The Biosfera, also known as 'Bolla' (bubble) designed by Renzo Piano, contributed to countering the issues of decay that permeated the legacy of the 1992 Specialist Expo (Gastaldi, 2012, p. 30).

The ECoC 2004 was another opportunity to continue the reconversion of Porto Antico and to regenerate the city centre. The core idea was to improve the connection among Porto Antico, the city's museums and Palazzi dei Rolli.[13] The focus on existing assets was a political choice rather than a matter of budget (interview, policy maker 5, June 2018). 200 million Euros were allocated for 'structural interventions' including the restoration of heritage buildings and the refurbishment of public spaces (Palmer–Rae Associates, 2004, p. 344). The focus of redevelopment works was on both continuing the restoration of built heritage in the city centre and further redeveloping the waterfront. Only one new cultural facility was built in relation to the event, namely the Galata Museo del Mare (Maritime Museum, Figure 3.12) on a dock owned by the City Council (Darsena Comunale).

Although the ECoC 2004 marked the end of the 'mega-event era', discussions continued around the future steps in the redevelopment of the waterfront. Renzo Piano delivered a vision called Affresco – meaning fresco, in three versions between 2004 and 2006 – for the redevelopment of the waterfront from the Fair area to Voltri (for a description of the project, see Gastaldi, 2010). The core vision included the relocation of the airport terminal on a floating platform, and a boundary to port expansion at Voltri. The project was abandoned in 2008 (Gastaldi & Camerin, 2016, p. 4). In 2015, a proposal by Renzo Piano in partnership with the City Council, the Provincial Council (now Metropolitan City Council), the Regional Council and the Port Authority, called Blueprint, focused on extending waterfront redevelopment to the east of Porto Antico (ibid., 2016).

In Valencia, the America's Cup 2007 led to a major transformation of the Dársena Histórica. The event, announced in 2003, was welcomed as an opportunity to complete the redevelopment of the waterfront, to regenerate the deprived maritime districts, to attract funding from central government and to boost tourism (Biot & Velert, 2003, in Tarazona Vento, 2017, p. 78). In 2004, Generalitat Valenciana approved the Council's Action Plan for the America's Cup, which revised the previous spatial vision of the Balcón al Mar project. In order to guarantee the safety of participants and to avoid the disruption of port traffic, the Dársena was physically separated from the working commercial

Figure 3.12 Galata Museo del Mare in Genoa's Darsena Comunale.

port, and a new port exit channel was created. 444 million Euros were budgeted for the redevelopment (Prytherch & Boira i Maiques, 2009, p. 112; Marrades, 2018, p. 192). Consorcio Valencia 2007, the event management body, applied for a 500 million Euros loan from the Instituto de Crédito Oficial (Sorribes i Monrabal, 2015, p. 270), while minor debts were contracted with Banco Santander and APV (Marrades, 2018, p. 192). A new marina and a superyacht marina were realised alongside the America's Cup team bases and a public park (Figure 3.13). The iconic Veles e Vents (Sails and Winds) designed by David Chipperfield was built at the beginning of the exit channel. Temporary exhibition spaces were arranged in the new building, where the trophy was displayed, as well as under the traditional tinglados (sheds).

The economic impact of the event in 2004–2007 was quantified in 5,748 million Euros – accounting for a 2.67% increase in the region's GDP – and generated 73,859 new jobs, that is a 3.29% increase in employment in the region (IVIE, 2007, p. 9; Parra Camacho et al., 2016, p. 326). Consorcio Valencia 2007 estimated an overall 2,476,300 visitor figure for the marina in the days of the America's Cup matches and of the Louis Vuitton Cup (IVIE, 2007, p. 42). The 2010 edition of the contest was not as successful as the previous one and attracted 200,000 visitors, in comparison with an average 2 million visitor figure for the annual traditional Falles festival (Del Romero Renau & Trudelle, 2011, p. 8). Nevertheless, the America's Cup also produced an 'irrecoverable' 486 million Euros debt for the City Council (Rius-Ulldemolins & Gisbert,

Figure 3.13 Port America's Cup in 2007.

2019, p. 387). The other institutions involved had similar financial issues. APV purchased a 4 million Euros yacht for the event, which was then rented in 2019 as its management had become unsustainable and its market value had decreased to a quarter of its original price (A.C.A., 2019). Generalitat Valenciana contracted an overall 1.5 billion debt to implement the city's megaprojects such as the Ciutat de les Arts i les Ciències (Fernández, 2014).

The Formula One European Grand Prix, which took place from 2008 to 2012, was the result of an agreement between Formula One Administration, Generalitat Valenciana and Ayuntamiento de Valencia. The event was anticipated in January 2007 by a show in the streets of Valencia involving Spanish driver Fernando Alonso to present McLaren's new Formula 1 challenger. Although Generalitat Valenciana claimed that the Grand Prix would self-finance itself (Ferrandis, 2010), the event's final estimated cost was 183 million Euros (Rius-Ulldemolins & Gisbert, 2019, p. 387), 98 million of which (Sierra, 2015) were allocated for the construction of Valencia Street Circuit. This accounted for an overall 627 million Euros investment in these international sporting events.

The short-term vision and the debts contracted to organise mega events meant that there was no legacy after 2012, and an abrupt cliff effect marked the experience of Valencia. There was no catalyst effect on sailing activities or the local motor industry, and the *ad hoc* sport facilities were not used for other large-scale events. Despite the claims about the potential societal benefits of mega events made by Generalitat Valenciana, such broader effects did not materialise (Tarazona Vento, 2017, p. 75).

After having explored more in depth the rationale for hosting mega events and how these occasions were embedded in urban regeneration strategies in the case-study cities, the next chapters examine the synergies between the events analysed and the spatial (Chapter 5), political (Chapter 6) and symbolic (Chapter 7) ties between these cities and their ports, with examples from other port cities hosting mega events.

Notes

1 Source: Travel to work area analysis in Great Britain, Office for National Statistics (2016).
2 For example, 41.0% of Hull's population is in the 0–29 age group in comparison with a figure of 36.7% in England. Source: Hull Data Observatory / ONS (2019).
3 The Referendum on the United Kingdom's membership of the European Union was held in June 2016. The ballot paper asked the following question: 'Should the United Kingdom remain a member of the European Union or leave the European Union?'. Voters could choose if they wished the UK to 'Remain a member of the European Union' or 'Leave the European Union'.
4 Source: OECD (2016).
5 Source: ISTAT (2018).
6 Horta (Huerta in Castilian Spanish) means 'vegetable garden' or 'orchard'.
7 Source: Oficina de Estadística del Ayuntamiento de Valencia (2017).
8 The Bethia, later HMS Bounty, was built along the River Hull in 1784.
9 Enterprise Zones are designated areas in England where businesses can access tax breaks and government support, and aim at attracting large companies and their supply chains (HM Government, 2019).

10 Eventually approved, the scheme raised socio-spatial tensions between the Port Authority and the local middle class (Atkinson, 2007, pp. 535–537). The Quay 2005 site was
later allocated for the development of Siemens manufacturing facility.

11 For example, the proportion of social housing against the city's overall housing stock in
1997 was 59% (Schutjens et al., 2002).

12 In the case of Barcelona, Avinguda Diagonal was included in the 1860 Cerdá Plan, by
breaking the regular grid of the design of the Example. It became a major urban road
running from the B-20 ring road to the seafront next to the mouth of the River Besòs.
The seafront area at the end of Avinguda Diagonal was redeveloped in relation to the
2004 Universal Forum of Cultures and transformed into a retail and residential complex
(known as Diagonal Mar) and an event space (Parc del Fòrum).

13 The Rolli Palaces are historic buildings in Genoa city centre. In the 16th and 17th centuries, these buildings were private palaces occasionally used to host state visits.

Bibliography

Aarts, M., Daamen, T., Huijs, M., & De Vries, W. (2012) Port-city development in Rotterdam: A true love story. *Urban-e – Revista Digital de Territorio, Urbanismo, Sostenibilidad,
Paisaje, Diseño Urbano*, 2(3), 1–28.

A.C.A. (2019). El puerto de Valencia alquila su yate después de tres subastas sin ofertas de
compra. *Expansión* [online], 18th November. Available at: www.expansion.com/valencia/
2019/11/18/5dd2bef9468aeb27618b4589.html [Accessed 27/11/2019].

Atkinson, D. (2007) Kitsch geographies and the everyday spaces of social memory. *Environment and Planning A*, 39, 521–540.

Atkinson, D., Cooke, S., & Spooner, D. J. (2002) Tales from the riverbank: Place-marketing
and maritime heritages. *International Journal of Heritage Studies*, 8(1), 25–40.

Baird, A. J. (1996) Containerization and the decline of the upstream urban port in Europe.
Maritime Policy & Management, 23(2), 145–156.

Bisio, L., & Bobbio, R. (2003) The Pulsar effect in Genoa: From big events to urban strategy. In
Beriatos, E., & Colman, J. (eds.) *The Pulsar Effect in Urban Planning*, Proceedings of the 38th
International ISoCaRP Congress, Athens, 21–26 September 2002. The Hague: ISoCaRP.

Bobbio, R. (2005) Re-shaping paces for a new economy: The case of Genoa. *41st ISoCaRP
Congress*, Bilbao, 17–20 October. Available at: www.isocarp.net/Data/case_studies/579.
pdf [Accessed 14/10/2018].

Boira i Maiques, J. V. (2013) Puerto y ciudad en Valencia. El tránsito hacia un modelo de uso
ciudadano (1986–2013). *Biblio 3W*, XVIII(1049–25). Available at: www.ub.es/geocrit/
b3w-1049/b3w-1049-25.htm [Accessed 04/10/2018].

Byrne, J. (2015) After the trawl: Memory and afterlife in the wake of Hull's distant-water
fishing industry. *The International Journal of Maritime History*, 27(4), 816–822.

Carrasco, J. S., & Pitarch-Garrido, M. D. (2017) Analysis of the impact on tourism of the
megaproject-based urban development strategy: The case of the city of Valencia. *Cuadernos de Turismo*, 40, 723–726.

Chen, Y. (2012) Urban regeneration through mega event: The case of Rotterdam. *Proceedings
of 2012 Shanghai International Conference of Social Science*, Shanghai, 14–17 August, 29–36.

City of Hull Development Committee (1937) *The City and the Port of Hull*. Hull and London:
H. Brown & Sons Ltd.

City Regeneration Strategy Group (1994a) *A City Regeneration Strategy for Hull: Background
Document*. Hull: Hull City Council.

City Regeneration Strategy Group (1994b) *A City Regeneration Strategy for Hull: Strategy and
Short Term Action Plan*. Hull: Hull City Council.

Culture, Place and Policy Institute (2018) *Cultural Transformations: The Impacts of Hull UK City of Culture 2017. Preliminary Outcomes Evaluation. March 2018.* Hull: University of Hull.

Daamen, T. A. (2010) *Strategy as Force: Towards Effective Strategies for Urban Development Projects: The Case of Rotterdam City Ports.* Amsterdam: IOS Press.

Dekker, R., Hemilsson, H., Krieger, B., & Scholten, P. (2015) A local dimension of integration policies? A comparative study of Berlin, Malmö, and Rotterdam. *International Migration Review*, 49(3), 633–658.

Del Álamo Andrés, M. (1999) Constructores Ferroviarios Valencianos: Construcciones Devis SA (1929–1947) y Material y Construcciones SA (1947–1989). In Vidal Olivares, J., Muñoz Rubio, M., & Sanz Fernández, J. (eds.) *Siglo y medio del ferrocarril en España, 1848–1998: Economía, industria y sociedad.* Alicante: Diputación Provincial de Alicante, Instituto Alicantino de Cultura Juan Gil-Albert.

Del Romero Renau, L., & Trudelle, C. (2011) Mega events and urban conflicts in Valencia, Spain: Contesting the new urban modernity. *Urban Studies Research*, 11. DOI: 10.1155/2011/587523.

Doucet, B. (2013) Variations of the entrepreneurial city: Goals, roles and visions in Rotterdam's Kop van Zuid and the Glasgow Harbour megaprojects. *International Journal of Urban and Regional Research*, 37(6), 2035–2051.

Entzinger, H., & Godfried, E. (2014) *Rotterdam: A Long-Time Port of Call and Home to Immigrants.* Washington, DC: Migration Policy Institute.

Erasmus Centre for Urban, Port and Transport Economics (2018) *Het Rotterdam Effect. De impact van Mainport Rotterdam op de Nederlandse economie.* Rotterdam: Havenbedrijf Rotterdam NV. Available at: www.portofrotterdam.com/sites/default/files/downloads/het-rotterdam-effect-pdf.pdf?token=y_mi09IN [Accessed 03/03/2020].

Evans, N. J. (2001) Work in progress: Indirect passage from Europe Transmigration via the UK, 1836–1914. *Journal for Maritime Research*, 3(1), 70–84.

Evans, N. J. (2017) The making of a mosaic: Migration and the port-city of Kingston upon Hull. In Starkey, D. J., Atkinson, D., McDonagh, B., McKeon, S., & Salter, E. (eds.) *Hull. Culture, History, Place.* Liverpool: University of Liverpool Press, 145–177.

Fernández, A. (2014) El Consell acumula 1.538 millones de sobrecostes en sus grandes proyectos. *Levante* [Online], 2nd October. Available at: www.levante-emv.com/comunitat-valenciana/2014/02/09/consell-acumula-1538-millones-sobrecostes/1077690.html [Accessed 24/08/2018].

Ferrandis, J. (2010) Del coste cero al circuito costoso. *El País* [Online], 18th January. Available at: https://elpais.com/diario/2010/01/18/cvalenciana/1263845883_850215.html [Accessed 12/11/2018].

Gastaldi, F. (2010) Genova. La riconversione del waterfront portuale. Un percorso con esiti rilevanti. Storia, accadimenti, dibattito. In Savino, M. (ed.) *Waterfront d'Italia. Piani politiche progetti.* Milano: Franco Angeli, 88–104.

Gastaldi, F. (2012) Grandi eventi e rigenerazione urbana negli anni della grande trasformazione di Genova: 1992–2004. *Territorio della Ricerca su Insediamenti e Ambiente*, 9, 23–35.

Gastaldi, F. (2017) Genova, a success story! In Porfyriou, H., & Sepe, M. (eds.) *Waterfronts Revisited: European Ports in a Historic and Global Perspective.* New York and London: Routledge, 123–133.

Gastaldi, F., & Camerin, F. (2016) El proceso de reconversion del waterfront de Génova después del período de los grandes eventos (2004–2014). *PortusPlus*, 6(6), 1–11.

Hajer, M. A. (1993) Rotterdam: Re-designing the public domain. In Bianchini, F., & Parkinson, M. (eds.) *Cultural Policy and Urban Regeneration: The Western European Experience.* Manchester: Manchester Press, 48–72.

Hernández i Martí, G. M., & Rius-Ulldemolins, J. (2016) La Política Cultural en las Grandes Ciudades. Giro emprendedor, globalización y espectacularización en la modernidad avanzada. In Rius-Ulldemolins, J., & Rubio Arostegui, J. A. (eds.) *Treinta años de políticas culturales en España: Participación cultural, gobernanza territorial e industrias culturales.* Valencia: Universitat de València, 45–87.

Hesse, M., & McDonough, E. (2018) Ports, cities and the global maritime infrastructure. In Kloosterman, R. C., Mamadouh, V., & Terhorst, P. (eds.) *Handbook on the Geographies of Globalization.* Cheltenham and Northampton, MA: Edward Elgar Publishing, 354–366.

Hitters, E. (2000) The social and political construction of a European cultural capital: Rotterdam 2001. *International Journal of Cultural Policy*, 6(2), 183–199.

HM Government (2019) Looking for a place to grow your business? *Enterprise Zones.* Available at: https://enterprisezones.communities.gov.uk/about-enterprise-zones/ [Accessed 07/11/2019].

Hull Citybuild (2003) *The Renaissance of Hull City Centre.* Hull: Hull City Council.

Hull City Council (n.d.) *Hull City Plan.* Available at: http://cityplanhull.co.uk/ [Accessed 31/07/2017].

Hull City Council (2000) *Hull Cityplan: Adopted May 2000.* Hull: Development Plans Team Transportation and Planning Division Regeneration and Development Directorate.

Hull City Council (2008) *City Centre Area Action Plan: Incorporating Citywide Policies: Submission Document: July 2008.* Hull: Hull City Council.

Hull City Council (2016) *EU Referendum.* Available at: www.hullcc.gov.uk/portal/page-_pageid=221,1543108&_dad=portal&_schema=PORTAL [Accessed 28/11/2017].

Hull UK City of Culture 2017 (2013) *Tell the World: Final Bid.* Hull: Hull City Council.

IVIE (2007) *Impacto Económico de la 32a America's Cup Valencia 2007. Informe final, diciembre 2007.* Available at: https://web2011.ivie.es/downloads/2008/01/PP_Ivie_impacto_Americas_Cup_2008.pdf [Accessed 21/08/2018].

Jansen, M., Brandellero, A., & van Houwelingen, R. (2021) Port-city transition: Past and emerging socio-spatial imaginaries and uses in Rotterdam's Makers District. *Urban Planning*, 6(3), 166–180.

Jauhiainen, J. S. (1995) Waterfront redevelopment and urban policy: The case of Barcelona, Cardiff and Genoa. *European Planning Studies*, 3(1), 3–23.

Jordison, S., & Kieran, D. (2003) *The Idler Book of Crap Towns: The 50 Worst Places to Live in the UK.* London: Boxtree.

Kerby, T. K., Cheung, W. W. L., & Engelhard, G. H. (2012) The United Kingdom's role in North Sea demersal fisheries: A hundred year perspective. *Reviews in Fish Biology and Fishing*, 22, 621–634.

Kirby, D., & Hinkkanen, M.-L. (2000) *The Baltic and the North Seas.* London and New York: Routledge.

Llavador, J. M. T. (2010) Valencia y el mar, un idilio hecho realidad. Valencia and the sea, a romance come true. *Portus*, 20, 30–35.

Marrades, R. (2018) La Marina de València: La apropiación ciudadana y la activación productiva del frente marítimo de la ciudad. In Baron, N., & Romero, J. (eds.) *Cultura territorial e innovación social. ¿Hacia un nuevo modelo metropolitano en Europa del sur?* Valencia: Universitat de València, 193–204.

McCarthy, J. (1999) The redevelopment of Rotterdam since 1945. *Planning Perspectives*, 14, 291–309.

Meyer, H. (1999) *City and Port: Urban Planning as a Cultural Venture in London, Barcelona, New York, and Rotterdam: Changing Relation between Public Urban Space and Large-Scale Infrastructure.* Rotterdam: International Books.

Palmer-Rae Associates (2004) *European Cities and Capitals of Culture: Study Prepared for the European Commission: PART II.* Available at: https://ec.europa.eu/programmes/creative-europe/sites/creative-europe/files/library/palmer-report-capitals-culture-1995-2004-ii_en.pdf [Accessed 09/07/2018].

Parra Camacho, D., Añó Sanz, V., & Calabuig Moreno, F. (2016) Percepción de los residentes sobre el legado de la America's Cup. Residents perceptions about the legacy of America's Cup Percepção dos moradores sobre o legado da Copa América. *Cuadernos de Psicología del Deporte*, 16(1), 325–338.

Platts-Fowler, D., & Robinson, D. (2015) A place for integration: Refugee experiences in Two English Cities. *Population, Space and Place*, 21, 476–491.

Prytherch, D. A., & Boira i Maiques, J. V. (2009) City profile: Valencia. *Cities*, 26, 103–115.

Regio Randstad (2017) *Randstad Monitor 2017: Randstad Region in Europe.* Brussels: Regio Randstad. Available at: www.nl-prov.eu/wp-content/uploads/2017/11/regio-randstad-monitor-2017.pdf [Accessed 15/02/2019].

Richards, G., & Wilson, J. (2004) The impact of cultural events on city image: Rotterdam, Cultural Capital of Europe 2001. *Urban Studies*, 41(10), 1931–1951.

Rius-Ulldemolins, J., & Gisbert, V. (2019) The costs of putting Valencia on the map: The hidden side of regional entrepreneurialism, 'creative city' and strategic projects. *European Planning Studies*, 27(2), 377–395.

Rius-Ulldemolins, J., Moreno, V. F., & Hernández i Martí, G. M. (2019) The dark side of cultural policy: Economic and political instrumentalisation, white elephants, and corruption in Valencian cultural institutions. *International Journal of Cultural Policy*, 25(3), 282–297.

Rizzini, M. (2008) Marta Vincenzi, la società civile sono io. *Il Foglio* [Online], 27th March. Available at: www.ilfoglio.it/articoli/2008/05/27/news/marta-vincenzi-la-societa-civile-sono-io-73142/ [Accessed 29/10/2019].

Romein, A. (2005) Leisure in waterfront redevelopment: An issue of urban planning in Rotterdam? *2005 AESOP Conference*, Vienna, 13–17 July. Available at: http://aesop2005.scix.net/data/papers/att/606.fullTextPrint.pdf [Accessed 27/11/2019].

Scholten, P., Crul, M., & Van de Laar, P. (eds.) (2019) *Coming to Terms with Superdiversity: The Case of Rotterdam.* Cham: Springer.

Schutjens, V. A. J. M., van Kempen, R., & van Weesep, J. (2002) The changing tenant profile of Dutch social rented housing. *Urban Studies*, 39(4), 643–664.

Sierra, J. (2015) El circuito de F1 costó 98 millones de los que 60 son un préstamo sin pagar. *Levante* [Online], 18th December. Available at: www.levante-emv.com/comunitat-valenciana/2015/12/18/circuito-f1-costo-98-millones/1356242.html [Accessed 19/11/2018].

Sorribes i Monrabal, J. (2015) *Valencia 1940–2014: Construcción y destrucción de la ciudad.* Valencia: Universitat de València.

Tarazona Vento, A. (2017) Mega-project meltdown: Post-politics, neoliberal urban regeneration and Valencia's fiscal crisis. *Urban Studies*, 54(1), 68–84.

Thomas, B. J. (1994) The privatization of United Kingdom seaports. *Maritime Policy & Management*, 21(2), 135–148.

Valenciaport (2018) The new terminal of Valenciaport will have 2 km. of berthing line. *Valenciaport*, 20th October. Available at: www.valenciaport.com/en/the-new-terminal-of-valenciaport-will-have-2-km-of-berthing-line/ [Accessed 30/10/2018].

Vries, I. (2014) From shipyard to brainyard: The redevelopment of RDM as an example of a contemporary port-city relationship. In Alix, Y., Delsalle, B., & Comtois, C. (eds.) *Port-City Governance.* Paris: Editions EMS, 107–126.

4 Port cities and event-led regeneration in ontologically insecure times

The political-economic context for event-led regeneration in the 21st century appears very different to that of economic restructuring and growth that characterised the rise of urban regeneration under emerging neoliberal capitalism in the 1980s and 1990s. The 2007–8 economic and financial crisis triggered by the aggressive behaviour of financial players and the devaluation of mortgage-based financial assets marked the beginning of more than a decade of austerity politics across Europe, where national governments have accelerated the contraction of public spending, in particular on welfare, and focused on the stability of state finances. Supranational institutions (such as the EU) and federal administrations have been imposing budget cuts and other cost-saving measures to national governments, sometimes through undemocratic processes and intimidating political discourses (e.g. 'sacrifice' and 'responsibility'). In turn, national governments have imposed similar measures on local authorities, generating a regime of austerity urbanism that has accelerated the dismantling of public services at the local level (Peck, 2012). A decade after the 2007–8 crisis, there was little evidence of recovery in Europe, as the impact of sustained austerity policies during the Great Recession became apparent. The rise of pro-Brexit parties in the UK and the Italian government's opposition to the EU's austerity rules show how established political equilibriums were undermined by widespread unemployment and anger. The 2007–8 crisis arguably turned into a deeper political-economic one, as demonstrated by the gradual disintegration of traditional political parties and the shift towards social conservativism. At that point, the COVID-19 pandemic hit European countries with devastated national healthcare systems, after decades of dismantling of welfare provision and more than ten years of reckless austerity (Hadjimichalis, 2020; Cooper & Szreter, 2021). The subsequent lockdown measures imposed to cope with grossly underprovisioned healthcare services have caused an even harsher economic recession. For example, in 2020, the UK experienced a record 9.8% decline in GDP,[1] the most pronounced economic downturn since the Great Frost.[2] Similar figures were recorded in other countries such as Germany (−5.4%), Italy (−9.2%), the US (−3.4%) and Brazil (−4.5%), while China's GDP grew by 2.3% (in comparison with 6.1% in 2019; International Monetary Fund, 2020), accounting for a 3.5% contraction of the global economy (International Monetary Fund, 2021).

DOI: 10.4324/9781003165811-4

The wave of unsettling news about COVID-19 and the aforementioned economic and societal impacts of extended lockdown measures arguably exacerbated existing widespread feelings of insecurity arising from contemporary societal issues such as the Great Recession, the rise of right-wing populism and authoritarianism, the disintegration of society, terrorism, climate breakdown, and more recently the cost of living crisis and geopolitical tensions with the risk of a new global war. Arguably, the combination and simultaneity of these crises, together with the prospect of recurrent pandemics, is undermining ontological security (Laing, 1990; Giddens, 1991). Giddens (1991, p. 37) understands ontological security as a person's 'fundamental sense of safety in the world', which is inherently linked to 'a basic trust of other people'. The lack of trust of others (e.g. neighbours, members of society, migrants, decision makers and experts), combined with unaddressed existential threats, fuels a deep sense of anxiety that hinders people's psychological wellbeing. Not only are today's politicians and decision makers unable to address this insecurity arising from the aforementioned threats and structural issues, but in fact ontological insecurity is often manipulated in the quest for power and money that characterises contemporary society, for example through populist political tactics (e.g. Steele & Homolar, 2019) and strategies to construct social acceptance around controversial policies.

The idea of the contemporary erosion of ontological security is also connected to the concept of postnormal times. In current, postnormal times, the 'normalcy' experienced in the second half of the 20th century is replaced by a world where uncertainty, complexity, competing interests within an unbridled capitalist economy, and the emergence of different forms of ignorance hamper decision making and pose increased risks to individuals (Sardar, 2010). The concept has been adopted in port city studies by Ramos (2020) to reflect on how port activity can adapt and be more resilient to increased complexity and uncertainty, in the light of the impacts of COVID-19 on maritime trade, supply chains and logistics worldwide.

This chapter problematises the role of mega events and their legacy in the early 21st century, with particular regard to maritime port cities, within the current socio-economic and political context portrayed earlier. Secondly, the chapter focuses on perceptions of and reactions to mega events in maritime port cities and on their long-term, sometimes unintended, impacts on the port-city interface.

Crisis, austerity and mega-event policies

Much of the literature on mega events tends to look at the rationale for and the impacts of hosting these events in contexts of economic restructuring under neoliberal forms of capitalism. However, a key question in the contemporary study of mega events and event-led regeneration is how the 2008 crash and subsequent rise of austerity impacted on the legacy of pre-2008 events and on the planning of those taking place since the 2010s. Even before the COVID-19 outbreak, in a context of reduced public finances, growing unemployment, rapidly decreasing living standards and political instability, it appeared increasingly difficult for local policy makers and coalitions of interest to seek public consensus around the considerable public spending that these events entail. This has resulted in a number of withdrawn and curtailed bids that failed to mobilise local stakeholders or to obtain political support from central governments. Policy makers in European port cities are still proactively seeking to secure mega events as part of their urban agendas; however, they are likely to concentrate their efforts on smaller-scale and more sustainable events that are perceived to be in line with the city's social profile and local meanings. An example is the number of bidding cities in the case of the ECoC and the replication of CoC schemes across the world.[3] In August 2021, a record number of 20 applicants submitted a bid for the UK City of Culture 2025 (BBC, 2021).

Impacts on event-led regeneration policies

The mega events which comprise the core case studies in the book took place during different timeframes in relation to the 2007–8 economic crisis and subsequent austerity measures. This is key to examining the different responses of the host cities. In Hull, the impact of the crisis on real estate markets and on the Council's finances contributed to halting the city's regeneration strategy in 2010. The UK City of Culture 2017 programme was planned and delivered in the period 2013–2017, when the limitations imposed by austerity policies and weaker economic growth were very clear to local policy makers. The event took place following a decade of austerity policies in a left-behind northern coastal city. UK coastal towns and cities, which had thrived as commercial, naval or fishing ports or seaside resorts in the 19th and 20th centuries (Shaw & Williams, 1997; Borsay & Walton, 2011), are now among the most deprived areas of the country. For example, in 2018, Hull displayed the fifth highest insolvency rate in England and Wales after Stoke-on-Trent and the coastal communities of Scarborough, Torbay and Plymouth (Elliott, 2019). These cities are geographically isolated, at the end of road and rail transport routes (Tommarchi & Cavalleri, 2020) and are acknowledged as part of the UK's 'rustbelt', in an unpleasant parallel with US deindustrialising cities (see e.g. Lehmann, 2016).

This may have been amongst the factors behind a considerable Leave vote in Hull in the 2016 EU Referendum.[4] This result was particularly significant considering the nature of Hull as a port city and its trade connections with continental Europe, as well as the investment that Siemens has made in the city since the early 2010s, and the contribution to local employment opportunities. The trend towards the rise of populist parties as in other European countries was visible in the case of the European Parliament elections in May 2019, where the Brexit Party – founded in November 2018 – obtained nearly 44% of the votes, and the UK Independence Party (UKIP) reached 6%; Labour was the second party with 18.6% of the votes.[5] In the General Elections in December 2019, the Labour Party experienced a considerable loss in their share of the votes, to the advantage of the Brexit Party (BBC, 2019a, 2019b, 2019c).[6] These results suggest that Labour, despite having supported the UKCoC bid, did not benefit from the celebration of the event. Nonetheless, it is worth mentioning that the UKCoC 2017 was not presented from the outset as a political project: dominant discourses concerned job creation and economic regeneration. The EU Referendum taking place in the middle of the planning phase of the event, together with this social and political climate, impacted on the role of the UKCoC and the activity of the event team:

> If you look back to, I suppose, the politics at the global scale or the European scale, obviously the Brexit Referendum was in the middle of 2016 and the kind of Trump agenda shall we say was kind of early 2017 . . . So, I think kind of the role for things like City of Culture is potentially different to how it was when we were thinking about what we were doing two years ago.
>
> (interview, event team member 1, January 2018)

The results of the EU Referendum and the following uncertainty arising from Brexit negotiations were perceived as a potential concern across bidding cities involved in the competition for the UK City of Culture 2021 (Cunningham & Platt, 2018). The title was eventually awarded to Coventry, where the Leave vote accounted for 55.6% (BBC, n.d.).

In Rotterdam, the legacy of the ECoC 2001 in relation to cultural programming and multicultural policies was impacted by the rise of Pim Fortuyn's list at national and local level (Van de Laar, 2018, p. 80). Liveable Rotterdam became the biggest party in the city after the Local Elections in March 2002 and deprioritised investment in arts and culture (Palmer-Rae Associates, 2004, p. 285). The 2008 crisis also led to a profound redefinition of port-city relationships. In the 1990s and 2000s the city's growing attractiveness and the diversification of the local economy had fuelled the idea that the port would play a less central economic role, as other economic activities including culture and tourism developed. This was rethought following the shock of the economic and financial crisis, when it was acknowledged that the city could not be seen as independent from its port. The economic role of the port was rediscovered, and planning strategies were readdressed (Aarts et al., 2016, pp. 27–28). This has contributed to tighter political and economic relationships, as port actors have increasingly taken part in the city's political and economic life. Rotterdam can be considered to be a city where austerity policies at national and local level affected decisions on future mega events. Although the Council's event policy, pursued by a dedicated team, continued until 2015, it is worth noting that the joint bid with Amsterdam for the 2028 Olympic Games did not get support from the Dutch government, while the idea of a bid for the 2025 World Expo raised by a group of entrepreneurs (Bikker & Co., 2016) failed to gain momentum (interview, expert 3, April 2018; interview, expert 4, February 2018). This happened after the Dutch-Belgian joint bid for the FIFA World Cup 2018 was rejected, raising questions about whether Rotterdam City Council should invest in such uncertain bids in a context of limited resources (Chen, 2012, p. 34).

In Genoa, the 2007–8 economic crisis came soon after the European Capital of Culture 2004 and was among the factors that negatively impacted its legacy, together with changes in the city's political agenda. The ECoC 2004 focused on the concept of durability, which was then undermined by Mayor Vincenzi's politics of discontinuity with the past. The 'era' of *grandi eventi*, from 1992 to 2004, was then considered over, as policy makers had no interest in bidding for other mega events.[7] Waterfront regeneration and gentrification were contained by the crisis and the related shock for the housing market, which also eased the pressure on port areas (interview, expert 9, May 2018; interview, port actor 4, June 2018; interview, expert 12, June 2018). However, waterfront redevelopment is still a key political discourse and is now focused on the redevelopment of the eastern edge of the port. The 2007–8 crisis and the following austerity policies contributed to intensifying problems of unemployment, poverty and crime in the city as well as throughout the country (Figure 4.1).

In Valencia, the 2007–8 crash interrupted a period of economic growth fuelled by real estate development and tourism, which had benefitted from permissive legal frameworks and corruption, and had been exacerbated by ongoing processes of capital accumulation through the construction sector (Sorribes i Monrabal, 2015). The 2007–8 crisis also coincided with a local economic crisis resulting from the debt contracted by the City Council to fund urban megaprojects and international sporting events. This, combined with the austerity policies that followed, radically changed local political values which in turn transformed the perception of new flagship cultural facilities from valued opportunities into white elephants whilst also blocking the redevelopment of Valencia Street Circuit (interview, policy maker 9, May 2018), as examined in the next chapter. The area of the circuit was scheduled to be transformed through the megaproject known as PAI del Grau (Grau Integrated Action Plan), whose implementation was also expected to pay back the costs of the circuit through developer contributions. However, this mechanism was envisioned in a period of economic growth, in which the real estate sector

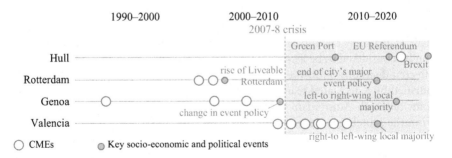

Figure 4.1 Major events and key socio-economic and political events in Hull, Rotterdam, Genoa and Valencia.

was thriving. The impacts of the crisis on the sector, together with episodes of corruption, contributed to the collapse of the operation. Moreover, the long-standing impacts of the crisis arguably contributed to the fall of the conservative political establishment in 2015 and marked the end of local coalitions of interests that had emerged around major sporting events (interview, expert 13, May 2018).

Growth machine theory is helpful in exploring the case of Valencia, where the Conservative-led City Council and Regional Government, the Port Authority and private organisations such as the Société Nautique de Genève and Formula One Group developed alliances around common goals. The local political agenda in the early 21st century can be interpreted using Phelps and Miao's (2019) concept of urban speculation, which portrays how aggressive urban policies are adopted to pursue economic growth and capital accumulation, in particular through the real estate sector. Culture- and event-led redevelopment projects, such as the Ciutat de les Arts i les Ciències or Port America's Cup, and major events more broadly, can be described as urban propaganda projects (Boyle, 1999), aimed at legitimising and supporting the activity of local pro-growth coalitions. Political propaganda and the manipulation of the media were also used by these coalitions. An example is the way in which Formula One Group's CEO Bernie Ecclestone made use of the media to subject the celebration of the Formula One European Grand Prix in Valencia to the electoral win of the People's Party at the 2007 local and regional elections (Ferrandis, 2007). In 2007, the party won regionally with a majority of 52.17% with Francisco Camps and locally with a majority of 56.67% for Mayor Rita Barberá (El País, n.d.).

A new model of large-scale events?

Policy makers in European cities appear inclined to focus on large-scale events that do not necessarily entail huge economic efforts to be delivered, such as City/Capital of Culture schemes. These events are perceived as more sustainable and suitable considering a city's social profile and specificity. This is in line with recent scholarship pointing at a crisis or downscaling of the largest mega events, such as the Olympics and the FIFA World Cup, and the rise of smaller-scale schemes (Gruneau & Horne, 2016; Jones & Ponzini, 2018; Jones, 2020; Di Vita & Wilson, 2020).

Despite this downscaling trend, mega events are still generally perceived to be as important by urban commentators despite the Great Recession. This can be explained by the increasing interurban competition where cities of any scale are promoted as exciting and safe places to live, visit, work and invest, as part of the range of efforts by local authorities that Phelps and Miao (2019) label as urban diplomacy. Policy makers in Rotterdam, Genoa and Valencia seem to have either little interest in or insufficient political support to bid for mega events. However, gaining a competitive advantage within interurban competition is still crucial, while cultural and sporting events are still an important feature of cultural urban policy more generally. It can be argued that local policy makers in these cities appear to be focusing on smaller-scale events, which are perceived as more compatible with local contexts and more sustainable in the long term. Smaller-scale events are opportunities for cities to benefit from the positive outcomes of culture- and event-led regeneration, without the negative impacts in terms of erosion of local finances, disruption and social conflict that the largest and well-known events, such as the Olympics or the FIFA World Cup, entail.

Much of the available research tends to categorise events on the basis of their (absolute) scale, for example by setting quantitative thresholds regarding budget and visitor figures. However, it needs to be underlined that the 'scale' of these events should be interpreted in relative terms (as suggested e.g. by Ponzini & Jones, 2020, p. 318), considering the context in which they are held. From this perspective, a year-round cultural festival such as the UK City of Culture held in a city such as Hull may well have transformative impacts of the kind visible in large cities hosting major international events.

In Rotterdam, the European Capital of Culture 2001 was followed by a series of themed year-round cultural programmes focusing on water (2003), sport (2005), architecture (2007) and youth (2009). Other events included Red Bull Air Race, the start of the Tour de France 2010, Rotterdam viert de stad[8] and the Innovation Expo 2018. Regular events include the Wereldhavendagen (World Port Days), the Port of Rotterdam North Sea Jazz Festival – which was moved to Rotterdam from The Hague in 2006 and is now funded by Rotterdam Port Authority – and the Architecture Biennale (IABR). Rotterdam will be the host city of the World Police and Fire Games in 2022, and there was an initial interest in hosting the Youth Olympics 2022. Policy makers in Rotterdam are thus focusing on smaller and selected events, which are considered in line with 'the DNA' of the city (interview, event team member 2, April 2018).[9]

A similar picture emerges in the case of Genoa, where the event 'era' is seen as 'a thing of the past' (interview, expert 9, May 2018), while local policy makers are now more interested in smaller-scale events such as the traditional Regata delle Repubbliche Marinare[10] or the 2018 Euroflora exhibition. In many Spanish cities, as observed by Carrasco and Pitarch-Garrido (2017, p. 724), events and urban projects have been perceived as a 'sign of modernity' until the 2007–8 crisis. In Valencia, this was coupled with the radical change in local politics in 2015 and with a trend to abandon elitist events (interview, policy maker 9, May 2018), pursuing a strategy of 'emotional and physical reconciliation with the city' (interview, event team member 6, June 2018).

Considering the case of Rotterdam, Genoa and Valencia, it can be suggested that policy makers in port cities where mega events have taken place tend to shift their attention towards smaller-scale events which are also better connected with local history and identity. On the one hand, this reframing is in part the natural consequence of hosting mega events, as they are 'one off' events. These events also present considerable issues of economic sustainability, which could be particularly relevant in structurally disadvantaged maritime port cities (for a definition of the concept, see Jonas et al., 2017, pp. 198–199), where there is often a contestation around the rebranding of the city's image. On the other hand, the number of withdrawn bids and rejected proposals – in both port and non-port cities – for the largest international schemes, such as the Olympics and the FIFA World Cup, also raises an open question about whether we are witnessing a crisis of mega events – or more specifically of the development model based on the largest and most well-known events – and whether this is linked to a broader and deeper crisis of neoliberal capitalism (or even capitalism itself, see Cooper & Szreter, 2021) and its model of urbanism.

Capitalism itself is questioned for being an adaptive system which is no longer able to adapt (Kotz, 2008; Mason, 2016), and for the striking social inequalities and the planetary-scale environmental destruction that it generates (Moore, 2016). As suggested by Gotham (2016), mega events can be understood as a means to perpetuate the Schumpeterian creative destruction that characterises capitalist accumulation. Destruction is associated with the systematic undermining of existing institutions, arrangements and social relationships (and meanings), while creation embodies the establishment of new institutions (e.g. permanent culture companies initially established to manage events), new infrastructures and urban spectacles (as well as meanings, Gotham, 2016, p. 33). The recent lack of public and political support around certain mega events may be a sign of the growing difficulty to legitimise the effort of hosting such events, as well as to exploit them as *panem et circensem* devices. If so this reflects the 2007–8 crash and the economic recession that followed, but also the growing insistence of discourses of environmental sustainability even within mega-event rhetoric (Hall, 2012). This also suggests a certain degree of weakness across coalitions of interest behind events, who fail to pursue their goals.

Thus, it appears possible to argue that events requiring huge investment – e.g. the Olympics – are today a game restricted to a few 'top' global cities. It is also worth noting that, as commented by Scherer (2011, p. 794), long-term and large-scale redevelopment projects are debt-financed and can therefore contribute to triggering local economic crises in moments of economic downturn. Conversely, smaller-scale events such as CoC schemes are more popular than ever across second-tier and medium-sized European cities that are trapped into destructive interurban competition. In port cities, smaller-scale events are considerably more appealing as a means to tackle the structural socio-economic decline generated by the restructuring of ports and by changing international trade patterns. However, many of these cities are still portrayed as working-class cities where huge spending in culture and events may be difficult to legitimise.

At the time of writing, the COVID-19 outbreak has been leading to the rescheduling or cancellation of a considerable number of events and mega events, including the 2020 Olympic Games and the EURO 2020 European football championships – both of which took place in 2021 – and virtually all cultural events involving mass gatherings. At this stage, it is not possible to predict when the celebration of large-scale events will be fully resumed or whether the aftermath of the pandemic will change the meaning of events themselves. However, it is worth suggesting that the current situation is likely to aggravate the crisis of the mega-event model.

Social reactions to event-led regeneration

Growing ontological insecurity means that the ability of event promoters to tap into local cultural traditions and meanings becomes even more important for the success, as well as the legitimation, of such initiatives.[11] Mega events in deindustrialising European maritime port cities may encounter relatively mild opposition in comparison with activism and protests against the largest international sporting events taking place in global cities across the world. On the one hand, the nature of the events being celebrated is key. On the other hand, the demise of the industrial port city model arguably plays a role. However, unintended and indirect outcomes of culture- and event-led regeneration may contribute to fuelling processes of touristification in the long term, which in turn may fuel opposition and conflict. These issues suggest that the way in which mega events are received locally and the reactions that they generate are of primary concern in contemporary mega-event studies.

Mega events are often understood in the literature as 'safety valves' (Smith, 2012, p. 31) or bread and circuses devices (as commented by Gotham, 2016), as they are often staged to control festivity in order to reduce demands for social transformation. These events may also be organised to construct public acceptance around controversial socio-political decisions and events, such as in the case of the divisive £120 million 'Festival of Brexit' (Quinn, 2019), initially called Festival UK★ 2022 and then rebranded as Unboxed. However, as mentioned in Chapter 2, mega events and event-led regeneration have often sparked criticisms and protests because of their very nature of urban spectacles and the huge public spending associated with them.

One could assume that mega events are more problematic in European maritime port cities, considering their outward-looking, yet rebellious character (e.g. Mah, 2014) and the fact that they are often home to a supposedly vast working-class population who may fiercely oppose large-scale projects that divert funding from social policies. High-profile cultural events may be felt as elitist and unnecessary because of their cost, accessibility and inability to meet the taste of the local general public. Urban conflicts may also arise from the fact that, waterfront redevelopment and culture- and event-led regeneration tend to transform areas of production into areas of consumption, through a 'port out, city in' strategy that attempts to transform the port city into a 'waterfront city'.

Yet, this assumption needs to be problematised from two perspectives: firstly, the rebellious and independent character of port cities described in the literature may not translate into stronger or organised activism and resistance against gentrifying creative city concepts specifically. Secondly, the 'working class' is no longer a straightforward concept. Economic restructuring due to automation produced a 'non-class of non-workers' (Gorz, 1997 [1980], p. 7). The tertiarisation – and the emergence of the quaternary sector – of the economy generated a heterogeneous service class (Savage et al., 1988), while the diversification of working arrangements and relationships led to the emergence of the 'precariat' as a new social class (Standing, 2011). An analysis of the social composition of the working class in European port cities is not the aim of the book. However, it is worth considering that what is traditionally described as the 'working class' in these cities might actually be a pulverised, highly heterogeneous mix of social groups – shaped by local meanings and volatile interest groups – including a range of low-skilled, underpaid or precarious workers employed in different sectors of the economy. As these workers display different backgrounds, values and lifestyles, they might also have rather different attitudes towards culture, sport and events. This section explores the criticisms and protests against major events, focusing in particular on issues related to their maritime nature, and examines the reactions to the transformation of waterfronts through event-led regeneration.

Protests and opposition against mega events in port cities

An element that distinguishes mega events in the 21st century is that promoters increasingly need to operate through subtle or controversial mechanisms in order to frame and adapt these events to local contexts and conditions. In the case of Hull, the designation as UK City of Culture 2017 was welcomed with initial scepticism, concerning in particular Hull's attitude to be a cultural city (see for instance Youngs, 2016) and the capability of local actors to deliver such a large-scale cultural event. The scale and pace of public ground works in 2016 also raised criticisms, although these were more about the inconvenience that such works generated, to the extent that Hull was sometimes labelled, for example on social media, as 'the City of Orange Barriers'.[12]

However, initial scepticism and criticisms faded away in early 2017. A key role in this was played by the opening event *Made in Hull* (interview, expert 2, January 2018), which made use of light shows and projections on the façades of iconic buildings – such as the Maritime Museum, the Ferens Art Gallery, the City Hall and The Deep – to create a sense of attachment to the event and to tell the story of Hull to its residents and visitors. On the one hand, the scale and spectacular character of the opening event cleared the doubts about the capability of local actors to deliver the UKCoC. On the other hand, local people felt connected with the event and with the history of their city, as images related to distant-water trawler fishing and the city's fishing past were displayed. In 2017 and 2018, the complaints about inconveniences due to public ground works also faded away and were replaced by a widespread feeling of pride arising from the visual impact of refurbished spaces (see e.g. Kemp, 2018). During and after 2017, criticisms focused on the fact that local artists were not given enough space within the UKCoC programme and that professional artists and cultural organisations sometimes had a problematic relationship with Hull 2017 Ltd (interview, expert 2, January 2018). Tension with residents was related to the fact that the UKCoC was conceived as a UK-wide event (interview, event team member 1, January 2018), in a city where many people felt that they had been 'left behind' by the state. More organised protests, albeit on a small scale, involved the role of British Petroleum (BP) as a major partner of Hull 2017 (Grove, 2017). BP, who run a chemical facility at the nearby Saltend Chemicals Park, contributed to funding the event. Hull 2017 Ltd was criticised for accepting sponsorship and, thus, legitimising BP's activity. Activists demonstrated during the event against BP's controversial exploitation of natural resources across the world, hoping to get more visibility. Broader political contestation is often a feature of mega events due to their visibility and media impact. For example, the 2014 Winter Olympics in Sochi were accompanied by widespread protests against Russian laws condemning homosexuality (Gotham, 2016, p. 9), which featured in international media as part of the coverage of the whole event.

In Rotterdam, scepticism about the fact that the city could be a cultural capital preceded the ECoC 2001 and then faded away as the event progressed (Palmer-Rae Associates, 2004). Although the ECoC 2001 was probably less effective in terms of repositioning in comparison with other events taking place in the city (Chen, 2012, p. 35), it contributed to boosting civic pride (interview, city planner 3, April 2018; interview, expert 4, February 2018). Marginal issues emerged due to a degree of opposition to attempts to celebrate diversity, which also involved future programming by Rotterdam Festival (interview, event team member 3, May 2018). However, these episodes had more to do with Rotterdam's political climate and issues of social cohesion within a multiethnic urban population rather than with the city's maritime nature.

In Genoa, the 1992 Specialist Expo did not generate substantial protests. However, attendance was far lower than expected. Criticisms concerned attempts to divert public funding to private companies, as well as the use of the event to unlock public investment in Northern Italy's transport infrastructure (see e.g. Negri, 1999). Uncertainty and criticisms about the reuse of cultural facilities after the event accompanied its celebration (CCR/PE/ADNKRONOS, 1992). Although the 2001 G8 summit is not explored in the book, it is important to mention that the event sadly monopolised national and international media due to the violent protests and clashes with the police that took place across the city: among the 200,000 protesters (Amnesty International, 2001), including black bloc anarchists, one died and hundreds were injured.

The European Capital of Culture 2004 was generally well received by the local population. Although Genoa was not necessarily a top cultural destination in the early 2000s, it was not thought surprising that the city could be a cultural capital, considering its history and rich heritage. No particular social tension accompanied the event (interview, policy maker 5, June 2018). Local stakeholders and residents – in particular young people – perceived the ECoC 2004 as a good opportunity to boost tourism and, ultimately, to help the local economy (interview, policy maker 6, June 2018). Event-led regeneration processes such as the construction of the new Galata Museo del Mare – and an increased and stable presence of people beyond school and office hours in

Porto Antico – were perceived as a means to discourage criminal activity in the area (interview, policy maker 5, June 2018).

Valencia presents a different picture. Del Romero Renau and Trudelle (2011) analysed 411 articles in local newspaper *El Levante* about 25 episodes of urban conflict in the city. Three of these episodes (12% of total) were related to the construction of Valencia Street Circuit, the impacts of the America's Cup and the development of the southern marina. 78 articles (19% of total) were about these three conflicts. However, a distinction should be made between the two kinds of international sporting events that were hosted in the city, namely the America's Cup (2007 and 2010) and the Formula One European Grand Prix (2008–2012). Despite being a niche sporting event addressed to a specialist audience, the America's Cup was free and open to everyone. Furthermore, the 2007 edition contributed to the opening of the old harbour and to its transformation into a public space. A study by the University of Valencia (UVEG, 2009) in the immediate aftermath of 2007 highlighted that the majority of residents recognised the positive impact of the event in terms of economic growth and international tourism and that 74% of residents felt proud about the fact that the event took place in Valencia. However, Parra Camacho et al. (2016) show how this perception changed soon after the event so that the socio-economic and socio-cultural legacy and even the impact of the event on urban development were reconsidered.

Conversely, Formula One races were expensively ticketed, and caused a lockdown of the area. The different use of public space was key, as while the America's Cup did enable the accessibility and permeability of the waterfront, Formula One races cut off the leisure port from the rest of the city. As noted by a local informant:

> Now I am speaking as a resident. I perceived Formula 1 and the America's Cup differently. The America's Cup was a recovery of the historic harbour for the city, it was free in the sense that you didn't need to pay to get in. There was greater permeability so that if one had come to the port to see the boats they could have done so. Formula 1 was a closed event, that you needed to pay for. Even physically. I clearly remember how the area was visually hidden from residents. If you hadn't paid, you couldn't see anything, just listen to the noise of the engines. This idea of two totally different events . . . An event which, so to speak, allowed integration between the port estate and the social and urban processes taking place in the city, such as the America's Cup, and which allowed residents to enter these spaces that until that moment were restricted, and another event, such as Formula 1, which on the contrary was a privatisation of [public] space.
>
> (interview, policy maker 8, June 2018, author's translation)

Given the nature of international motorsport events, some extent of closure was necessary for safety and security reasons. However, in the case of Formula One, the specific measures that were taken to isolate the track from the rest of the city suggest the intention to maximise ticket sales and to protect the elit-ist and lavish F1 environment from the typical port city context in which the races took place. For example, the surrounding deprived district of Natzaret was visually hidden from those inside the perimeter of the circuit (Del Romero Renau & Trudelle, 2011, p. 9).

The privatisation, commodification and, in some cases, militarisation of public space is a recurrent element in the experience of port cities across the world where high-profile international sporting events have been held. In Baku, where the Formula One Azerbaijan Grand Prix has been hosted since 2017 (except for the 2020 edition which was cancelled due to COVID-19), simi-lar arrangements were put in place to prevent unauthorised viewings and to hide areas of urban decay from visitors, while military ships patrolled the Cas-pian Sea coast (Gogishvili, 2018, pp. 172–173). The Formula One Singapore Grand Prix has been hosted in the Marina Bay Street Circuit since 2008 (with the exception of the 2020 and 2021 editions due to COVID-19). This is an example where aggressive privatisation and commodification of public space to host temporary events of international appeal may result in the local com-munity being disengaged with the event and retreating from the waterfront. Henderson et al. (2010, p. 65 and 68) reports that the disruption caused by the race led to reduced revenues for retailers and restaurants, as disappointed residents avoided the area. In the case of Cape Town, where the FIFA World Cup was held for the first time in the African continent in 2010, Alegi (2008, p. 402) reports that FIFA delegates pressured the City Council to move the new stadium from its proposed location in a social housing area to its final loca-tion next to the redeveloped waterfront, so that television viewers would see pleasant images of the city rather than its periphery. In Rio de Janeiro, attempts were made to hide *favelas* from event audiences. Duignan and McGillivray (2019) note that specific measures, that were hardly recognisable as 'law' were issued to enforce public order and restrict citizens' rights, in order to deliver the 2016 Olympics. The authors recount the militarisation of event venues in the run up to the Olympics, which included warships patrolling Copacabana beach. Many scholars have commented on the degree of coercion and violence that were deployed by the Brazilian government in the *favelas* in relation to mega events (e.g. Rekow, 2016; Talbot & Carter, 2018). This was not limited to the FIFA World Cup and the Olympics. Police actions resulted in the killing of several residents in the Complexo de Alemão in the run up to the 2007 Pan American Games as well (Gaffney, 2010, p. 18). According to Faulhaber and Azevedo (2015), between 2009 and 2012, approximately 20,000 people were displaced due to event-led urban transformation.

Returning to the case of Valencia, a study of residents' perception (Añó Sanz et al., 2012) shows how F1 races in the city were positively rated in terms of economic growth and the city's image, while they were negatively rated as regards employment, return on public investment and civic pride. Formula One events also generated largely negative reactions. Collectives were estab-lished to oppose the event, such as Fórmula Verda[13] and Circuit Urbà No,[14] pointing out in particular its considerable infrastructure and social costs. Environmental concerns were raised in relation to the waste of fossil fuels and noise pollution, as F1 cars in 2008–2012 were equipped with loud V8 aspirated engines burning high-octane petrol. Public spending on the event was a crucial issue, considering the spark of the 2007–8 crisis and its immediate impact on employment, nationally and locally. As in many other host cities, public spending on the event was criticised for absorbing resources which could be used in other areas of the city and other policy domains. Fórmula Verda used the slogan 'Formula 1 – Barris 0'[15] to highlight how the city's maritime districts would not benefit from the investment (Vázquez, 2017), while protests also denounced the lack of investment in social policies (EFE, 2012; Govan, 2012). Tension concerned public spending and the lack of consultation. As noted by Tarazona Vento (2017, pp. 77–78), mega events in Valencia – as well as mega urban projects – were managed through two mechanisms: exceptionality measures and public-private organisations, depriving citizens of any decision-making capabilities. This had a considerable impact on the port-city interface and the city's maritime districts. As recalled by a city planner in the case of urban transformation along Avenida del Puerto:

> we could have sought citizens' consensus around these projects. For instance, [in the case of] Avenida del Puerto, we could have established a debate with the city about . . . the investment that this implied and [we could have] managed it. The problem is that the implementation schedule was very tight and did not allow this type of contact.
> (interview, city planner 5, May 2018, author's translation)

The role of private organisations further reduced the chances for citizens' involvement in the process of transformation of the inner harbour. In the case of the America's Cup:

> The America's Cup Management (ACM), a private consortium collaborating with the national and local administrations, designed the renewal project and managed the organization in a way that excluded the possibility of participation of local urban-based movements. No social, cultural, or ecological local associations in Poblats Marítims were given the chance to participate in the decision-making process in any way, and their demands were completely ignored by the ACM forum.
> (Del Romero Renau & Trudelle, 2011, p. 7)

Relationships underpinned by corruption between certain policy makers and Formula One Group was also a key element of opposition. All these aspects contributed to generating a 'sense of rejection' for international sporting events and event-led regeneration (interview, city planner 5, May 2018) among the population of the maritime districts, as a result of event-led urban conflicts, privatisation of public space, increasing land values and evictions (Del Romero

Renau & Trudelle, 2011, p. 2). Interviews with a small group of residents in Natzaret confirmed the negative perception of Formula One events, in particular in relation to noise pollution and reduced permeability of the area.

Populist political strategies were deployed to corral local discourses to stifle opposition around sporting events. For example, contesters were labelled as 'un-Valencians', while the events were claimed to be good for 'the Valencian people' (Tarazona Vento, 2017, p. 79). Some local PP members claimed that citizens *had* to be in favour of Formula One since the party had prevailed in the Local Elections (Del Romero Renau & Trudelle, 2011, p. 8). These strategies implemented by local coalitions of interest were effective in repressing opposition. As noted by a local informant:

> this is the terrible thing about Valencia. It seems to me that the problem is that they used these mega events in order to generate a social and cultural hegemony. . . . They deactivated all the antibodies that could have existed. Social movements fell silent, to a certain extent, syndicates fell silent, neighbourhood associations fell silent. As far as I know, there weren't great protests. Of course, there were people who were critical. I would like to say that there was the problem that . . . I think it was clear, Zaplana and then Camps used Formula One as a means to win the elections and they also said it explicitly. And this should be . . . I think this should be a scandal or should have been a scandal leading to the exclusion of these people and their teams. But no, on the contrary, even during the crisis, they kept gaining vote shares higher than 50%.
>
> (interview, expert 14, interview, May 2018, author's translation)

In other port cities, *ad hoc* legal tools were deployed to stifle opposition against Formula One events in a similar fashion. Hall (2006, p. 65) reports that the Victorian Grand Prix Act exempted the construction of Melbourne's F1 track from environmental impact, pollution and planning assessments and controls, and that the agreements with (private) event promoters would not be accessible under the Freedom of Information Act.

It is also worth considering the attempts to maximise engagement with mega events in port cities through participation and engagement programmes. Although the nature of the intention behind these initiatives might be rather diverse and difficult to demonstrate, two of the case-study cities provide examples of such efforts. In Hull, except for protests against the involvement of BP, there was no substantial opposition to the UKCoC. A key role in this might have been played by engagement, especially considering the social composition of Hull's population. As mentioned by a senior officer from the City Council:

> I think that [opposition] could easily have happened, but it didn't. And I think the reason why it didn't was we were very careful to say . . . because art and culture on one level can be conceived as very highbrow, so it's classical music, it's ballet, it's things that lots of people enjoy, but actually

in more working-class cities like Hull it's not the natural environment for people to attend. And we were very clear that our City of Culture year was not all about that. We had some of that, because you want to mix, but actually it was about engaging communities.

(interview, policy maker 1, interview, February 2018)

An example is Hull's Volunteer Programme, which involved about 2,400 volunteers from different age groups and from across the city in a range of supporting activities (Culture, Place and Policy Institute, 2018, p. 162). The even spatial distribution of volunteers was 'very calculated' (interview, policy maker 1, February 2018) by the City Council, with the aim of maximising engagement through word of mouth. In Rotterdam, the Opzomeeren programme was run in preparation of hosting EURO 2000 and it generated engagement and interest around the event (Chen, 2012, p. 33; interview, expert 6, April 2018). The programme was named after Opzomeerstraat near Delftshaven, where, in the 1980s, residents proactively worked together – for example by wiping the street and installing street lighting – in order to discourage drug dealing in the area. However, despite being initially envisioned as a bottom-up initiative to promote social cohesion, the Opzomeeren programme was later described as a city-wide tool of social control, in a context of revanchist urban policies (see e.g. Uitermark & Duyvendak, 2008).

In the light of this variegated picture of opposition against large-scale events, a key question is whether event-led regeneration in (at least some European) maritime port cities is less opposed than in other contexts because of the collapse of the 20th century industrial port city model, or as a result of a more or less subtle mobilisation of local discourses and meanings. Although a comparative analysis of port and non-port host cities would be necessary to further explore this hypothesis, it is possible to point out a few aspects. Informants across the four case-study cities agreed that there was no substantial tension or conflict in relation to event-led regeneration, apart from fear of gentrification and touristification in some of these cities and the aforementioned issues of waste of public money and corruption. Nevertheless, a distinction should be made in relation to these cities' history and economic trajectories as maritime port cities. The cases of Hull and Genoa are examples of industrial port cities hit by economic decline due to deindustrialisation, where conventional urban policies have failed and culture- and event-led regeneration are seen as an alternative. Rotterdam did display, until the 1990s, some of the typical features of deindustrialising port cities. However, despite the shocks that occurred in the 1970s and late 2000s, it is difficult to argue that a similar structural socio-economic decline as in Hull has taken place. Culture- and event-led urban regeneration can be considered more as a supportive strategy for assisting the development of a competitive port. In this case, although culture is far from being the alternative and worst-case-scenario strategy, it does contribute to the economic competitiveness of the port and to the city's wealth. The question is more about the extent to which residents are aware of this connection and how this builds acceptance of event-led regeneration. Valencia represents an exception, due to the traditional separation between the city and its port and to the fact that port activity has not necessarily been the undisputed core of the local economy. It is not the case that event-led regeneration is more accepted in the Spanish city because of the failure of the industrial port city model. Furthermore, despite the underuse of the Zona de Actividades Logísticas (ZAL, logistics zone) and the competition with the nearby port of Sagunto, it cannot be asserted that Valencia's port had been declining before mega events took place. Notwithstanding the protests against Formula One events, Valencia displays a different picture in comparison to Barcelona:

> Unlike Barcelona, where 'strategic cultural events' such as The Forum of Cultures 2004 sparked growing opposition, the Valencia Local Council and Regional Government could do much as they pleased in re-zoning the Port area and in gentrifying the south-eastern quarter of the city on the pretext of carrying out strategic projects. Most of Valencia's citizens either approved of these projects or simply let the plans go through without demur (Cucó i Giner, 2013).
>
> (Rius-Ulldemolins & Gisbert, 2019, p. 382)

This can be explained considering the role of populist propaganda and pro-growth coalitions around events – and how these coalitions manipulated local policy discourses and meanings – rather than the failure of the socio-economic model of the industrial port city.

Another aspect to consider in commenting on the apparent 'acceptance' of event-led regeneration in European port cities is the typical rhythms of the industrial port city. Up until the 1980s or even 1990s, Rotterdam and Genoa were dormitories and service areas for port workers and were thus largely 'closed' and empty in the evening and on weekends. In this context, culture- and event-led regeneration have undoubtedly revitalised central areas beyond the normal working hours of the industrial port city:

> Even in the early 1990s, mid-1990s, there was absolutely nothing to do [in Rotterdam]. After 6 o'clock, the city was empty, the heart of the city. There were shops there, yeah, sure, but . . . And the bars and the clubs were completely scattered around, in dodgy places. There was a saying in Rotterdam that you could fire a cannon in the heart of the city at Saturday night and nobody would care.
>
> (interview, expert 4, February 2018)

> Here in the city [of Genoa], you know, tourists have always been welcome because the city became livelier, because they brought new activities, because this is a city . . . I can tell you [that] on Saturdays and Sundays, this was a completely closed city, with all shutters closed. There was nobody around. On non-working days, the city was closed, there weren't any open

bars. In the city centre, I couldn't even have a coffee. [Now] this has completely changed. Residents are happy about this.

(interview, expert 9, May 2018, author's translation)

It appears possible to argue that certain mega events may encounter less opposition in deindustrialising port cities, where residents may welcome such events as devices to sustain local economies in a context of structural decline. However, it should also be noted that context-specificity plays a key role. In order to portray a more complete picture, it is also worth exploring the reactions to the – direct and indirect – long-term impacts of event-led regeneration, which are presented in the next section.

A waterfront city for whom? The long-term socio-economic and urban restructuring of European port cities

Although most of the mega events held in the case-study cities of the book were celebrated without strong opposition, it can be argued that they contributed to a long-term transformation of urban port areas and waterfronts and a restructuring of local economies that has produced social opposition and conflicts. In other words, it appears possible to suggest that event-led regeneration may – contingently – stimulate a range of socio-economic and spatial transformations – namely gentrification, touristification and overtourism, socio-spatial disparities and environmental issues – so that an event appears accepted in the short run, but generates tension and conflict in the long term.

On the one hand, waterfront redevelopment has introduced an unprecedented distinction between some urban areas at the water's edge and the rest of the city (Porfyriou & Sepe, 2017, p. 3). On the other hand, however, it can be suggested that culture- and event-led regeneration in European port cities emphasise such differences in the long term. This appears to be a particular case of the 'spatial dilemmas' – namely the centre-periphery disparity – generated by culture-led regeneration that were first mentioned by Bianchini (1993, p. 201). However, it must be clarified that it may be impossible to isolate the specific direct impacts of mega events and event-led regeneration, as they operate in the context of processes of economic restructuring. Nonetheless, the *contingent* impacts of these initiatives are of interest.

Mega events have displayed different relationships with local trajectories of culture-led urban regeneration across the core case-study cities. In Hull, although direct event-led physical transformation was marginal, the UKCoC 2017 did contribute to accelerating or sustaining processes of urban regeneration, helping to resume the regeneration of the city centre which had been halted due to the Great Recession. As mentioned, mega events in Rotterdam did not have much direct physical or economic impact. Nonetheless, they arguably encouraged the Council's subsequent event policy until the mid-2010s. This has shown an increasing awareness of the role of culture as a place-making device and its potential for urban planning.[16] In Genoa and Valencia, major events kick-started the redevelopment of inner harbours and contributed to boosting tourism figures.

Gentrification and touristification in European port cities are complex phenomena, which in some cases elude direct causal relationships. In relation to culture and events, these phenomena have to do with both the way in which culture is produced – that is local cultural offer, facilities and amenities – and the way in which it is consumed. Cultural consumption patterns may develop in unintended ways, especially in the long term, generating different meanings and social practices. In the case of Hull, the redevelopment of the Fruit Market area – which did not happen because of the event – involved the opening of a number of bars and restaurants, art galleries and shops, which helped revitalise the area and create a new centrality. The social groups who use the area (i.e. young people and professionals) appear different from those using other areas such as Queen Victoria Square (e.g. young parents with their children, elderly people). In this case, the concept of gentrification does not fully explain the socio-spatial processes triggered by urban regeneration, as it refers to the displacement of original urban populations and the concentration of new, wealthier dwellers. As there was no original population in the area, the concept of retail gentrification (Gonzalez & Waley, 2013; Hubbard, 2018) – the replacement of retail activities and urban amenities with new ones that are beyond the reach of previous customers – better describes the ongoing transformation of the urban environment and its impact on the social profile of the area (Figure 4.2).

Figure 4.2 Bars and restaurants on Humber Street in the Fruit Market area.

In Rotterdam, gentrification can be considered as a relatively recent phenomenon (see e.g. Likku & Mandias, 2016). Architecture, culture-led regeneration and cultural and sporting events have been elements of the City Council's strategy to make Rotterdam more attractive. Mega events have played a marginal role in this, as increased tourism and gentrification in Rotterdam appears more as a result of a range of processes and of the City Council's social and urban policy. As noted by Romein (2005, p. 2) in relation to tourism growth:

> It is no question that the number of visits to Rotterdam for leisure purposes has rapidly increased during the past few years: from 12,4 million in 1999 to 17,5 million in 2003 (OBR, 2004a). The city's modern high-rise architecture, fun shopping zones, extended agenda of summer festivals, sports events, rock concerts and museums attract more and more people.

This trend has continued in recent years, with the number of overnight stays in the city growing from 1.06 million in 2012 to 1.73 million in 2018[17] (Figure 4.3).

It appears possible to argue that the Council's event and cultural policy since the 1990s has played a role, by acting on the national and international image of Rotterdam as an attractive and dynamic 'waterfront city'. It is important to note that social tension is neither necessarily the outcome of the city's increased attractiveness, nor specifically maritime related. Rather, it could be related to the diversity of the local population and to social fragmentation. The policy of attracting high-income and high-skilled urbanites is changing the city's social composition, while problems of poverty and education remain, in particular in

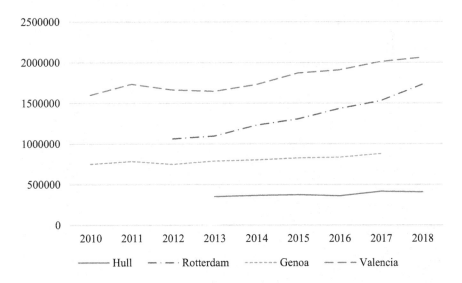

Figure 4.3 Overnight stays in the four case-study cities. Author's work.

Sources: Hull – Visit Hull and East Yorkshire (VHEY); Rotterdam – Gemeente Rotterdam, Centraal Bureau voor de Statistiek; Genoa – Comune di Genova; Valencia – Turismo Valencia.

southern districts and among Moroccan and Antillean groups (interview, port actor 3, April 2018).

Genoa provides an opportunity to analyse how the actual outcomes of the complex and interrelated processes triggered by event-led regeneration might be different from initial expectations or external predictions. The redevelopment of Porto Antico, which introduced a range of retail and leisure functions (Figure 4.4), could be expected to foster gentrification.

As a matter of fact, a certain degree of gentrification was initially visible since the mid-1990s. This phenomenon appeared in contrast with the established tendency of middle- and upper-class groups to move to the suburbs and emerged after a period of sustained immigration which, together with problems of waste collection, crime and prostitution, had contributed to the stigmatisation of the city centre as a dangerous area (Gastaldi, 2013, 2017). However, the changes in the social composition of the city centre appear more complex than the mere displacement of lower-class groups in favour of middle- and upper-class groups, and they are difficult to ascribe solely to culture- and event-led regeneration (for a description of these changes, see Gastaldi, 2013). Furthermore, social groups with a foreign background consolidated their presence in the city centre, which to some extent continues to be stigmatised as run down and dangerous. Social tension takes place between regenerated and non-regenerated areas (interview, expert 11, June 2018) – as for instance

Figure 4.4 Shops and restaurants in Porto Antico.

in the case of Porto Antico and areas such as Via di Prè or the Maddalena neighbourhood – as a result of urban fragmentation (Hillmann, 2008).

It is also relevant to note that initial event-led gentrification and the related rise in real estate values (interview, expert 10, June 2018; interview, port actor 7, June 2018) have more recently been impacted by broader processes of economic decline. This has hampered real estate development, contributed to the spatial concentration of migrants in the city centre, and thus reinforced the stigmatisation of the area and allowed the aforementioned historic tendencies emerge once again.

> Of course land values increased somehow in relation to the [leisure] port, though this phenomenon is more complex because in the 90s the city centre saw land values increasing substantially because there was this important renewal, linked to the public investment for these mega events, but also to the fact that private investment began to concentrate in these areas due to their potential. And then, nonetheless, there was a period of decay due to phenomena of economic decline, including that of migration. . . . Of course, when you put people . . . with very limited economic resources in an area with possibly higher needs in terms of renewal . . . it's clear that the result could be further decay, as it was. And then, that phenomenon of attraction, the appeal of this area to high-income people faded away because, of course, this area became a bit more difficult, a bit riskier . . . a bit less pleasant, so to speak, then of course the rich . . . now retreat to more traditional and established [location] options.
>
> (interview, expert 12, June 2018, author's translation)

This more nuanced phenomenon is also visible in Porto Antico. As reported by a local academic:

> And I would say the same for the Porto Antico area, which actually is used, as expected, by tourists, students, wealthy residents who use this area as a service area, but it is also intensively used by residents living in the city centre. So, it's common, especially in the evenings on weekdays, to see many migrant children and people from the city centre and, as soon as this space is less crowded, as it is on weekdays, they take control of it.
>
> (interview, expert 11, June 2018, author's translation)

Gastaldi (2013, p. 72) suggests that the city centre became more attractive to those seeking proximity and close relations with other people, which were possible because of the distinctive urban fabric of the area. Arguably, the increased porosity of Porto Antico as a public space, played a role in this. In addition, its redevelopment was aimed at creating a new centrality without causing a parallel decline of the city centre. An example is the redevelopment of Magazzini del Cotone, which were not transformed into a retail space and now host a conference centre and a public library. Local policy makers also targeted promoting legacy and the reuse of such facilities in the long term, prioritising cultural functions and public space. For example, the project of a 200-metre tower including office spaces, restaurants and a conference centre on a triangular-shaped platform, known as Cono di Portman, was rejected (Gastaldi, 2010). Nonetheless, it is worth noting that the transition from event-related to permanent cultural functions had been uncertain immediately after the 1992 Specialist Expo and was overcome with the work of Porto Antico Spa (Mastropietro, 2007, p. 180).

The case of Valencia offers a different perspective. One could argue that in the 1990s and early 21st century gentrification and touristification were to some extent planned goals, which were pursued with the reconversion of the Dársena for the America's Cup 2007. This transformation implied that:

> two marinas for megayachts were constructed and the former docks, which had remarkable heritage buildings, among them tinglados (port warehouses) from the beginning of the 20th century, were closed and replaced by the bases of the regatta teams. Trendy cafés and restaurants and Louis Vuitton boutiques were opened, and a brand new pavilion designed by star architect David Chipperfield was constructed for 35 million euros to accommodate the press and visitors during the competition, along with the five-star luxury spa hotel Las Arenas, which was built next to the old fishing houses of El Cabanyal.
>
> (Del Romero Renau & Trudelle, 2011, p. 6)

In contrast with the case of Barcelona, where Port Vell was redeveloped as a new centrality and public space for middle-class residents and tourists, Valencia's leisure port specifically targeted wealthy people (interview, expert 14, May 2018). This can be considered one of the reasons why the new leisure port failed to become a centrality immediately after the hosting of mega events had taken place (see Chapters 5 and 7). Similarly, international sporting events hosted in the leisure port were largely perceived as elitist and 'for the rich' (interview, policy maker 9, May 2018).

If it is true that gentrification is a likely outcome of culture- and event-led regeneration, these processes can also contribute to fostering touristification in the long term. Waterfront redevelopment and flagship cultural facilities have played a pivotal role in launching some European port cities as tourist destinations, as for example in the case of post-1992 Barcelona. Before the COVID-19 outbreak, anti-tourism sentiments in Barcelona had developed as a response to the remarkable increase in tourist numbers, to the extent that Papathanassis (2017, p. 288) reports the appearance of murals saying 'If it is tourist season, why can't we shoot them?' or 'Tourists go home'. Similar sentiments and opposition grew in other European port cities where touristification had been a planned goal even in the absence of mega events, such as in Venice or Dubrovnik.

In the four case-study cities, with the exception of Valencia's El Cabanyal-El Canyamelar district as explored later, surveyed residents suggested that there was no substantial tension in relation to the presence of tourists. In Genoa, residents have some awareness that the steady growth of tourism in the last fifteen years has been positive for the city's economy, but also for the different atmosphere it has created. The reason why this increase in tourism, resulting from events and even led regeneration, has been tolerated so far is arguably related, as in the case of events and event-led regeneration more broadly, to the phenomena of deindustrialisation and socio-economic decline that had hit the city since the 1970s (as reported by expert 12, June 2018). As in many other cities and tourist spots in Italy, the gradual touristification of Porto Antico has also encouraged informal economies and street vending, as in the case of Barcelona's Port Vell.

However, media narratives about tourism in Genoa portray a rather different picture. A 2018 newspaper article points to the Genoese's 'right of intolerance' towards tourists, despite their nature of 'people of the sea' (see Cubeddu, 2018). Similarly, online media give account of the 'assault' to the city and the region in 2019 (Redazione ANSA, 2019), despite a sharp decrease in tourist numbers after fifteen years of steady growth (Il Secolo XIX, 2019). Of course, this perception was challenged in 2020 due to COVID-19 lockdowns and travel restrictions.

In Valencia, the recent rapid growth of tourism led the regional government to issue a new tourism law to give local authorities more powers to control tourist rentals (Govan, 2018; Zafra, 2018), in particular Airbnb apartments, whose proliferation has been generating tension with the local population (Sampedro, 2020). The case of El Cabanyal-El Canyamelar is particularly interesting from the perspective of touristification. The district was at the heart of a long-lasting urban conflict in relation to the project of extending Avenida de Blasco Ibañez towards the sea, which threatened to destroy the neighbourhood's historic urban fabric (see e.g. Webster, 2010). As mega events and culture-led regeneration projected Valencia as a tourist destination, they indirectly encouraged a rapid gentrification and touristification of Poblats Marítims (Del Romero Renau & Trudelle, 2011), to the extent that the City Council tried to limit tourism development in the area (Toledo, 2018). The neighbourhood has been witnessing increasing land values and a sharp growth in the number of hotels, bars, restaurants, luxury student housing (EFE & Ferrer, 2018) and, in particular, Airbnb apartments (about touristification and digital platforms, see Del Romero Renau, 2018), fuelling resentment among residents (Figure 4.5).

As reported by a local informant:

> Nowadays that Valencia, not only for the America's Cup but also because of global trends, is getting more tourists and this generates some tension related to real estate prices, housing, use of public space. So, we, not as much as it's happening in Venice or in Barcelona, but we are having this kind of public discussion about how much tourism we can handle.
>
> (interview, event team member 6, June 2018)

Figure 4.5 Mural in El Cabanyal-El Canyamelar against gentrification in the neighbourhood. It says, in Valencian: 'We all are Cabanyal. Stop gentrification'. The drawing of a rich man driving an early 1900s luxury car is probably inspired by the popular board game Monopoly.

For this reason, local institutions have been pursuing a strategy of 'reconciliation' with the local population, focused on participatory projects that could help change the idea of public space and cultural events (interview, event team member 6, June 2018) after years of aggressive city branding.

Although this is only marginally related to mega events and event-led regeneration, it is worth noting that, in all the core case-study cities, cruise tourism was raising port-city conflicts before 2020. According to a report for the Cruise Lines International Association, cruise passengers' expenditure in Europe in 2017 accounted for $4.41 billion, against a total $21.34 billion of direct cruise expenditure which was 3.2% higher than in 2016 (Business Research & Economic Advisors, 2018, p. 20). Such an increase in cruise tourism meant that port cities that were calling points along cruise routes had experienced a rapid and substantial growth in tourist numbers, which represented a threat to their local identity (Andrade Marques, 2018). Urban regeneration on the waterfront and in city centres, together with the improvement of local cultural offerings, have contributed to an increased attractiveness of such cities, and to encouraging cruise tourism (Andrade & Costa, 2020, p. 191). Nonetheless, cruise tourism appears to be driven more by broader tourism dynamics and structural processes than by event-led regeneration. Before 2020, cruise tourism has raised criticisms and opposition in relation to a range of negative externalities, including congestion, pollution, potential damage to physical heritage. In particular, the increase in cruise ships' size and the spread of low-cost tourist offerings meant that cities along cruise routes were invaded by mass tourism (ibid., p. 191). Activist collectives operating in a range of European port cities including Barcelona, Lisbon, Málaga, Palma, Valencia, Valletta and Venice established the Network of Southern European Cities against Touristification (Eagan, 2018), asking national and local governments to take action to regulate tourism. For example, in Venice, the *No Grandi Navi* campaign (Vianello, 2017) gained momentum after a number of incidents involving cruise ships sailing through the Canale della Giudecca. However, it is worth noting that these trends could be reversed as the cruise sector is being severely hit by COVID-19.

In Hull, residents of Victoria Dock Village are opposing the proposed cruise terminal, which is planned to be built at Sammy's Point. In Rotterdam, the cruise terminal does generate congestion on Wilhelminakade, where key functions such as City Council offices and the headquarters of the Port Authority share a narrow space. However, residents have not massively opposed cruise tourism (interview, expert 5, April 2018). Problems of congestion, mobility issues and environmental concerns are being raised in Genoa in relation to ferry and cruise traffic, as Stazione Marittima (cruise/ferry terminal) is located in the heart of Porto Antico. After peaking at 480,233 passengers in 2013 (Sanz Blas & Zhelyazkova Buzova, 2014, p. 81) and declining in 2014, cruise tourism in Valencia grew again reaching a figure of 422,000 passengers in 2018 (Valenciaport, 2019). Opposition to cruise tourism in Valencia is related in particular to pollution and to the planned expansion of the port, which includes the relocation of the cruise terminal (Martínez, 2019).

Assuming that the global tourist industry will resume these trends after the COVID-19 pandemic, one of the risks that event-led regeneration and touristification pose in the long term is that residents may not react to these processes and may be forced to become tourism entrepreneurs. As in the case of world-famous tourist destinations in Italy such as Venice or Cinque Terre (next to Genoa), regenerated districts in port cities may see their original population moving out to rent their homes to tourists and live on the resulting private income. For example, residents feared that gentrification and touristification could transform Valencia's El Cabanyal-El Canyamelar into an 'Airbnb district', due to the extent and pace of such changes.

Lessons from port cities of culture and events in ontologically insecure times

Mega events, and in particular the largest among these schemes, continue to be highly contested occasions. The growing ontological insecurity amongst the public arising from unaddressed existential challenges and the ravages of unbridled capitalism is forcing event promoters to operate through subtler mechanisms to seek legitimation. These mechanisms include the greenwashing of events, controversial political and communication tactics to stifle opposition or construct acceptance, and attempts to tailor these events in order to mobilise local cultural and social conditions and meanings. The very role of mega events has been changing in a context of pervasive economic recession and austerity. In this chapter, it has been argued that events have retained their pivotal role in urban policies after the 2007–8 crisis. However, it has been suggested that policy makers in many towns and cities appear to be focusing on smaller-scale, more sustainable, events, in particular where these are in line with the city's profile or the image that is being promoted and with local traditions and cultures.

The independent and rebellious attitude commonly associated with European maritime port cities could be seen as a factor contributing to exacerbating opposition. However, especially in relation to large-scale events that are nonetheless smaller than the Olympics or the FIFA World Cup, such as City/Capital of Culture schemes, this is not necessarily the case. The experience of the four cities examined in the book suggests that events have encountered relatively mild opposition, in comparison with other host cities. This appears particularly the case with industrial port cities where maritime activities represented the core of the economic base. Although some of these cities, employed a range of mechanisms to construct acceptance of mega events and contain opposition, it has been suggested that this milder opposition might be better explained by the perception that culture could be used as a response to the failure of the industrial port city model.

Even where mega events are mildly opposed, for example as a result of the aforementioned mechanisms to legitimise such initiatives, the direct or contingent outcomes of mega events and event-led regeneration may lead to opposition and conflict in the long term. It has been argued that the concentration of investment in certain areas due to events and event-led regeneration might foster spatial disparities and urban fragmentation between waterfronts and the rest of the city. Touristification is also a possible outcome to take into account, as it could generate urban and port-city conflict in the long term despite little initial opposition in contexts of deindustrialisation and economic decline.

Notes

1 Source: Office for National Statistics, GDP quarterly national accounts, UK: October to December 2020 (2020).

2 The extraordinary cold winter that hit Europe in 1708–1709 as a consequence of reduced solar activity.

3 For example, Green (2018) reported that twenty-three cities across the world had delivered a CoC scheme in 2017.

4 Leave vote in Hull accounted for 67.6% (Hull City Council, 2016) in comparison with 51.9% nationally. Hull was the 24th area in the country by percentage of Leave vote; Boston was the city with the highest proportion of Leave vote (75.6%, see BBC, 2016). The five districts with the highest percentages of Leave vote are all port or coastal communities: apart from Boston, Leave vote accounted for 73.6% in South Holland, 72.7% in Castle Point,

72.3% in Thurrock and 71.5% in Great Yarmouth (Electoral Commission, 2016). How-ever, it is important to stress that the EU Referendum in Hull was also characterised by a relatively low turnout (62.9%, Hull City Council, 2016). Colantone and Stanig (2018) have observed a correlation between the spatial distribution of Leave vote across the UK and the hardest negative impacts of economic globalisation across UK regions.

5 In commenting the results of the 2019 European Elections in the UK, it is important to note that the Brexit Party arguably undertook an aggressive electoral campaign in a con-text of weak electoral campaigning by major parties. Turnout in Hull was 24% (Young & Cocoran, 2019).

6 Turnout in Hull was particularly low in the 2019 General Elections as well: the three parliamentary constituencies of Hull ranked first, third and fourth among the constitu-encies displaying the lowest turnout in the country (House of Commons Library, 2020).

7 As emerged from interviews with local officers, mega events are not widely perceived by policy makers in Genoa as a prominent aspect in contemporary urban agendas.

8 In 2015, *Rotterdam celebrates the city* commemorated 75 years of reconstruction in Rot-terdam. A stairway was installed in front of the Central Station to connect the square to the top of Groot Handelsgebouw.

9 Architecture and sport were stressed by a number of informants in Rotterdam as key areas for the city's cultural policy.

10 The *Regatta of the Maritime Republics* is a boating contest established in the 1950s and symbolically involving four Italian maritime powers of the Middle Age and Renaissance, namely Genoa, Venice, Pisa and Amalfi. The event is held every year in one of these cities, so that it is celebrated in the same city every four years. It was celebrated in Genoa in 2018.

11 For a discussion of the reframing of urban cultural policies more broadly in the current socio-political climate, see Bianchini and Tommarchi (2020).

12 In the UK, temporary pedestrian safety barriers are painted in orange.

13 Fórmula Verda (Green Formula) contested the event from a range of perspectives (for a full manifesto, see Fórmula Verda, n.d.), including infrastructure and social cost, safety, lack of participation, impact on urban development and, in particular, environmental exter-nalities and noise pollution. The collective included residents' associations, and contested the issues of isolation and noise in the case of Natzaret (Del Romero Renau & Trudelle, 2011, p. 8).

14 Circuit Urbá No (Valencian for 'no street circuit') wrote an open letter to Spanish F1 driver Fernando Alonso to oppose the construction of the circuit.

15 *Barris* is Valencian for neighbourhoods.

16 An example is urban regeneration in Katendrecht (formerly a sailortown and red-light district on the south bank of the River Maas), where the Theater Walhalla, along with the Fenix Food Factory and many bars and restaurants, are key elements of a regenera-tion strategy that is being implemented by the City Council. The 'rough' character of the neighbourhood is being mobilised – in combination with its new cultural offer – to target specific potential households, that is young people, creative professionals.

17 Source: Gemeente Rotterdam, Centraal Bureau voor de Statistiek (2018).

Bibliography

Aarts, M., Huijs, M., & Vries, I. (2016) How to develop an unprecedented port-city syn-ergy. *Urban Design*, 138, 27–29.

Alegi, P. (2008) 'A nation to be reckoned with': The politics of World Cup stadium con-struction in Cape Town and Durban, South Africa. *African Studies*, 67(3), 397–422.

Amnesty International (2001) *G8 Genoa Policing Operation of July 2001: A Summary of Con-cerns*. Available at: https://web.archive.org/web/20050506053406/http://web.amnesty.org/library/index/engeur300122001 [Accessed 06/03/2020].

Andrade, M. J., & Costa, P. J. (2020) Touristification of European port-cities: Impacts on local populations and cultural heritage. In Carpenter, A., & Lozano, R. (eds.) *European Port Cities in Transition: Moving Towards More Sustainable Sea Transport Hubs.* Cham: Springer, 187–204.

Andrade Marques, M. J. (2018) The port-city in the post-crisis context: Identity and humanisation in the process of touristification. *25th APDR Congress 'Circular Economy: Urban Metabolism and Regional Development'*, Lisbon, 5–8 July.

Añó Sanz, V., Calabuig Moreno, F., & Parra Camacho, D. (2012) Impacto social de un gran evento deportivo: El Gran Premio de Europa de Fórmula 1. *Cultura, Ciencia y Deporte*, 8(7), 53–65.

BBC (n.d.) Local results. *EU Referendum.* Available at: www.bbc.co.uk/news/politics/eu_referendum/results/local/c [Accessed 06/04/2019].

BBC (2016) EU referendum: The result in maps and charts. *BBC*, 24th June. Available at: www.bbc.co.uk/news/uk-politics-36616028 [Accessed 08/08/2019].

BBC (2019a) Hull East Parliamentary constituency. *BBC*. Available at: www.bbc.co.uk/news/politics/constituencies/E14000771 [Accessed 02/04/2020].

BBC (2019b) Hull North Parliamentary constituency. *BBC*. Available at: www.bbc.co.uk/news/politics/constituencies/E14000772 [Accessed 02/04/2020]

BBC (2019c) Hull West & Hessle Parliamentary constituency. *BBC*. Available at: www.bbc.co.uk/news/politics/constituencies/E14000773 [Accessed 02/04/2020].

BBC (2021) Record number of bids for UK City of Culture 2025. *BBC*, 20th August. Available at: www.bbc.co.uk/news/uk-england-58272630 [Accessed 20/08/2021].

Bianchini, F. (1993) Culture, conflict and cities: Issues and prospects for the 1990s. In Bianchini, F., & Parkinson, M. (eds.) *Cultural Policy and Urban Regeneration: The West European Experience.* Manchester: Manchester Press, 199–213.

Bianchini, F., & Tommarchi, E. (2020) Urban activism and the rethinking of cities' cultural policies in Europe. In Wimmer, M. (ed.) *Kann Kultur Politik? – Kann Politik Kultur? Warum wir wieder mehr über Kulturpolitik sprechen sollten.* Vienna: De Gruyter, 156–166.

Bikker & Co. (2016) World Expo 2025 Rotterdam. *Bikker & Company.* Available at: www.bikker.com/portfolios/world-expo-2025-rotterdam/ [Accessed 26/03/2018].

Borsay, P., & Walton, J. K. (2011) Introduction: The resort-port relationship. In Borsay, P., & Walton, J. K. (eds.) *Resorts and Ports: European Seaside Towns since 1700.* Bristol: Channel View Publications, 1–17.

Boyle, M. (1999) Growth machines and propaganda projects: A review of readings of the role of civic boosterism in the politics of local economic development. In Jonas, A. E. G., & Wilson, D. (eds.) *The Urban Growth Machine: Critical Perspectives Two Decades Later.* Albany: State University of New York Press, 55–70.

Business Research & Economic Advisors (2018) *The Contribution of the International Cruise Industry to the Global Economy in 2017.* Phillipsburg: CLIA. Available at: https://cruising.org/-/media/CLIA/Research/Global%202018%20EIS [31/10/2019].

Carrasco, J. S., & Pitarch-Garrido, M. D. (2017) Analysis of the impact on tourism of the megaproject-based urban development strategy: The case of the city of Valencia. *Cuadernos de Turismo*, 40, 723–726.

CCR/PE/ADNKRONOS (1992) Colombiadi: È polemica sul futuro dell'antico porto di Genova. *AdnKronos*, 14th March. Available at: www1.adnkronos.com/Archivio/AdnAgenzia/1992/03/14/Altro/COLOMBIADI-E-POLEMICA-SUL-FUTURO-DELLANTICO-PORTO-DI-GENOVA_182100.php [Accessed 19/08/2019].

Chen, Y. (2012) Urban regeneration through mega event: The case of Rotterdam. *Proceedings of 2012 Shanghai International Conference of Social Science*, Shanghai, 14–17 August, 29–36.

Colantone, I., & Stanig, P. (2018) Global competition and Brexit. *American Political Science Review*, 112(2), 201–2018.

Cooper, H., & Szreter, S. (2021) *After the Virus: Lessons from the Past for a Better Future*. Cambridge: Cambridge University Press.

Cubeddu, M. (2018) Benvenuti a Genova, la città che odia i turisti. *Linkiesta*, 28th July. Available at: www.linkiesta.it/it/article/2018/07/28/benvenuti-a-genova-la-citta-che-odia-i-turisti/38979/ [Accessed 13/07/2019].

Culture, Place and Policy Institute (2018) *Cultural Transformations: The Impacts of Hull UK City of Culture 2017. Preliminary Outcomes Evaluation. March 2018*. Hull: University of Hull.

Cunningham, I., & Platt, L. (2018) Bidding for UK city of culture: Challenges of delivering a bottom-up approach 'in place' for a top-down strategy led scheme. *Journal of Place Management and Development*. https://doi.org/10.1108/JPMD-01-2018-0005.

Del Romero Renau, L. (2018) Touristification, sharing economies and the new geography of urban conflicts. *Urban Science*, 2(104), 1–17.

Del Romero Renau, L., & Trudelle, C. (2011) Mega events and urban conflicts in Valencia, Spain: Contesting the new urban modernity. *Urban Studies Research*, 11. DOI: 10.1155/2011/587523.

Di Vita, S., & Wilson, M. (eds.) (2020) *Planning and Managing Smaller Events: Downsizing the Urban Spectacle*. London and New York: Routledge.

Duignan, M. B., & McGillivray, D. (2019) Disorganised host community touristic-event spaces: Revealing Rio's fault lines at the 2016 Olympic Games. *Leisure Studies*, 38(5), 692–711.

Eagan, K. (2018) Anti-tourism movement rising around European cities. *Tourism Review*, 30th April. Available at: www.tourism-review.com/anti-tourism-organization-launched-news10572 [Accessed 24/07/2019].

EFE (2012) Vecinos protestan contra el 'despilfarro' de la Fórmula 1. *Las Provincias* [Online], 24th June. Available at: www.lasprovincias.es/20120624/comunitatvalenciana/valencia/protesta-formula1-valencia-201206241336.html [Accessed 12/06/2018].

EFE, & Ferrer, J. (2018) Así es la lujosa residencia de estudiantes del Cabanyal. *Las Provincias* [Online], 16th May. Available at: www.lasprovincias.es/valencia-ciudad/cabanyal-lujosa-residencia-estudiantes-20180515180652-nt.html [Accessed 24/07/2019].

Electoral Commission (2016) *EU Referendum Results: UK Government*. Available at: https://data.gov.uk/dataset/be2f2aec-11d8-4bfe-9800-649e5b8ec044/eu-referendum-results [Accessed 09/01/2020].

Elliott, L. (2019) Coastal towns hit hardest by soaring level of insolvencies. *The Guardian* [Online], 18th July. Available at: www.theguardian.com/money/2019/jul/17/insolvencies-grow-in-england-and-wales-for-third-year-running [Accessed 01/11/2019].

El País (n.d.) Resultados electorales 2007. *El País*. Available at: https://resultados.elpais.com/elecciones/2007/ [Accessed 05/03/2020].

Faulhaber, L., & Azevedo, L. (2015) *SMH 2016: Removals on the Olympic City* (translated by E. H. Oscar). Rio de Janeiro: Mórula.

Ferrandis, J. (2007) Ecclestone condiciona que Valencia albergue el Gran Premio a que el PP gane las elecciones. *El País* [Online], 5th October. Available at: https://elpais.com/deportes/2007/05/10/actualidad/1178781715_850215.html [Accessed 12/04/2018].

Fórmula Verda (n.d.) *10 raons contra el circuit urbà de Fórmula 1 a València i a favor d'una ciutat sostenible i una nova cultura urbana*. Available at: www.ecologistasenaccion.org/IMG/pdf_MANIFEST_F1.pdf [Accessed 12/06/2018].

Gaffney, C. (2010) Mega-events and socio-spatial dynamics in Rio de Janeiro, 1919–2016. *Journal of Latin American Geography*, 9(1), 7–29.

Gastaldi, F. (2010) Genova. La riconversione del waterfront portuale. Un percorso con esiti rilevanti. Storia, accadimenti, dibattito. In Savino, M. (ed.) *Waterfront d'Italia. Piani politiche progetti*. Milano: Franco Angeli, 88–104.

Gastaldi, F. (2013) Event-based urban regeneration and gentrification in the historic centre of Genoa. *Journal of Urban Regeneration and Renewal*, 7(1), 67–78.

Gastaldi, F. (2017) Genova, a success story! In Porfyriou, H., & Sepe, M. (eds.) *Waterfronts Revisited: European Ports in a Historic and Global Perspective*. New York and London: Routledge, 123–133.

Giddens, A. (1991) *Modernity and Self-Identity*. New York: Polity Press.

Gogishvili, D. (2018) Baku formula 1 city circuit: Exploring the temporary spaces of exception. *Cities*, 74, 169–178.

Gonzalez, S., & Waley, P. (2013) Traditional retail markets: The new gentrification frontier? *Antipode*, 45(4), 965–983.

Gorz, A. (1997 [1980]) *Farewell to the Working Class: An Essay on Post-Industrial Socialism* (translated by M. Sonenscher). New York: Pluto Press.

Gotham, K. F. (2016) Beyond bread and circuses: Mega-events as forces of creative destruction. In Gruneau, R., & Horne, J. (eds.) *Mega-Events and Globalization: Capital and Spectacle in a Changing World Order*. Abingdon and New York: Routledge, 31–47.

Govan, F. (2012) Valencia: The ghost city that's become a symbol of Spain's spending woes. *The Telegraph* [Online], 29th September. Available at: www.telegraph.co.uk/finance/financialcrisis/9573568/Valencia-the-ghost-city-thats-become-a-symbol-of-Spains-spending-woes.html [Accessed 05/04/2018].

Govan, F. (2018) Valencia joins the battle against mass tourism with ban on rooms with a view. *The Local*, 9th May. Available at: www.thelocal.es/20180509/valencia-joins-the-battle-against-mass-tourism-with-ban-on-rooms-with-a-view [Accessed 07/01/2020].

Green, S. (2018) Capitals of Culture in 2018. *Prasino*. Steve Green's Cultural Chronicle. Available at: http://prasino.eu/ [Accessed 03/08/2018].

Grove, A. (2017) Anti-BP protesters gatecrash Hull 2017 lecture to campaign against oil firm and hold minute's vigil. *Hull Daily Mail* [Online], 20th July. Available at: www.hulldailymail.co.uk/news/hull-east-yorkshire-news/anti-bp-protesters-gatecrash-hull-222761 [Accessed 06/12/2017].

Gruneau, R., & Horne, J. (2016) Mega-events and globalization: A critical introduction. In Gruneau, R., & Horne, J. (eds.) *Mega-Events and Globalization: Capital and Spectacle in a Changing World Order*. London and New York: Routledge, 1–28.

Hadjimichalis, C. (2020) An uncertain future for the post-Brexit, post-COVID-19 European Union. *European Urban and Regional Studies*. DOI: 10.1177/0969776420968961.

Hall, M. C. (2006) Urban entrepreneurship, corporate interests and sports mega-events: The thin policies of competitiveness within the hard outcomes of neoliberalism. *The Sociological Review*, 54(s2), 59–70.

Hall, M. C. (2012) Sustainable mega-events: Beyond the myth of balanced approaches to mega-event sustainability. *Event Management*, 16, 119–121.

Henderson, J. C., Foo, K., Lim, H., & Yip, S. (2010) Sports events and tourism: The Singapore Formula One Grand Prix. *International Journal of Event and Festival Management*, 1(1), 60–73.

Hillmann, F. (2008) Big ships on the horizon and growing fragmentation at home: Genoa's transformation of the urban landscape. *Erdkunde*, 62(4), 301–316.

House of Commons Library (2020) General election 2019: Turnout. *House of Commons Library*, 7th January. Available at: https://commonslibrary.parliament.uk/insights/general-election-2019-turnout/ [Accessed 31/01/2020].

Hubbard, P. (2018) Retail gentrification. In Lees, L., & Phillips, M. (eds.) *Handbook of Gentrification Studies*. Cheltenham and Northampton, MA: Edward Elgar Publishing, 294–309.

Hull City Council (2016) *EU Referendum*. Available at: www.hullcc.gov.uk/portal/page-_pageid=221,1543108&_dad=portal&_schema=PORTAL [Accessed 28/11/2017].

Il Secolo XIX (2019) Turismo in Liguria, dati negativi per il 2019. Crollano le prenotazioni degli stranieri e scoppia la polemica. *Il Secolo XIX* [Online], 17th July. Available at: www.ilsecoloxix.it/genova/2019/07/17/news/turismo-in-liguria-dati-negativi-per-il-2019-e-crollano-le-prenotazioni-degli-stranieri-scoppia-la-polemica-1.37091260 [Accessed 24/07/2019].

International Monetary Fund (2020) *World Economic Outlook Update*. Available at: www.imf.org/en/Publications/WEO/Issues/2020/01/20/weo-update-january2020 [Accessed 10/05/2021].

International Monetary Fund (2021) *World Economic Outlook Update*. Available at: www.imf.org/en/Publications/WEO/Issues/2021/01/26/2021-world-economic-outlook-update [Accessed 10/05/2021].

Jonas, A. E. G., Wurzel, R. K. W., Monaghan, E., & Osthorst, W. (2017) Climate change, the green economy and reimagining the city: The case of structurally disadvantaged European maritime port cities. *Die Erde*, 148(4), 197–2011.

Jones, Z. M. (2020) *Cultural Mega-Events: Opportunities and Risks for Heritage Cities*. London: Routledge.

Jones, Z. M., and Ponzini, D. (2018) Mega-events and the preservation of urban heritage: Literature gaps, potential overlaps, and a call for further research. *Journal of Planning Literature*, 33(4), 433–450.

Kemp, D. (2018) Hull's orange barriers went nearly a year ago: Here's what you think of the city centre now. *Hull Daily Mail* [Online], 15th April. Available at: www.hulldailymail.co.uk/news/hull-east-yorkshire-news/hulls-orange-barriers-went-nearly-1459676 [Accessed 04/06/2019].

Kotz, D. M. (2008) The financial and economic crisis of 2008: A systemic crisis of neoliberal capitalism. *Review of Radical Political Economics*, 41(3), 305–317.

Laing, R. D. (1990) *The Divided Self*. Penguin: London.

Lehmann, A. (2016) The rise of Trump comes as no surprise on England's disaffected east coast. *The Guardian* [Online], 11th December. Available at: www.theguardian.com/uk-news/2016/nov/12/trumps-rise-no-surprise-englands-disaffected-east-coast-hull-grimsby [Accessed 08/11/2019].

Likku, E., & Mandias, S. (eds.) (2016) *Help, we zijn populair. Rotterdam stad in verandering*. Rotterdam: Nai Publishers.

Mah, A. (2014) *Port Cities and Global Legacies: Urban Identity, Waterfront Work, and Radicalism*. Basingstoke: Palgrave MacMillan.

Martínez, L. (2019) Grupos ecologistas y ciudadanos y el alcalde Ribó presionan para frenar la ampliación del puerto de Valencia. *El Diario*, 23rd July. Available at: www.eldiario.es/cv/Movilizacion-ecologista-ampliacion-puerto-Valencia_0_923558026.html [Accessed 24/07/2019].

Mason, P. (2016) *PostCapitalism: A Guide to Our Future*. London: Penguin.

Mastropietro, E. (2007) I grandi eventi come occasione di riqualificazione e valorizzazione urbana. Il caso di Genova. *ACME – Annali Della Facoltà Di Lettere e Filosofia Dell'Università Degli Studi Di Milano*, 60(1), 207.

Moore, J. W. (ed.) (2016) *Anthropocene or Capitalocene? Nature, History and the Crisis of Capitalism*. Oakland, CA: PM Press.

Negri, G. (1999) *Il paese del non fare. Dal ponte sullo stretto al Giubileo, viaggio nell'Italia delle occasioni mancate*. Florence: Ponte alle Grazie.

Palmer-Rae Associates (2004) *European Cities and Capitals of Culture: Study Prepared for the European Commission. PART II*. Available at: https://ec.europa.eu/programmes/

creative-europe/sites/creative-europe/files/library/palmer-report-capitals-culture-1995-2004-ii_en.pdf [Accessed 09/07/2018].

Papathanassis, A. (2017) Over-tourism and anti-tourist sentiment: An exploratory analysis and discussion. *"Ovidius" University Annals*, 17(2), 288–293.

Parra Camacho, D., Añó Sanz, V., & Calabuig Moreno, F. (2016) Percepción de los residentes sobre el legado de la America's Cup Residents perceptions about the legacy of America's Cup Percepção dos moradores sobre o legado da Copa América. *Cuadernos de Psicología del Deporte*, 16(1), 325–338.

Peck, J. (2012) Austerity urbanism American cities under extreme economy. *City*, 16(6), 626–655.

Phelps, N. A., & Miao, J. T. (2019) Varieties of urban entrepreneurialism. *Dialogues in Human Geography*. https://doi.org/10.1177/2043820619890438.

Ponzini, D., & Jones, Z. M. (2020) Emerging issues, opportunities and threats and how to deal with them. In Ponzini, D., Bianchini, F., Georgi-Tzortzi, J.-N., & Sanetra-Szeliga, J. (eds.) *Mega-Events and Heritage: The Experience of Five European Cities*. Krakow: International Cultural Centre, 316–343. Available at: www.tau-lab.polimi.it [Accessed 26/03/2020].

Porfyriou, H., & Sepe, M. (2017) Introduction: Port cities and waterfront developments: From the re-actualization of history to a new city image. In Porfyriou, H., & Sepe, M. (eds.) *Waterfront Revisited: European Ports in a Historic and Global Perspective*. New York and London: Routledge, 1–16.

Quinn, B. (2019) Government pushes ahead with plans for 'festival of Brexit'. *The Guardian* [Online], 5th November. Available at: www.theguardian.com/politics/2019/nov/05/government-pushes-ahead-plans-festival-of-brexit [Accessed 08/04/2020].

Ramos, S. J. (2020) Port futures in Postnormal Time(s). *Portus*, 40.

Redazione ANSA (2019) Assalto turisti in Liguria, code. *ANSA*, 29th June. www.ansa.it/liguria/notizie/2019/06/29/assalto-turisti-in-liguria-code_1a76e2ee-274b-4cd5-9b0f-e2d9b034c5fb.html [Accessed 24/07/2019].

Rekow, R. (2016) Rio De Janeiro's Olympic legacy: Public security for whom? *Journal of Human Security*, 12(1), 74–90.

Rius-Ulldemolins, J., & Gisbert, V. (2019) The costs of putting Valencia on the map: The hidden side of regional entrepreneurialism, 'creative city' and strategic projects. *European Planning Studies*, 27(2), 377–395.

Romein, A. (2005) Leisure in waterfront redevelopment: An issue of urban planning in Rotterdam? *2005 AESOP Conference*, Vienna, 13–17 July. Available at: http://aesop2005.scix.net/data/papers/att/606.fullTextPrint.pdf [Accessed 27/11/2019].

Sampedro, S. (2020) La Comunidad Valenciana dobla su registro de pisos turísticos en solo cuatro años. *El Mundo* [Online], 5th January. Available at: www.elmundo.es/comunidad-valenciana/alicante/2020/01/05/5e108047fc6c83f16a8b464a.html [Accessed 07/01/2020].

Sanz Blas, S., & Zhelyazkova Buzova, D. (2014) Situación actual del turismo de cruceros en la ciudad de Valencia. *Papers de Turisme*, 56, 81–100.

Sardar, Z. (2010) Welcome to Postnormal Times. *Futures*, 42, 435–444.

Savage, M., Dickens, P., & Fielding, T. (1988) Some social and political implications of the contemporary fragmentation of the 'service class' in Britain. *International Journal of Urban and Regional Research*, 12(3), 455–476.

Scherer, J. (2011) Olympic villages and large-scale urban development: Crises of capitalism, deficits of democracy? *Urban Studies*, 45(5) 782–797.

Shaw, G., & Williams, A. M. (eds.) (1997) *The Rise and Fall of British Coastal Resorts: Cultural and Economic Perspectives*. London: Mansell.

Smith, A. (2012) *Events and Urban Regeneration: The Strategic Use of Events to Revitalise Cities.* London and New York: Routledge.

Sorribes i Monrabal, J. (2015) *Valencia 1940–2014: Construcción y destrucción de la ciudad.* Valencia: Universitat de València.

Standing, G. (2011) *The Precariat: The New Dangerous Class.* London: Bloomsbury.

Steele, B. J., & Homolar, A. (2019) Ontological insecurities and the politics of contemporary populism. *Cambridge Review of International Affairs*, 32(3), 214–221.

Talbot, A., & Carter, T. F. (2018) Human rights abuses at the Rio 2016 Olympics: Activism and the media. *Leisure Studies*, 37(1), 77–88.

Tarazona Vento, A. (2017) Mega-project meltdown: Post-politics, neoliberal urban regeneration and Valencia's fiscal crisis. *Urban Studies*, 54(1), 68–84.

Toledo, C. (2018) Valencia estudia ya límites al turismo en Ruzafa, Ciutat Vella y El Cabanyal. *El Mundo* [Online], 5th October. Available at: www.elmundo.es/comunidad-valencia na/2018/05/10/5af34cedca474163638b458e.html [Accessed 06/12/2018].

Tommarchi, E., & Cavalleri, F. (2020) City/Capital of Culture schemes in European medium-sized coastal cities: The cases of Hull (UK) and Pafos (Cyprus). In Di Vita, S., & Wilson, M. (eds.) *Planning and Managing Smaller Events: Downsizing the Urban Spectacle.* London and New York: Routledge.

Uitermark, J., & Duyvendak, W. (2008) Civilising the city: Populism and revanchist urbanism in Rotterdam. *Urban Studies*, 45(7), 1485–1503.

Universitat de València-Estudi General (UVEG) (2009) *Informe sociológico sobre la Gestión Deportiva Municipal en Valencia.* Valencia: Universitat de València.

Valenciaport (2019) Pasajeros. *Valenciaport.* Available at: www.valenciaport.com/autoridad-portuaria/estadisticas-de-trafico/pasajeros/ [Accessed 24/07/2019].

Van de Laar, P. T. (2018) Rotterdam migratiestad: Op zoek naar een nieuw narratief. *History @ Erasmus*, 78–81. Available at: http://hdl.handle.net/1765/115427 [Accessed 13/06/2019].

Vázquez, C. (2017) El plan urbanístico del Grau de Valencia absorberá el circuito de F1. *El País* [Online], 27th March. Available at: https://elpais.com/ccaa/2017/03/27/valencia/1490631755_212001.html [Accessed 04/12/2018].

Vianello, M. (2017) The No Grandi Navi campaign: Protests against cruise tourism in Venice. In Colomb, C. & Novy, J. (eds.) *Protest and Resistance in the Tourist City.* London and New York: Routledge, 171–190.

Webster, J. (2010) Head for Valencia's fishermen's quarter–before the bulldozers get there. *The Guardian* [Online], 5th August. Available at: www.theguardian.com/travel/2010/may/08/valencia-el-cabanyal-neighbourhood-spain [Accessed 30/05/2018].

Young, A., & Cocoran, S. (2019) European elections turnout: How many people in Hull and East Yorkshire voted. *Hull Daily Mail* [Online], 26th May. Available at: www.hulldailymail.co.uk/news/hull-east-yorkshire-news/european-elections-turnout-how-many-2909984 [Accessed 09/01/2020].

Youngs, I. (2016) Culture? In Hull? UK City of Culture 2017 aims to win over sceptics. *BBC*, 30th December. Available at: www.bbc.co.uk/news/entertainment-arts-38358407 [Accessed 04/06/2019].

Zafra, I. (2018) Valencia joins the fight against holiday rentals. *El País* [Online], 9th May. Available at: https://elpais.com/elpais/2018/05/09/inenglish/1525851010_505130.html [Accessed 07/01/2020].

5 The spatiality of event-led regeneration at the port-city interface

Whether directly through *ad hoc* urban transformations or indirectly through their regenerative spillovers, large-scale cultural and sporting events have long played a role in reshaping the spatial relations between ports and cities. This chapter focuses on the spatial outcomes of these events on the waterfront and on how culture- and event-led regeneration contribute to transforming the port-city interface. Certain aspects of the spatial relationships between ports and cities in the context of event-led regeneration are explored, such as the introduction of permanent cultural functions in urban port areas, the competition with residual or developing maritime activities, the rapid transformation of the port-city interface, the porosity of waterfront areas before and after event-led regeneration and the governance of the port-city interface. Event-led regeneration needs to be problematised considering the impact of permanent cultural activities in urban port areas and their potential to intensify socio-spatial disparities between redeveloped waterfronts and other areas of the city.

Firstly, this chapters looks at how urban and cultural functions have gradually occupied former port areas, and it shows how certain light industrial and maritime-related activities are moving back into urban port areas. Secondly, it focuses on specific aspects of this spatial tension on the waterfront, namely deterritorialisation, the role of property rights, porosity and spatial disparities.

Ports and cities back to the waterfront

The physical separation between ports and cities triggered by technological developments and changing maritime trade patterns in the second half of the 20th century built the rationale for waterfront redevelopment schemes, particularly in North America and Europe. In his model of the evolution of port-city relationships, Hoyle (2000) acknowledges that, since the 1980s, waterfront redevelopment processes have marked a new phase of renewal of port-city links, where abandoned urban port areas have become strategic assets for both the city and the port. Since the 1990s, event-led regeneration has been deployed to trigger and sustain large-scale waterfront redevelopments in many port cities across Europe, such as Barcelona, Glasgow, Genoa and Liverpool, and beyond.

The experiences of the case-study cities of the book are examples of the appeal of waterfront areas to city policy makers and, at the same time, of

DOI: 10.4324/9781003165811-5

the renewed centrality of cities from the perspective of port actors. Abandoned port areas and waterfronts in central city locations were redeveloped and opened to residents and visitors for leisure purposes, albeit in different moments and timeframes. Mega events and event-led regeneration played different roles in these processes, ranging from being the main trigger, a catalyst or a means to celebrate urban regeneration.

The 'urban takeover' of port areas driven by culture and events

Many port cities across the world display a gradual transformation of port areas and waterfronts in central city locations, which implies a shift from maritime-related uses to urban functions such as housing, office complexes and cultural facilities. These urban functions may combine culture and leisure with light maritime uses. However, most port functions, in particular heavy and industrial port activities that are deemed as incompatible with urban uses, tend to be pushed out. This 'port out, city in' strategy portrays the transformation of many port cities into 'waterfront cities'. This is in line with the idea that cities, rather than ports alone, are now the driving force of urban development (Wiegmans & Louw, 2011, p. 582).

Mega events may act as accelerators of these processes, although this depends on the extent of the planned urban transformation. On the one hand, in port cities such as Hull and Rotterdam, these events produced very little direct physical impacts on the port-city interface. However, they did play a pivotal role in the redevelopment of vast portions of inner harbours in Genoa and Valencia. This can be explained by considering that inner harbours in Hull and Rotterdam had already undergone redevelopment since the 1970s and 1980s respectively, well before policy makers decided to bid for the mega events analysed. This is in contrast with the experience of Genoa and Valencia, where inner harbours were – completely or in part – abandoned and inaccessible before mega events took place.

In the case of Hull, the UK City of Culture 2017 had spatially contingent outcomes, for example in the redevelopment of the Fruit Market area. This transformation had been planned independently from the event itself. However, the UK City of Culture brand arguably contributed to boosting the attractiveness of this area. In Rotterdam, the European Capital of Culture 2001 was less focused on regeneration – in comparison for instance with Glasgow European City of Culture 1990 – and more on city branding. Nevertheless, the event did engage with ultramodern architecture in Kop van Zuid and contributed to celebrating this redevelopment. In addition, it can be argued that the twenty years' experience in organising cultural and sporting events and mega events that policy makers have developed has played a role in raising awareness of the role of culture-led regeneration and of culture in terms of place making within waterfront redevelopment schemes such as in Kop van Zuid, Katendrecht and Delftshaven. Urban regeneration in Katendrecht is an example of how maritime-related industrial functions are gradually being pushed out by urban functions, which in turn are encouraged to locate in the area using culture as a place-making device.

Conversely, mega events implied extensive physical transformation in the case of Genoa and Valencia, following trajectories more closely aligned with the event-led reconversion of Barcelona's Port Vell. Nonetheless, the outcomes of these processes were rather different in the two cities. In the case of Genoa, as observed by one informant:

> [mega events] were crucial. I mean, hadn't they taken place, it would have been impossible to implement what was done. . . . [F]rom the transformation of Porto Antico in 1992 to the regeneration of the city centre, or at least of part of the city centre, through the G8 [summit] and [the ECoC] 2004 and the museum network. . . . Well, of course, without those occasions, it would not have been possible to do all that.
>
> (interview, event team member 4, June 2018, author's translation)

Event-led transformation in the inner harbour should be interpreted as a series of single interventions which contributed to implementing a broader vision of redevelopment (Gastaldi, 2012, p. 32). Apart from the transformation driven by the 1992 Specialist Expo, the case of Darsena Comunale is a good example. Prior to the European Capital of Culture 2004, unauthorised fishing-related activities used to take place (interview, policy maker 5, June 2018) alongside a newly built residential development – known as Il Cembalo – and institutions such as the Faculty of Economics of the University of Genoa and Istituto Nautico San Giorgio (a nautical college). This meant that the area was populated only in the morning from Monday to Saturday, allowing then space for criminal activity and forms of anti-social behaviour. The European Capital of Culture 2004 was the chance to address this issue, ceasing unauthorised fishing practices and encouraging a prolonged presence of people thanks to shops and restaurants in the area. Galata Museo del Mare (the Maritime Museum) was the flagship project implemented to sustain this transformation, albeit some tension remains, as licensed fishing practices share the same space with residents and visitors who walk along the dock. The G8 summit and the European Capital of Culture 2004 contributed to the transformation of the old harbour. Porto Antico is now a large pedestrian zone, much appreciated by both residents and visitors. It has become a new city centre of a polycentric city, as a result of the long-standing policy goal of regenerating both the city centre and the waterfront.

The case of Valencia shows how a similar strategy led to very different outcomes, due to a range of factors including geographical settings, urban design choices and popularity of events held. More than ten years after the 32nd America's Cup took place in 2007, event facilities and spaces still needed to be fully repurposed and incorporated into the city. The underuse and decay of event facilities is a common negative outcome of hosting mega events. As suggested by Cavalcanti et al. (2016) in the case of the 2016 Olympic Games in Rio de Janeiro, mega events entail the production of 'ruins'. These 'mega-event ruins' may precede the event itself, in the form of evictions and demolitions to make room for event-led physical regeneration, and may endure after the event in the form of white elephants. In early 2020, Rio's Olympic facilities at Barra da Tijuca, which had been abandoned right after the event (The Guardian, 2017), were closed due to safety concerns (BBC, 2020). Sport facilities were built near the Olympic Village, on an area formerly occupied by the Jacarepaguá Circuit, where the Formula One Brazilian Grand Prix was held in 1978 and from 1981 to 1989.

Albeit to a less dramatic extent, event facilities in Valencia did suffer from underuse and contributed to fuelling a general feeling of urban decay, together with the lack of maintenance of certain permanent cultural facilities:

> [w]hen [the event] is over, it leaves a space that looks Dantesque to me. There is the area of the Marina, the area of the City of Arts and Sciences . . . There is the area of Formula 1. Now, some [areas] have been regenerated, but sometimes it seems we are in a post-apocalyptic city, so to speak. Everything is quite run down. All that once looked new, now is old. It is a very rapid consumption of space. Once the event has consumed the space, the area is abandoned because there is no prescribed use [for it].
> (interview, expert 14, May 2018, author's translation)

The state of Valencia's old harbour can be interpreted as the result of two processes of 'deindustrialisation', namely port migration and the decay and abandonment of event facilities:

> [i]n 2015 . . . the inner harbour looked like it was in 2012. A 1 million square meters space, taking into account both land and water surfaces, which included unused buildings and infrastructure that could be reimagined. An urban vacuum resulting from two deindustrialisation processes. Firstly, the deindustrialisation of traditional port industry, which left the inner harbour unsuitable for trade functions. Secondly, the late deindustrialisation of mega events and of the leisure and spectacle industry, which has left several buildings and spaces with no use too quickly.
> (Marrades, 2018, p. 193, author's translation)

The legacy of the Formula One European Grand Prix held in Valencia from 2008 to 2012 is arguably perceived as the low point in this trajectory of neglect of cultural/sporting facilities. The reuse of Valencia Street Circuit proved to be difficult to the extent that, in 2017, Generalitat Valenciana abandoned the idea of reusing the facility to host other motorsport events (Navarro Castelló, 2017). This, together with the problematic implementation of PAI del Grau, implied the inability of generating revenues to pay back construction costs. In addition, the expected spillovers in terms of regeneration, which should be driven by the attractiveness of the area in relation to the event, did not materialise. Large swathes of the circuit area still laid abandoned and fenced off, while some areas are occupied by informal settlements hosting a community of migrants (see e.g. Bono, 2021). As summarised by one informant:

> First, there is a tremendous economic debt upon the city. This is important. Then, all the infrastructure . . . It was untrue that we could reuse it. That is to say that all the tarmac surface that was laid down in the construction of the

circuit did not follow a design of urban roads, right? It was a mistake to think that this could be readapted later. . . . [T]he trap, that fiction they crafted, was to say that [the circuit] would pay for itself with the revenues generated by urban development in the area, by real estate speculation. . . . So, this falls upon the city . . . to overestimate urban development expectations in order to pay for such piece of infrastructure that has proved to be utterly useless.

(interview, policy maker 9, May 2018, author's translation)

Of course, the fact that mega events may trigger or sustain the reconversion of former industrial port areas into sites for cultural consumption, with different extents of 'takeover' of existing port functions, is not a European-specific phenomenon. Looking outside Europe, the already mentioned case of the 2016 Olympic Games in Rio de Janeiro accelerated the implementation of Porto Maravilha, the largest redevelopment project undertaken in Latin America (Sardinha Lopes & Pauletto Fragalle, 2016) as well as the largest public-private partnership in the history of Brazil (Broudehoux & Carvalhaes, 2017). The project involved a formerly dynamic port district, which failed to adapt to containerisation and suffered competition with a new port facility built approximately 70 kilometres away, at Itaguaí, in the early 1980s (Silvestre, 2017). The redevelopment of this waterfront area next to Rio city centre was first envisioned in the 2001 Plano de Recuperação e Revitalização da Zona Portuária (Redevelopment and Revitalisation Plan for the Port Area) and was informed by internationally known cases of waterfront redevelopment such as Barcelona's Port Vell, London Docklands and Buenos Aires' Puerto Madero (Sardinha Lopes & Pauletto Fragalle, 2016). In this case, the model based on the wholesale replacement of port functions was not fully applied, as certain maritime-related activities were retained (Andreatta & Herce, 2012). Despite having been initiated in the early 2000s, Porto Maravilha was then framed as a key legacy project of the 2016 Olympics (Silvestre, 2017) and entailed 'the largest Live Site ever developed in Olympic history' (Duignan & McGillivray, 2019, p. 696). The implementation of the project nonetheless implied the displacement of some economic activities traditionally located in the area, such as local recycling centres (Broudehoux & Carvalhaes, 2017), contributing to the transformation of the neighbourhood's job market as well.

The Expo 2010 in Shanghai provides another example of how the exceptionality of mega events can be a key factor in triggering the redevelopment of former port areas and waterfronts (see e.g. Chan & Li, 2017). Initially, the Expo site was envisioned to be developed in the outskirts of the city, with the aim of stimulating urban development in the area. However, a large site on the bank of the Huangpu River in central Shanghai, occupied by industrial functions and shantytowns, was eventually selected. In order to build the Expo site, shipyards owned by the Chinese navy and approximately 27,000 housing units were demolished (den Hartog, 2021, p. 184). The area remained underused after the Expo and has been redeveloped only after 2015, with a combination of office, retail and cultural functions (ibid., pp. 184 and 188; Chen, 2020).

Maritime functions in redeveloped urban port areas

The past decade has witnessed a renewed interested from port authorities and companies in formerly abandoned urban port areas, especially for light maritime industries or maritime-related activities. It is worth highlighting how this tendency of repopulating urban port areas with maritime activities is present in the four case-study cities and how these functions relate to cultural uses.

In Hull, maritime-related industry and cultural tourism represent two pillars of the 2013 City Plan, the planning document envisioning the city's long-term vision of future development. Through the Green Port Hull agreement, Siemens Gamesa located a wind turbine manufacturing plant at Alexandra Dock. This new use did not generate substantial tension with cultural facilities and functions – although there was tension with nearby residential uses – and played a role within the UK City of Culture programme itself, as discussed in Chapter 6.

In Rotterdam, the traditional 'port out, city in' strategy that has dominated port-city relationships since the 1970s is gradually being replaced by a more balanced strategy of waterfront redevelopment (interview, city planner 3, April 2018). On the one hand, since the economy – before the COVID-19 outbreak – was growing again after the shock of the 2008 crisis, the Port Authority appeared to be more conservative in giving port land away for redevelopment (interview, city planner 3, April 2018; interview, city planner 4, April 2018). On the other hand, the Port Authority appeared to be more interested in being involved in the development of the city. For example, the Port Authority decided to locate its headquarters, the World Port Center, on Wilhelminapier, one of the most iconic areas of Rotterdam. As noted by two informants:

the Port [Authority] has never talked about redeveloping the Kop van Zuid or the southern bank, for example. [Now] they put their headquarters on that spot, to be [once] again present in the city.

(interview, city planner 3, April 2018)

And having this new bridge with the Kop van Zuid architectural development and port redevelopment. . . . [It] may be insignificant, but [the fact that] the World Port Center was created there is very strategically chosen, because it was a symbol for 'look, we are the Port Authority and we are building an institutional bridge; we invest in the new city of Rotterdam'.

(interview, expert 5, April 2018)

In this context, urban port areas are attractive to a range of new businesses, such as light maritime activities and hi-tech businesses, because of their proximity to the city centre. As summarised by an officer from the Port Authority:

the port connects maritime services, small businesses, start-ups, grown–ups, innovative industries together with education institutes. We try to create for them an attracting environment in the eastern part of the port. . . . These are smaller-scale areas, and they are very interesting for new businesses, also for the port. These are knowledge-based or knowledge-intensive [businesses] and, of course, a lot of people work there. They're not going to settle on the Maasvlakte, because, you know, that's a sort of desert with terminals, fully automated. That's nice, as a port, for the whole logistic cluster of Europe. But for the city, those old port city areas are much more interesting, actually, to renew. And the Port Authority itself is also interested in investing in those kinds of areas.

(interview, port actor 3, April 2018)

A similar process is affecting the M4H area. Light maritime-related activities, for example related to fruit distribution, are present on the waterfront. This is an appealing location for these innovative businesses, as the high-skilled professionals that they require may be interested in the area's distinctive environment in proximity to the city centre. This edgy urban environment attracts artists, who choose M4H to locate their studios (interview, city planner 4, April 2018), as well as a range of professionals – in particular but not only from the creative class – who are attracted by the area's 'people climate' (as understood by Florida, 2004 [2002]). These processes appear to be a new facet of waterfront redevelopment in Rotterdam and are supported by the Port Authority in the prospect of the transition to a low-carbon economy (interview, city planner 3, April 2018), in a similar way as cultural activity helped compensate for the negative impacts of port migration and restructuring in the late 20th century. This richer blend of functions is not only related to more balanced port-city relationships, but could be pivotal to the dynamism of waterfront areas in a moment when established regeneration strategies relying on cultural consumption and leisure are questioned. The case of waterfront redevelopment in Singapore shows how local policy makers, who had initially tried to import successful consumption-oriented regeneration templates from other port cities, diversified their strategies by incorporated managerial and business functions when the impacts on the local tourism market of events such as terrorist attacks (e.g. September 11, Bali) and the SARS outbreak became apparent (Chang & Huang, 2011).

Future trends in high-skilled workers' location choices also need to be problematised. Assuming that the local economy recovers swiftly after the COVID-19 shock, extended and reiterated lockdown measures are likely to have an impact. Further research should examine whether high-skilled workers are still interested in locating in these central city areas. Perhaps, it is too early to say whether Rotterdam is a pioneering example of how waterfront redevelopment processes worldwide will work in the near future. Other port cities display different trends from this perspective. For example, the redeveloped Porto Maravilha in Rio de Janeiro is attracting businesses operating in the still growing oil and gas cluster, fuelling an increasing demand for office space (Silvestre, 2017).

Although, at the time of writing, cruise tourism seems much less of an issue than it was before 2020, it is worth mentioning the tension at the port-city interface generated by cruise and ferry terminals. Cruise terminals may have a mutual relation with event-led regeneration. On the one hand, they impact on cultural and sporting events, as existing open venues near these facilities may need to be moved elsewhere for safety and security reasons. On the other hand, it could be argued that culture contributes – albeit contingently – to the development of cruise tourism itself, by increasing the city's attractiveness and raising local ambition in terms of tourism development. There is a direct relationship between cultural tourism and port activity. Cruise and ferry terminals are present (or planned to be built) in many port cities, and are often acknowledged as one of the primary sources of spatial port-city tension in these places. In Rotterdam and Hull, these facilities are subjected to political tension, as discussions regarding their relocation are fuelled by the struggle of local actors and institutions to agree on a common strategy. Key issues preventing agreement among such stakeholders include congestion, as a large number of people gather at the same time in 'restricted' port areas, clash with other functions (such as administrative functions and housing), pollution and accessibility, property rights and management responsibilities.

Hull is an example of how cruise terminals are managed in relation to higher ambition in terms of tourism development. The City Plan acknowledged the UK City of Culture 2017 as a pivotal element of a strategy aimed at making Hull a world-class visitor destination. As part of this strategy, the plan includes the construction of an offshore cruise terminal at Sammy's Point, opposite The Deep aquarium. Currently, ferry passengers travelling through the port of Hull do not necessarily visit the city, as it happens for example in Calais or Civitavecchia. A cruise terminal at walking distance from the Old Town, and in proximity to an iconic modern building such as The Deep, is believed to be more effective in encouraging passengers to visit the city, rather than travelling directly to other parts of the country. As discussed in Chapter 7, the *Hull: Yorkshire's Maritime City* project aims to create a maritime cultural offer and to attract visitors and cruise tourists.

In Rotterdam, the cruise terminal is located on Wilhelminapier in Kop van Zuid, where the former Holland America Line's arrival and departure building was located. Many different functions, including cultural facilities, are concentrated in the – relatively small – area, where the little physical transformation related to the European Capital of Culture 2001 was concentrated. Rotterdam's cruise terminal saw a considerable increase in vessel and passenger flows, from approximately 50 ships and 38,550 passengers between 1998 and 2004 to 80 ships and more than 213,000 passengers between 2005 and 2010 (McCarthy & Romein, 2012, p. 2043). In 2019 alone, 102 cruise ships called at Rotterdam, while approximately 255,000 people travelled through the port.[1] In relation to this increase, Rotterdam Festival needed to reduce the activity of the World Port Days – the flagship cultural festival celebrating the port – and to move some cultural events to other venues to avoid congestion in the area, albeit this was not a critical problem for local cultural organisations (interview, event team member 3, May 2018). Due to issues of congestion and pollution, other location options for this facility were being discussed at the time of fieldwork (interview, event team member 2, April 2018).

In Genoa, the cruise/ferry terminal is located within the old harbour, yet it is physically separated from the redeveloped section of it, generating no substantial tension with cultural uses. A similar situation is visible in Valencia, where the cruise terminal was separated from the Dársena by Moll de Ponent in the mid-2000s. As in the case of Rotterdam, before the spreading of COVID-19 halted the industry, a rapid increase in the number of ships and passengers was generating tension in relation to mobility issues in both Genoa and Valencia.

Spatial tension at the port-city interface

The 'urban takeover' of former port areas is largely understood as a phenomenon generating tension with existing maritime uses. Similarly, one could expect that the introduction of temporary or permanent cultural functions at the port-city interface raises similar issues. However, when it comes to culture and leisure, the picture appears to be different. The little tension between cultural and port uses can be explained considering that heavy port functions were no longer present in inner harbours and waterfronts that were transformed in relation to mega events. In other words, event-related uses were welcomed as an opportunity to reconvert derelict port and industrial spaces. In the case of Genoa, for instance, the 1992 Columbus Expo was the catalyst for the reconversion of the abandoned Porto Antico. As suggested by an informant:

> When [the University] came here [to Porto Antico], nobody wanted to come here, because this was a no man's land. . . . If you think about it, twenty years ago they created this thing relatively out of nothing. I mean, they did not throw out a working port. The port was working, but in another site. There was almost nothing here.
>
> (interview, expert 12, June 2018, author's translation)

The Port Authority retained those areas within the harbour that were considered crucial for maritime purposes, such as the cruise and ferry terminals, and gave other unused port areas to the city. From the perspective of the Port Authority, current working port areas are deemed to be sufficient to manage inward traffic, while event-led regeneration taking place since the 1990s has not hampered the growth of the port (interview, port actor 3, June 2018).

The case of Valencia is not dissimilar, as redundant areas were used for the America's Cup. In addition, the new port exit channel physically separated leisure spaces from working port areas. However, considering that mega events in Valencia also involved the use of part of the port estate, tension *was* generated by road closures and security measures and by heavier workloads for port staff to manage these special occasions. As illustrated by a senior officer from the Port Authority:

> [t]o the port as such, if we are here to move ships and freights, doing sailing contests and motor races is an inconvenience. It implies inconvenience for what [our] work is. It implies inconvenience for port work, and it implies more work for our technical and legal services who need to accommodate these unusual practices in relation to what the law allows. Because if you look at the law, it disciplines how to give concessions, how to move ships,

how to move freights. Then, you need a lot of work to understand what is the legal framework to do sailing contests or motor races. This is the [kind of extra] work. It implied much work, and I don't think this generated any more containers.

(interview, port actor 5, May 2018, author's translation)

In Hull, too, a few events in 2017 were held within the port estate, despite the security arrangements in place and the fact that a physical separation between the port and the rest of the city is present. However, little spatial tension was visible in relation to the UK City of Culture 2017 and to permanent cultural facilities. This is largely due to the fact that indoor and outdoor event venues on or in proximity to the waterfront were actually located in areas that had already been fully transformed and incorporated into the city, as in the case of Victoria Dock.

In Rotterdam, the Port Authority still retains areas in relatively central city locations and is more oriented towards mixed-use developments in waterfront areas – albeit heavy port industries are of course hard to blend with other uses – and therefore welcome cultural uses and facilities. While the pressure of urbanisation – of housing in particular – on port areas does produce tension between the Port Authority and the City Council (interview, port actor 3, April 2018), a different attitude is visible in relation to culture-related uses (interview, expert 5, April 2018). The experience of the European Capital of Culture 2001 and the following event policy reinforced policy makers' idea that culture can be a powerful tool for place making, especially at the port-city interface. This view is shared by the Port Authority:

[t]ogether with the Municipality we [the Port Authority] are making a new zoning plan in which most of the old port activities are moved away gradually. It takes a lot of time and [it] costs a lot of money. Those areas [are] being regenerated into a new business area, but also combinations of housing and urban ways of living. . . . Of course, [people] want a café or a bar or some place-making [functions], and they want to take their friends out in the area. So, for the marketing branding, the place making, but also for, you know, the vitality of those areas, the cultural aspects are very important. Cultural activities, events . . . And of course, these areas are also very exciting because you have space, it's not a dense urban [area], so [there's] also space to experiment. For instance, next year we have a street art festival or [next] summer we have the International Architecture Biennale. We had an Art Rotterdam Week in the area, which took place in old industrial buildings, heritage you could say. So, there's a lot going on and I think specifically in those areas which are bits of the port-city interface, as we call it, [and which] are very rough, so [this] attracts a specific kind of people. And artists are working there.

(interview, port actor 3, April 2018)

Socio-spatial conflicts at the port-city interface may be associated with the negative externalities of port expansion, for example in the case of Prà and Voltri in Genoa and of Natzaret in Valencia. In both cases, port authorities and local councils are cooperating to pursue urban regeneration at the port-city interface as compensation for such negative externalities. Examples are Genoa's Fascia di Rispetto (buffer zone) in Prà and Valencia's Parque de Desembocadura (rivermouth park), both public parks at the port-city interface. The case of Valencia is particularly worth mentioning here. Event-led regeneration arguably exacerbated the existing port-city socio-spatial conflicts generated by port expansion (Figures 5.1, 5.2 and 5.3).

> Today, we have a post-conflict space, consisting of some huge areas in the south part of the port [which are] totally empty, where they destroyed, I think, more than 600 dwellings, which in part were heritage. . . . They completely altered an agricultural landscape that was part of the Valencian identity and, clearly, part of the society didn't like this.
>
> (interview, expert 13, May 2018)

This conflict was arguably fuelled by the idea that such port facilities were not necessary, as the growth of international trade had been overestimated (interview, expert 13, May 2018). The ZAL (logistics zone) is not fully used, while the 'natural' growth of the port is expected to take place at Sagunto (Sorribes i Monrabal, 2015), which offers more space for future growth. Up until early January 2019, the port-city interface in Natzaret was demarcated by what was called *el muro de la vergüenza* (the wall of shame, Figures 5.1 and 5.2). In this context of port-city conflict, the construction of Valencia Street Circuit arguably worsened the accessibility of Natzaret and its connection to the city centre.

In recent years, the Cuc de Llum footbridge, initially envisioned to access the circuit, has provided a connection with the Grau area. More broadly, this conflict is being addressed by the Ayuntamiento and APV (Valencia Port Authority) through a *convenio* aimed at realising the aforementioned Parque de Desembocadura, intended as compensation for residents who suffered the negative externalities of port expansion and had no benefit from the impacts of mega events (interview, policy maker 8, June 2018). In 2021, the Plan Especial Zona Sur 1 (Special Plan South Zone 1) of the port has provisionally been approved, in order to devote 230,000 sqm of port land to urban uses. The park, located at the port-city interface between Natzaret and the working commercial port and initially envisioned in the mid-1990s, includes an 86,000 sqm park, 18,000 sqm of tertiary uses, 99.000 sqm of port facilities and the base of Levante football club, a new metro connection to the city centre, with the aim of regenerating the area and incorporate it into the city. In Spain, these schemes are encouraged by the law, which disciplines non-port uses at the port-city interface. Thus, local policy makers and city planners have planning tools at their disposal to act on spatial port-city relationships. It is as part of this agreement that the 'wall of shame' was torn down in mid-January 2019 (Navarro Castelló, 2019), with a ceremony

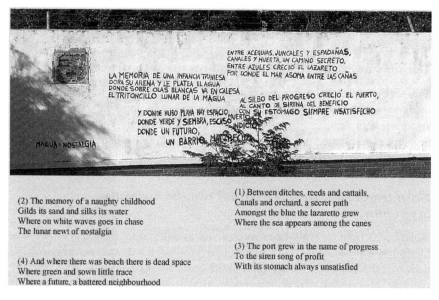

Figure 5.1 Poem on the 'wall of shame' in June 2018.

Figure 5.2 Murals on the 'wall of shame' in June 2018.[2]

involving Mayor Joan Ribó. In addition, public realm works associated with PAI del Grau have begun, with the aim of improving permeability and therefore alleviating the isolation of Natzaret resulting from the F1 circuit.

Tensions in event-led regeneration on the waterfront

This second part of the chapter expands on the socio-spatial tension generated or influenced by event-led urban regeneration, examining a range of issues that are either generative processes or outcomes of this tension. These are the role of property rights at the port-city interface, the issue of permeability and accessibility of waterfront areas, questions of spatial disparities in event-led urban regeneration.

Deterritorialisation, property rights and event-led regeneration in port cities

Waterfronts have recently been interpreted as deterritorialised spaces (see e.g. Desfor & Laidley, 2011). As mentioned in Chapter 2, the deterritorialised nature of waterfronts is understood in the book from two perspectives, namely the role of external actors (e.g. transnational companies and state-run port authorities) and the disengagement between place and culture. With regard to the aforementioned first dimension of deterritorialisation, one might consider event-led urban regeneration on the waterfront as more easily achievable in continental Europe (than for instance in the UK) and more generally in those ports that display a lower degree of interconnection with international trade patterns. This is because in many countries in mainland Europe, unlike in the UK, port authorities are public institutions and the port land is owned either by the state or directly by local councils (as examined later in relation to property rights). Private or corporatised port authorities – especially where they also own the land – are likely to operate according to different business models, in which the city is a contingency, a 'risk' that needs to be managed (interview, expert 3, April 2018). However, this hypothesis needs to be problematised.

One crucial aspect concerns institutional settings, which may vary substantially. For example, the port authority is a private organisation in Hull, a public yet corporatised organisation in Rotterdam and an extra-territorial entity governed by the State in Genoa and Valencia (Table 5.1). In Hull, the port land is owned by the Crown and leased to ABP, who is a private company. In Rotterdam, the Port Authority used to be directly controlled by the state and the City Council. Although it is a public organisation, the Port Authority was corporatised and depoliticised through the 2004 port reform and now works as an independent company. This led to a greater tension, as the role of the Port Authority in the development of spatial visions and the role of the City Council in port visions have changed (interview, expert 3, April 2018; interview, expert 5, April 2018; interview, city planner 4, April 2018).

The President of the Port Authority is nominated by the Ministry of Infrastructure and Transports in the case of Genoa and by Generalitat Valenciana in

Table 5.1 Nature of the Port Authority across the four cities.

	Hull	Rotterdam	Genoa	Valencia
Port Authority	Associated British Ports (ABP)	Havenbedrijf Rotterdam N.V.	Autorità di Sistema Portuale del Mar Ligure Occidentale	Autoridad Portuaria de Valencia (APV)
Status	Private organisation	Public – State/city corporatised since 2004	Public – State (Ministry of Infrastructure and Transports)	public – State (Ministry of Public Works – Ports of the State)
Leadership	CEO	CEO	President nominated by the Minister	President nominated by the Regional Council
Political connection with the city	Informal discussions with the City Council	City Council's political representatives in the board	More centralisation with recent reforms (Delrio Act)	Since 2015 – Port-City Commission led by the Mayor

Valencia. Decision making is then further centralised by the state. In the case of Valencia, one informant stressed this strong centralisation as follows:

> Who takes the decisions? On the basis of what criteria? And also, what objectives of public interest do they serve? Because . . . one of the problems of ports in the case of Spain is that they are managed by the state, the General Administration of the State, whose decisions are taken in Madrid, 500 km away from here . . . the headquarters of Ports of the State are located 500 km away from any port, in Madrid.
>
> (interview, May 2018, author's translation)

An informant in Genoa raised concerns in relation to the connection of Italian port authorities with transnational companies:

> there is the risk for port authorities, in particular the Mediterranean ones, that with megaships and the direct intervention of shipowners, they have no power, in my opinion. And on a future perspective, I don't know whether they are going to have a great future.
>
> (interview, port actor 5, June 2018, author's translation)

These global pressures are coupled with rigid institutional and legal frameworks, which make negotiations between local councils and public port authorities rather lengthy and complex. This aspect has considerable impacts in terms of opportunities for event-led urban regeneration on the waterfront. For example, in Italy, waterfront areas are usually owned by the state, as part of Demanio Marittimo, which is the whole of state-controlled coastal and marine areas across the country. In addition, these areas are landscape heritage items, which are protected by the Superintendence responsible for cultural and natural heritage conservation. This means that the regeneration of waterfront areas implies negotiations with a range of national institutions. A member of Genoa's City Council underlined that this had contributed to hampering urban regeneration in the case of the Hennebique area, in a context where public resources were insufficient:

> as regards urban regeneration, there are problems not necessarily with the Port Authority but with the Superintendence. . . . We should give more freedom to the private sector to try to . . . give new life to certain areas that could not thrive again without any money. And we, as the Council, have no money to regenerate them, neither does the Port Authority.
> (interview, policy maker 4, June 2018, author's translation)

In Genoa, Ponte Parodi, a large pier next to the Maritime Museum, was initially envisioned as the main venue for the ECoC 2004. However, due to uncertainties about the institutional framework and the suitable planning procedure to follow for its redevelopment, the area remained in a state of decay:

> The conflict wasn't of the kind that the Port Authority wanted to do something there and the City Council wanted to do something else. It was a legal problem about who had the right [to transform that area]. . . . So, this could be pointed at as a case of lacking or ineffective cooperation among the institutions involved in this matter.
> (interview, expert 12, June 2018, author's translation)

In this case, the exceptionality of a mega event (the European Capital of Culture 2004) was not sufficient to overcome problems of negotiation with the state. Conversely, for example, the Expo 2010 made it possible for Shanghai City Council to relocate a number of state-owned industrial plants away from the riverside docklands chosen to host the event, a task that would have been difficult to implement under normal circumstances (Chan & Li, 2017, p. 676).

Land ownership is a crucial factor for event-led regeneration in port cities. Informants in Hull, from both the city and the port side, suggested that private ownership or lease of port land by private organisations may hamper processes of this kind (interview, policy maker 1, February 2018; interview, port actor 1, December 2017). This is assumed by local city and port policy makers to be a peculiar feature of event-led urban regeneration in the UK, in comparison with mainland Europe (with the case of Barcelona's Port Vell often mentioned as an example). This assumption should be problematised. On the one hand, it is true that, in the case of Hull, the UKCoC 2017 did not cause much tension with ABP because – with the exception of ancillary events organised by ABP themselves – most events did not take place within the port estate. On the other hand, even though port authorities do not exclude in principle to borrow land for cultural uses, they do not appear keen on conceding their land to the city either. This is due to the fact that port authorities try to avoid the pressure generated by housing and by the permanent presence of people, which may be encouraged by event-led regeneration. In the case of Rotterdam, as suggested by one informant, 'the ugly word for port planners is "housing", residential development; . . . cultural things are sort of in a grey area' (interview, expert 3, April 2018). In Valencia, the fact that the inner harbour is still predominantly owned by the state led to difficult negotiations between the city and the state, as reported by a policy maker:

> Do you know Valencia's inner harbour? The tinglados and all of that . . . It 'costed some blood' [*i.e. it was very hard*] to get a minimal concession of land. So, this was a remarkable limitation in terms of the expectation that the city had about the port and its seafront. The port still retains the ownership of these areas, apart from the tinglados and a little more.
> (interview, policy maker 9, May 2018, author's translation)

This reluctance by the state to give port land to the city was explained as followed by a senior officer from APV:

> The thing is that, if this [land] is mine, planning powers are mine. If I give [this land] to the city, planning powers will be held by the [C]ity [Council]. And I could give this to the city, to a mayor whom I agree with, but it's not given that there will be the same mayor for ten years. If the [P]ort [Authority] loses its ownership, it cannot be sure than in ten years' time there won't be a local government putting houses over here. So, we will have the same problem again. The best option is to create a zone of culture, which remains [port] property or which remains within the port public domain, and to discuss its use with the Council.
> (interview, port actor 5, May 2018, author's translation)

Rotterdam's experience shows that such discussions on land ownership continue well after mega events have indirectly contributed to boosting regeneration at the port–city interface, although there has been no substantial friction between the port and the city because of mega events themselves (interview, expert 6, April 2018). Ongoing waterfront redevelopment schemes such as in Katendrecht generate discussions and negotiations about port land, which needs to be sold to the City Council (interview, city planner 4, April 2018).

Porosity, security, safety and culture on the waterfront

The accessibility of redeveloped waterfronts is a crucial factor for the effectiveness of these schemes. Waterfronts in European port cities present critical issues of porosity (see e.g. Hein, 2021). Porosity is understood in the book as the permeability/accessibility and the degree of physical connection between the city and the waterfront, as a legacy of the latter's past or actual maritime role and the related security concerns. Ports and cities are separated by tangible and intangible borders, arising from physical barriers but also from different regulatory regimes.

Event-led regeneration has often contributed to improving the porosity of these areas, where former international and restricted port areas have been transformed into urban areas and public spaces, as happened in Genoa and Valencia. As explored in Chapter 7, this helped restore, or establish, a relationship with the sea, which had been interrupted or prevented by the presence of a fenced-off industrial port area. However, constraints to porosity remain. For example, whether still used by ports or for urban traffic, port ring roads may represent a key constraint to the permeability of waterfronts. Waterfront redevelopment schemes across Europe have sometimes included the redesign of these roads, as in the case of Passeig de Colom in Barcelona, where the ring road was moved underground, and a promenade was created.

In Hull, Humber Street Gallery and Fruit Market were key venues of UK City of Culture events in 2017 and have retained their role as cultural poles after that. The area is nonetheless separated from the Old Town and the city centre by Castle Street, that is the section of the A63 – a major road connecting Leeds to the port of Hull – that runs through the city. Castle Street is a rather busy road, which is also used by trucks and lorries to transport goods from and to the port (Figure 5.3).

Figure 5.3 Weekday traffic on Castle Street.

The redevelopment of Fruit Market and the UK City of Culture 2017 gave momentum to the ambition of reconnecting this waterfront area with the city centre. In the event bid, £170 million were budgeted for 'Major Road improvement – critical to festival venues – funded by Government' (Hull UK City of Culture 2017, 2013, p. 77) on Castle Street. Similarly, the City Plan included a proposal for an iconic footbridge (see Hull City Council, n.d.), which was completed in 2021. This implied the redesign of a road that is key for port activity. A city planner discussed this tension as follows:

> the idea of connecting the Fruit Market around the Marina back into the sort of retail core of the city centre is a real priority. So, we've been working very, very closely with Highways England to get a road scheme designed up, which doesn't just improve speed of getting into the port, but also brings the Marina and the retail core closely together. Now, I am aware the port operators actually don't really bother about the Fruit Market and the city centre working well. They are more interested in getting their vehicles in the port as quickly as possible. Which does mean they'd probably prefer a scheme that could be built much more quickly, something like a flyover that could go in there, but the impact a flyover would have in sort of segregating the Marina and the rest of the city . . . it'd be awful, it'd be horrific. To be fair to them, I think they . . . We have, I think, a good relationship with ABP. They do understand why, as a Council, we are pushing for that longer-term solution.
>
> (interview, city planner 3, January 2018)

In Rotterdam, waterfront areas in central city locations display different extents of permeability. Accessibility on foot is influenced by major roads such as Vasteland and Blaak. Leisure waterfronts are nonetheless easily accessible by public transport (e.g. Veerhaven, the Wereldmuseum and the Maritime Museum). The permeability of waterfronts was not affected by the little direct physical outcomes of cultural and sporting events and mega events, and it is more the result of urban development, whether or not culture led. In the case of Oude Haven, Rotterdam's old harbour, the world-famous Kijk-Kubus complex built in the late 1970s as an example of innovation in architecture has reorganised the space and created a different relationship with the waterfront, as visitors need to walk through the complex to get there (Figure 5.4).

In Genoa, event-led regeneration contributed to radically changing the picture in terms of permeability. While the growth of the industrial port had led to the closure of Porto Antico, interrupting traditional relationships between the old port and the city centre, mega events offered a chance to give back to the city some of the iconic port areas that were abandoned as the port migrated and grew. Today, there is little perception that Porto Antico was – and in part still is – an international area (interview, port actor 4, June 2018). The waterfront is easily accessible on foot from the city centre and most of it is pedestrianised. This was possible also because of the presence of a flyover (Sopraelevata) built in the 1960s to improve port accessibility (Figure 5.5).

Figure 5.4 Kijk-kubus on Rotterdam's Oude Haven.

Figure 5.5 Sopraelevata in Genoa's Porto Antico.

However, due to its visual impact, there is the willingness to replace this infrastructure with a tunnel (interview, policy maker 4, June 2018), as in the case of Barcelona's Passeig de Colom. This will nonetheless imply discussions with the Port Authority and central government regarding port accessibility for passengers and goods. The importance – and fragility – of accessibility of port areas by road and rail, and its impact on the local economy, was exposed by the collapse of Ponte Morandi in August 2018, which blocked the railway line connecting the port of Genoa with Northern Italy and France (see e.g. Zaccariello, 2018; Capuzzo, 2019). In Rio de Janeiro, a similar flyover (Elevado da Perimetral) was demolished as part of the Porto Maravilha redevelopment project in 2014. This intervention made it possible to open the waterfront promenade Orla Pref. Luiz Paulo Conde and the Olympic Boulevard. Together with the repaving of Praça Mauá, it contributed to connecting the city with the pier where the futuristic Museu do Amanhã (Museum of Tomorrow) was built, next to the cruise terminal.

Finally, event-led regeneration in Valencia displays mixed outcomes in terms of permeability of waterfront areas. On the one hand, the America's Cup 2007 was crucial to separate the harbour from the working port, enabling the former to be fully devoted to leisure and urban uses. On the other hand, unlike other port cities such as Barcelona, Genoa and Rio de Janeiro, the redeveloped harbour was not fully pedestrianised and connected to the city. Avinguda de l'Enginyer Manuel Soto and Carrer Marina Real Juan Carlos I still represent a physical barrier. These roads were retained as they were used as the main straight and the pit lane of Valencia Street Circuit (Figure 5.6). Mega events also had a negative impact on the permeability of waterfront areas and were missed opportunities to reorganise the port-city interface.

> It's true that the port-city relationship was not optimised, because Formula 1 prevented the road that every port city has, or used to have, between the city and the port [from being pedestrianised] . . . This road ring was kept because it formed part of the [F1] circuit. So, it wasn't pedestrianised. . . . [A]fter Formula 1, in that period, you still had road traffic through this area and that wasn't a direct relationship.
>
> (interview, expert 15, May 2018, author's translation)

Similar issues of permeability can be found in the case of Baku, where the Formula One Azerbaijan Gran Prix has been held since 2017 (with the exception of the cancelled 2020 edition) using a temporary street circuit in the heart of the city and in proximity to the main cargo terminal. As noted by Gogishvili (2018), 'leftovers' from F1 remained: these include concrete barriers scattered throughout the track and most notably the Paddock Club – F1 VIP hospitality – which is expected to remain in its current location in Azadliq Square, between the House of Government and Dənizkənarı Milli Park on the seafront, until the event is hosted in the city.

Figure 5.6 Harbour ring road in Valencia and former main straight and pit lane of Valencia Street Circuit.

Other issues impact on the permeability of Valencia's Dársena. If it is true that the city used to 'give its back to the sea', the port also used to – and still does – give its back to the city. This, together with the fact that the port is managed by the state, prevented a full permeability to be achieved, as port–city 'borders' remained.

> Historically, in Valencia we say that the city has been living giving its back to the sea. And that's true, because it is far away from the sea. And nowadays the port lives giving its back to the city as well. And that causes a lot of problems to the extent that, even though we had many mega events, even though [the port] was in part opened, the port is still fenced off. In fact, there is a part [of it], the commercial part, which is fenced off. And the part that was given to the city . . . still has a series of boundaries that clearly mark a jurisdictional border between a port entity and the city.
>
> (interview, expert 13, May 2018, author's translation)

[T]he first question that should have been asked, so to speak, or that should have been thought about is: how do we connect the port, in terms of urban uses, with the rest of the city? Up until a little time ago, there was a wall that divided completely and enclosed the port from the rest [of the city]. People needed to pass through a series of filters.

(interview, policy maker 7, May 2018, author's translation)

Port-city 'borders and filters' are also coupled with the presence of spaces and facilities that, ten years after the events, still lack a clear function.

And [the redeveloped port] is a fantastic space, which has much potential. But it should be opened to the city, because it is full of fences, full of impediments to have a walk. There are many areas that are semi-industrial or semi-I-don't-know-what, which are odd to visit. In this sense, I think there is quite a barrier for citizens to use these spaces.

(interview, expert 14, May 2018, author's translation)

While aspects of security in relation to spatial port-city relationships may be relatively obvious, issues of safety are perhaps less immediate to appreciate. On the one hand, ports are international areas which raise particular risks in terms of trafficking, international crime and terrorism. On the other hand, contemporary ports are also 'dangerous' places due to their complexity and degree of automation. This affects both the use of the port-city interface and the possibility of hosting events within the port estate. As noted by informants from the Port Authority in Hull and Valencia:

Port aren't safe places, there is a risk around them. And people who work for us when they go there, they go there with training, they go there with specialist protective equipment, they are there to be doing a job, and the general public coming onto that creates a risk for them and for us.

(interview, port actor 2, February 2018)

Considering that ports have been growing more and more and more in terms of complexity, it is really dangerous to roam a commercial port. You can only open to the city those areas of the port that are no longer used for commercial purposes.

(interview, port actor 5, May 2018, author's translation)

As mentioned earlier, in Hull, a few events in 2017 took place within the port estate. Although these events were incorporated into the programme, they were organised and managed by ABP rather than by Hull 2017 Ltd. The exhibition *In-Port Stories* was held in the Grade-II listed Pump House at Alexandra Dock, and was the chance for residents and visitors to access a heritage building within the port estate. The 1885 building which hosted the exhibition has occasionally been used as a cultural venue after the UK City of Culture 2017 as well. Rotterdam's World Port Days, the annual maritime festival, is another example of this tension. Most events are celebrated along the river and on

Wilhelminapier. However, a few events take place within the port estate, as companies operating in the port such as Shell organise guided tours of their plants (Van Tuijl & Van den Berg, 2016, pp. 6–7). In both cases, part of the port estate is made visible in relation to very ephemeral events and to small number of visitors, so that safety and security measures can be put in place in these settings.

Waterfronts and cities: 'culture-led' spatial disparities

To different extents, mega events have contributed to the 'opening' or 'reopening' of waterfronts to the city, by regenerating abandoned port areas. However, culture-led regeneration may also produce spatial contradictions where the concentration of investment and activity in city centres generates spatial disparities to the detriment of the periphery (Bianchini, 1993, p. 201). Transforming an area into a cultural quarter may produce gentrification and displacement (Miles, 2005, p. 890), as land values tend to increase due to the greater attractiveness of the area. Conversely, peripheral areas may become less attractive and may lose existing activities as a result of a renewed city centre. This process can also be viewed from another perspective, considering that culture- and event-led regeneration schemes may be unable – or not intended – to produce regenerative impacts on the city as a whole.

Although many community arts events and social projects were held in the periphery, UK City of Culture events in Hull tended to concentrate in the city centre and in the newly redeveloped Fruit Market creative hub. Capital investment and public realm improvements were also concentrated in the city centre. This was in line with the Council's strategy of prioritising regeneration in this area. Waterfront areas benefitted from public and private investment, in part fostered by the UK City of Culture 2017, such as in the case of the redevelopment of Humber Street and Fruit Market. The concentration of public realm improvements and cultural activity in the city centre has had regenerative impacts, as well, especially in terms of increased footfall. However, the nationwide crisis of retail, which is unrelated to the specificity of Hull and its trajectory of culture-led urban regeneration, is affecting the city centre. The closure of local branches of national chains such as Marks & Spencer, Boots, House of Fraser and, more recently, Debenhams are examples of this trend. This appears to be a structural tendency that event-led regeneration was arguably not able to contrast. In addition, social distancing measures and the alarming news related to COVID-19 were arguably the *coup de grace* accelerating the ongoing demise of high streets across the country. In terms of spatial disparities between the city centre and the rest of the city, further research is needed to assess whether the concentration of activity and regeneration has negatively affected other cultural poles beyond the city centre, such as Beverley Road.

In Rotterdam, although cultural and sporting events and mega events did not engage extensively with urban regeneration, the EURO 2000 final match took place in Feyenoord Stadium, in the southern peripheral Feyenoord district, where a metro connection with the city centre was provided. The ECoC 2001 celebrated the redevelopment of Kop van Zuid, by concentrating events along the river. Since then, though, it appears possible to argue that the location of cultural facilities and the celebration of (smaller-scale) cultural and sporting events have displayed a more even spatial distribution. For example, the North Sea Jazz Festival takes place in Rotterdam Ahoy in Zuiderpark, near Feyenoord. The International Architecture Biennale is held primarily in the M4H area. The Wereldhavendagen include events along the river, but also excursions to Futureland or Rozenburg Peninsula. The World Police and Fire Games 2022 will be hosted in a range of indoor and outdoor sporting facilities, venues and locations in and around the city, such as Rotterdam Ahoy, Neptunus, Boezembocht, Zoetermeer.

Genoa's Porto Antico was redeveloped with the aim of creating a new *centrality* without damaging existing poles such as the city centre. As mentioned, Magazzini del Cotone were not transformed into a retail centre – as it was done for instance in Barcelona's Port Vell – to avoid damaging existing businesses (interview, policy maker 5, June 2018). A concentration of investment and events characterised the city's mega-event policy, as a specific strategy targeting the city centre and the waterfront in Porto Antico. As noted by one informant, this choice helped generate and sustain the necessary momentum to implement such an ambitious vision and to coordinate different projects and initiatives:

> [i]n Genoa, this [*common effort around a shared vision*] has happened, because as regards the central area of Genoa, the waterfront, there certainly was a specific choice of investing resources and concentrate the effort in this area. Maybe to the detriment of other areas, maybe to the detriment of the peripheries, which represent another area of possible intervention that on the contrary was not prioritised.
>
> (interview, expert 11, June 2018, author's translation)

As pointed out by another informant, this was also supported by the idea that such a powerful transformation would contribute to the regeneration of the city as a whole:

> they haven't done a single thing for the peripheries. But the decision of concentrating everything in that part of the city was a precise, strategic and targeted choice. Because Gabrielli[3] used to say 'this is the richest part of the city in terms of potential [so] if this goes well, all the city will do well'.
>
> (interview, expert 10, June 2018, author's translation)

However, the extent to which these regenerative spillovers took place is questionable. Porto Antico, the Aquarium and the Maritime Museum produced visible positive effects locally, but arguably failed to connect with the rest of the city, just behind the harbour. As suggested by one informant, one reason behind this is that parts of the city centre are still run down and retain the traditional 'edginess' of Mediterranean port cities.

> the city centre is still really run down, and people do not go there. . . . If only the visit of the city centre were pleasant! Without that feeling of dirtiness, bad pavements if you go there in the winter, poor quality or lacking lighting, drug dealing, prostitution, thus a set of things that do not help, let's say.
>
> (interview, event team member 5, June 2018, author's translation)

It is worth noting that the current local plan (Piano Urbanistico Comunale) sets amongst its strategic priorities a spatial 'rebalancing' in terms of facilities and services across the city, by ensuring at least one high-profile public facility in every neighbourhood, with the aim of creating a city 'without peripheries'.

Finally, in Valencia, event-led regeneration also had quite localised impacts, which failed to affect the city as a whole (interview, policy maker 7, May 2018; interview, policy maker 9, May 2018). Two issues need to be mentioned. Firstly, the fact that Valencia city centre is located 5 kilometres inland, appears as a key constraint in terms of spillovers from the regeneration of the harbour. Arguably, the construction of Jardín del Túria, which runs through the very heart of the city, was much more important a factor in the overall regeneration of Valencia. As in the case of Barcelona's Parc del Fòrum – the waterfront site at the end of Avinguda Diagonal where the 2004 Universal Forum of Cultures was held – localised regenerative impacts have only been visible in the long term. Secondly, the America's Cup and Formula One events produced very different outcomes. The former event, albeit generating criticisms, contributed to opening the Dársena to visitors and citizens. The Marina Real Juan Carlos I is becoming a new leisure hub. However, there is no evidence that this is negatively impacting on other areas of the city in terms of reduced attractiveness and cultural activity. This did produce regenerative effects in nearby areas, but also contributed to strengthening speculative pressures on maritime districts such as El Cabanyal-El Canyamelar. The latter event, on the contrary, produced negative outcomes in nearby areas, such as Grau and Natzaret, in terms of permeability and urban decay.

The spatiality of event-led regeneration in port cities: open questions

Event-led urban regeneration is one of the aspects that allows us to question the narrative of port-city separation. One key lesson is that port-city relationships are rapidly evolving and retightening, as also emerged from recent scholarship (Wiegmans & Louw, 2011; Daamen & Louw, 2016). Culture plays a relevant role in this evolution, in particular where it is associated with large-scale infrastructural and urban projects, as in the case of mega events. However, its contribution tends to be overlooked in the analysis of port-city relationships.

Mega events have generated either little or substantial spatial impacts. The extent of these impacts was closely related to geographical contexts and, more importantly, to the evolution of port-city relationships in these cities. In either case, a relationship between culture and port activity is present. Mega events were backed by port actors in Rotterdam, as an indirect means to increase port competitiveness. They played a role in increasing the attractiveness of the analysed host cities, producing a tangible impact in terms of growth of cruise tourism. Cultural activity appears to indirectly contribute to an increased urban pressure on ports, which cannot afford a permanent and sustained presence of people at the port-city interface.

These processes raised policy implications and further research questions about the future evolution of port-city relationships and the role that culture might play in it. In terms of governance and policy implications, it is worth noting that former port areas in central city locations have become strategic assets for both culture-led urban regeneration and light maritime industries. Waterfront areas such as M4H in Rotterdam are pioneering examples of urban environments characterised by a blend of innovative maritime activities – which tend to locate in proximity to the city centre to attract high-skilled professionals and artists, who appreciate the distinctive character of these areas – and cultural uses. The analysed mega events have generally not produced substantial spatial tension for two reasons: firstly, event-led regeneration has in most cases involved former port areas, where port activities were no longer present; secondly, mega events are by definition special occasions, lasting for a limited period of time. However, a subsequent permanent presence of cultural activities and people, generated by more mature culture-led regeneration processes after mega events have taken place, may generate tension between port and city actors where the former are interested in retaining urban port areas for maritime activity. In addition, it is worth stressing that touristification and other phenomena such as the growth of cruise tourism should be taken into account.

One key challenge for port-city governance and policy making is whether cultural and maritime functions can coexist and represent a model for future waterfront redevelopment schemes. This also in the light of the incoming post-oil transition, which may lead to a new process of port restructuring. Whether directly or indirectly, culture- and event-led regeneration have proved to contribute to the regeneration of the port-city interface and – at least in some cases – of nearby areas. However, their broader impact on the city as a whole still raises 'spatial dilemmas' in relation to the uneven spatial distribution of investment, events and regeneration.

Notes

1 Source: Cruise Europe, see www.cruiseeurope.com/statistics/.
2 On the top left picture, 'Catalogo de vallas' means 'fence catalogue', while the sentence below says 'Beyond the stone blocks, [there's] the beach'. In the top right picture, we can read 'Capitalism [is] marvellously cool' and 'hot summer'. The mural in the bottom right picture portrays a 'Museum of the Rivermouth Park' and says 'We want the park.

Always' (author's translations). All murals are references to the former beach and seafront of Natzaret and recall ideas of freedom and nostalgia. 'Hot summer' may also refer to the allegedly warmer microclimate created by the expansion of the port blocking the breeze coming from the sea, which was mentioned by one informant (interview, policy maker 9, May 2018).

3 Bruno Gabrielli was Assessore (Deputy Mayor) for urban planning in Genoa from 1997 to 2006.

Bibliography

Andreatta, V., & Herce, M. (2012) Rio de Janeiro and the 2016 Olympics: The city center revitalization on the conjugation of the project 'Porto Maravilha' and 'Porto Olympic'. *PortusPlus*, 2, 1–24.

BBC (2020) Rio Olympic Park: Judge orders closure of site over safety concerns. *BBC News*, 16th January. Available at: www.bbc.co.uk/news/world-latin-america-51133312 [Accessed 22/01/2021].

Bianchini, F. (1993) Culture, conflict and cities: Issues and prospects for the 1990s. In Bianchini, F., & Parkinson, M. (eds.) *Cultural Policy and Urban Regeneration: The West European Experience*. Manchester: Manchester Press, 199–213.

Bono, F. (2021) Las chabolas se asientan en el fiasco inmobiliario del circuito de Fórmula 1 de Valencia. *El País* [online], 3rd August. Available at: https://elpais.com/espana/2021-08-03/las-chabolas-se-asientan-en-el-fiasco-inmobiliario-del-circuito-de-formula-1-de-valencia.html [Accessed 18/08/2021].

Broudehoux, A., and Carvalhaes dos Santos Monteiro, J. C. (2017) Reinventing Rio de Janeiro's old port: Territorial stigmatization, symbolic re-signification, and planned repopulation in Porto Maravilha. *Revista Brasileira de Estudos Urbanos e Regionais*, 19(3), 493–512. DOI: 10.22296/2317-1529.2017v19n3p493.

Capuzzo, N. (2019) Morandi bridge impact on Genoa port: Here are final figures. *Ship 2 Shore: On Line Magazine of Maritime and Transport Economics*, 23rd April. Available at: www.ship2shore.it/en/ports/morandi-bridge-impact-on-genoa-port-here-are-final-figures_70585.htm [Accessed 02/08/2019].

Cavalcanti, M., O'Donnell, J., & Sampaio, L. (2016) Futures and ruins of an Olympic city. In Carvalho, B., Cavalcanti, M., & Rao, V. V. (eds.) *Occupy All Streets: Olympic Urbanism and Contested Futures in Rio de Janeiro*. New York: Terreform, 60–89. DOI: 10.1080/02665433.2018.1453282.

Chan, R. C. K., & Li, L. (2017) Entrepreneurial city and the restructuring of urban space in Shanghai Expo. *Urban Geography*, 38(5), 666–686.

Chang, T. C., & Huang, S. (2011) Reclaiming the city: Waterfront development in Singapore. *Urban Studies*, 48(10), 2085–2100.

Chen, Y. (2020) Financialising urban development: Transforming Shanghai's waterfront. *Land Use Policy*. DOI: 10.1016/j.landusepol.2020.105126.

Daamen, T. A., & Louw, E. (2016) The challenge of the Dutch port-city interface. *Tijdschrift Voor Economische En Sociale Geografie*, 107(5), 642–651. DOI: 10.1111/tesg.12219.

Den Hartog, H. (2021) Shanghai's regenerated industrial waterfronts: Urban lab for sustainability transitions? *Urban Planning*, 6(3), 181–196.

Desfor, G., & Laidley, J. (2011) Introduction: Fixity and flow of urban waterfront change. In Desfor, G., Laidley, J., Stevens, Q., & Schubert, D. (eds.) *Transforming Urban Waterfronts: Fixity and Flow*. London and New York: Routledge, 1–13. DOI: 10.4324/9780203841297.

Duignan, M. B., & McGillivray, D. (2019) Disorganised host community touristic-event spaces: Revealing Rio's fault lines at the 2016 Olympic Games. *Leisure Studies*, 38(5), 692–711.

Florida, R. (2004 [2002]) *The Rise of the Creative Class: And How It's Transforming Work, Leisure, Community, and Everyday Life*. New York: Basic Books.

Gastaldi, F. (2012) Grandi eventi e rigenerazione urbana negli anni della grande trasformazione di Genova: 1992–2004. *Territorio Della Ricerca Su Insediamenti e Ambiente*, 9, 23–35.

Gogishvili, D. (2018) Baku formula 1 city circuit: Exploring the temporary spaces of exception. *Cities*, 74, 169–178.

The Guardian (2017) Rio Olympic venues already falling into a state of disrepair. *The Guardian*, 10th February. Available at: www.theguardian.com/sport/2017/feb/10/rio-olympic-venues-already-falling-into-a-state-of-disrepair#:~:text=Just%20six%20months%20on%20from,Olympic%20golf%20course%20is%20struggling [Accessed 22/01/2021].

Hein, C. (ed.) (2021) Planning for porosity: Exploring port city development through the lens of boundaries and flows [Special issue]. *Urban Planning*, 6(3).

Hoyle, B. (2000) Global and local change on the port-city waterfront. *The Geographical Review*, 90(3), 395–417. DOI: 10.6092/2281-4574/1254.

Hull City Council (n.d.) A63 iconic footbridge. *Hull City Plan*. Available at: http://cityplanhull.co.uk/index.php/a63-bridge/ [Accessed 17/04/2019].

Hull UK City of Culture 2017 (2013) *Tell the World: Final Bid*. Hull: Hull City Council.

Marrades, R. (2018) La Marina de València: La apropiación ciudadana y la activación productiva del frente marítimo de la ciudad. In Baron, N., & Romero, J. (eds.) *Cultura territorial e innovación social. ¿Hacia un nuevo modelo metropolitano en Europa del sur?*. Valencia: Universitat de València, 193–204.

McCarthy, J. P., & Romein, A. (2012) Cruise passenger terminals, spatial planning and regeneration: The cases of Amsterdam and Rotterdam. *European Planning Studies*, 20(12), 2033–2052. DOI: 10.1080/09654313.2012.722914.

Miles, M. (2005) Interruptions: Testing the rhetoric of culturally led urban development. *Urban Studies*, 42(5–6), 889–911. DOI: 10.1080/00420980500107375.

Navarro Castelló, C. (2017) Valencia ve imposible recuperar el coste del circuito de F1 con el PAI del Grao. *El Diario*, 27th March. Available at: www.eldiario.es/cv/Ayuntamiento-imposible-recuperar-circuito-F1_0_626787731.html [Accessed 24/08/2018].

Navarro Castelló, C. (2019) Adiós al muro de la vergüenza de Natzaret: El barrio marinero recupera parte del terreno que le arrebató el puerto. *El Diario*, 15th January. Available at: www.eldiario.es/cv/Natzaret-simboliza-recuperacion-ampliacion-Valencia_0_857414493.html [Accessed 10/04/2019].

Sardinha Lopes, R., & Pauletto Fragalle, N. (2016) Rio Criativo. O projeto Porto Maravilha em questão. *E-metropolis*, 7(26), 15–24.

Silvestre, G. (2017) Rio de Janeiro 2016. In Gold, J. R., & Gold, M. (eds.) *Olympic Cities: City Agendas, Planning, and the World's Games, 1896–2020*. London and New York: Routledge, 400–423.

Sorribes i Monrabal, J. (2015) *Valencia 1940–2014: Construcción y destrucción de la ciudad*. Valencia: Universitat de València.

Van Tuijl, E., & Van den Berg, L. (2016) Annual city festivals as tools for sustainable competitiveness: The world port days Rotterdam. *Economies*, 4(11), 1–13. DOI: 10.3390/economies4020011.

Wiegmans, B. W., & Louw, E. (2011) Changing port-city relations at Amsterdam: A new phase at the interface? *Journal of Transport Geography*, 19, 575–583. DOI: 10.1016/j.jtrangeo.2010.06.007.

Zaccariello, G. (2018) Ponte Morandi, il crollo mette in ginocchio il porto: 'Così muore l'economia della città'. *Il Fatto Quotidiano* [Online], 17th August. Available at: www.ilfattoquotidiano.it/2018/08/17/ponte-morandi-il-crollo-mette-in-ginocchio-il-porto-cosi-muore-leconomia-della-citta/4562089/ [Accessed 18/08/2018].

6 The politics of event-led regeneration in port cities

As any other process of urban or socio-economic transformation, event-led regeneration is far from being apolitical. Event bids, whether or not successful, are often the product of complex, sometimes innovative governance processes involving a number of local stakeholders, as well as the local community. Discourses of change, hope and alternative visions for the future of the city may dominate the local political debate (e.g. Anderson & Holden, 2008). Although top-down governance structures with little room for inclusive processes tend to emerge in the planning and delivery of mega events due to the 'impossibility to fail' associated with them (Tommarchi et al., 2018), intense discussions and negotiations between key institutions and actors are fundamental. However, political struggle, in particular around the use of public resources or the displacement of local populations, often arises. After a mega event is held, managing its legacy for the city is again a moment that may witness the re-emergence of inclusive governance processes, provided that there is any legacy to speak of.

Mega events and event-led regeneration in port cities do present a further element of complexity, namely their interconnection with the relationships between city institutions (city councils, but also other entities such as regional councils) and port actors (port authorities, port operators, businesses in local maritime clusters). This chapter therefore engages with the political aspects of event-led regeneration in the context of port-city relationships. This interest stems from the fact that much of the research on mega events and event-led regeneration tends to emphasise their economic and spatial dimensions, to some extent overlooking the politics behind these processes. Firstly, the chapter explores the role and involvement of port authorities in the city's cultural activity, especially in the planning and delivery of mega events. If it is true that, on the one hand, port policy makers are aware that mega events and event-led regeneration may contribute to port competitiveness and therefore to the economic prosperity of the city, on the other hand, port authorities increasingly engage with the city's cultural life. Nevertheless, port authorities display different roles and approaches in relation to their involvement in local cultural activity, which depend on their institutional nature and framework, as well as on their established practices. Secondly, the chapter looks at policy discourses and urban imaginaries of the 'port city' and the 'city of culture' that emerge in

DOI: 10.4324/9781003165811-6

event programming and other policy documents. These ideas may be competing urban imaginaries, albeit maritime economic activities generally play more important a role in local economies in comparison with cultural activities, which act as catalysts for urban development.

The 'cultural' role of port authorities

Port authorities are key institutional actors in port cities, as they run the port infrastructure and yield considerable revenues from acting as mediators within maritime operations. However, their role in the city's cultural life is often overlooked. Whether public, corporatised or private organisations, port authorities may be interested in culture for a number of reasons. These include the awareness that an attractive city generally helps port competitiveness, the possibility of engaging or reconciling citizens with ports and thus gaining public support for port activity, the willingness to attract educated people for a range of new port-related jobs, and finally the opportunity of educating and getting young people (i.e. the potential port workforce of the future) interested in port activity. The involvement of port authorities in the city's cultural life can be examined by considering their understanding of the port city environment and of the role of culture in urban policy. On the one hand, port authorities can display an instrumental approach to culture and interpret their cultural involvement as a tool to gain public support around their activity. On the other hand, they can understand the city as an 'ecosystem' and recognise the importance of culture for the vitality of the port city as a whole.

From landlords to developers

As suggested by Vries (2014, pp. 111–112), port authorities may play different roles in the city's economic, cultural and political life by acting as 'landlords' or 'developers'. Vries builds on the idea of port authorities' attitudes 'beyond the landlord' proposed by van der Lugt and de Langen (2007; see also van der Lugt et al., 2015, 2017). At one end of this spectrum, port authorities act as 'landlords' where they run the port infrastructure with no specific involvement in the city's affairs. Such a position may be a response to the growing involvement of private companies in seaports across the world (van der Lugt et al., 2017, p. 412). At the other end, port authorities may act as 'developers' where they are directly interested and involved in a range of aspects such as local development, urban governance, spatial planning or cultural programming.

Port authorities may transition from a landlord position to a developer attitude, depending on their status (i.e. public, corporatised or private), their scope in relation to the expectations of their stakeholders (Vries, 2014) and on the changes in their commercial and operational environment (van der Lugt et al., 2015, pp. 571–572). Such a shift generates a greater involvement in a range of other activities beyond their landlord role, especially where port authorities are corporatised rather than embedded into government structures (ibid., p. 588).

Although a developer attitude may potentially arise from a greater awareness of port authorities of their social responsibility, or from forms of enlightened capitalism, such a behaviour is more likely to be a proactive response to their 'local dependence', which may be understood as an unavoidable dependence of local institutions and businesses on the local context in which they operate (Cox, 1993, p. 434). Port actors are subjected to regime politics arising from the interaction of a multiplicity of stakeholders locally (Jacobs, 2007; Dooms et al., 2013; Notteboom et al., 2013). They still need to access the local labour market and to gain their 'licence to operate' from the public opinion. In the aforementioned literature, the idea of port authorities acting either as landlords or developers is not necessarily related to cultural activity. However, port authorities can be considered as developers also where they contribute to funding research, education and cultural events (Table 6.1).

At least before 2017, the role of ABP in Hull appeared closer to the landlord extreme, displaying a limited involvement in culture. As commented by a senior official, ABP used to have no interest 'in the fluffy things of culture' (interview, port actor 2, February 2018). Nonetheless, there were signs of tighter political relationships with the City Council, arguably facilitated by the role of former port director Matt Jukes, who at the time of writing is the CEO of Hull City Council (interview, city planner 1, February 2018; interview, event team member 1, January 2018). In 2017, as explored in this chapter, ABP appeared more interested in Hull's cultural life. It seems possible to argue that the UK City of Culture 2017 has played a role in this, opening the door for ABP's future engagement with culture and the city (interview, expert 2, interview, January 2018). An open question remains about whether ABP's cultural engagement will be a feature of port-city relations in Hull or whether it should be considered as an episode occurred under the umbrella of the UK City of Culture. This also in the light of the uncertainties for maritime trade generated by Brexit and the development of so-called 'free ports' across the country.

In Rotterdam, the role of the Port Authority as developer appears more evident. Rotterdam's Port Authority – which is publicly owned, yet corporatised since 2004 – has traditionally been committed to supporting the arts as a means to support port-city relationships (see e.g. the description of the 1980 cultural project Ponton 010 in Van Ulzen, 2007, pp. 143–151), in particular by supplying empty buildings to local artists (interview, expert 7, April 2018). Similarly,

Table 6.1 Role of port authorities in the analysed cities according to Vries' model (2014).

Hull	Rotterdam	Genoa	Valencia
Landlord	*Developer*	*Mixed position*	*Landlord*
Landlord position; recent interest in culture	Established effort in culture-led regeneration and innovation	Attempts to innovate; institutional constraints	Port-city separation; recent interest in cultural events

local port champions – the CEOs of port companies – also used to invest in culture (interview, port actor 3, April 2018). The gradual relocation of port companies' headquarters elsewhere in the world has arguably contributed to weakening this connection (interview, port actor 3, April 2018), to the extent that, in the early 2000s, there was little cooperation from the perspective of cultural activity (interview, event team member 2, April 2018).

This picture has gradually been changing as Rotterdam, as a *city*, became more international. The Port Authority has increasingly been interested in the city's cultural and political life (interview, event team member 2, April 2018), as it recognised the importance of culture for the local business climate, as well as its social responsibility (interview, port actor 3, April 2018). The Wereldhaven-dagen (World Port Days) are organised by the Port Authority, who also sponsors the Port of Rotterdam North Sea Jazz Festival, another key event of the city's cultural programme. Established sponsoring relationships link the Port Authority with Rotterdam Festivals (interview, event team member 3, May 2018), the permanent culture company responsible for the planning and delivery of cultural festivals, as in the case of the Eurovision Song Contest 2021. Indirect sponsorships involve a range of local cultural organisations, including the Phil-harmonic Orchestra. In addition, the Port Authority funds small-scale cultural events and participatory projects in the surrounding municipalities. An example is DeltaPORT Donatiefonds, a funding scheme to support activities in schools, hobbies and creative initiatives proposed and developed by citizens (DeltaPORT Donatiefonds, 2020). Similarly, port companies and the Port Authority are now eager to invest in the 'software of the port' (interview, port actor 3, April 2018), that is in education, research, innovation, branding, marketing and so forth.

As mentioned, the Port Authority recognises the importance of culture and cultural events in terms of place making and branding, in particular in the case of former port areas. Examples are the redevelopment of the RDM Campus (for a description of the scheme, see Vries, 2014), where a submarine wharf is used as a venue for business and cultural events, and Makers District, where artists were involved as place makers (interview, port actor 3, April 2018). The case of Makers District is particularly relevant. The area is being transformed through a joint development initiative involving the City Council and the Port Authority, who aim to create a vibrant urban district where innovative manu-facturing, cultural activities and new forms of urban living coexist. Start-ups and professionals can benefit from specialist training provided for example by the Erasmus Centre for Entrepreneurship and by Port XL (specialising in maritime businesses), both located in the M4H area. Culture and events play an impor-tant role, as they contribute to fuelling the creative and innovative atmosphere that is sought by the City Council and the Port Authority as the key aspect of the 'character' of the district. For example, the International Architecture Biennale is held primarily in the M4H area. Facilities where light industrial, residential and cultural functions share the same space are also being intro-duced in the area as a result of this joint strategy, as in the case of the Kunst & Complex in Keileweg.

In addition, since 2014, the Port Authority, Erasmus University Rotterdam, the City Council and Rotterdam Partners – an organisation managing networks of local companies and institutions – have also been involved in the Rotterdam Make It Happen partnership, with the aim of consolidating Rotterdam's external image and to attract companies, students and visitors. The Port Authority – along with key actors including Rotterdam City Council, Rotterdam Partners, the Drechtsteden Regional Council, the Province of Zuid-Holland and Rotterdam Maritime Board – is also working on the branding campaign Rotterdam Maritime Capital of Europe. This initiative launched in 2018 focuses on maritime innovation and competitiveness, although it also considers cultural amenities and events as key components of a positive business climate, in line with the Port Authority's established approach to culture.

The case of Genoa, where the port is owned and run by the State, shows how national institutional frameworks influence the cultural role of port authorities. Genoa's Port Authority has traditionally played a role in the city's cultural life, for example by funding small-scale cultural initiatives (interview, policy maker 5, June 2018) and by organising lectures, conferences and events for students (interview, port actor 5, June 2018). As observed by a former official, the Port Authority 'had become a cultural point of reference for the local population' (interview, port actor 5, June 2018, author's translation) in the 1990s and early 2000s. Nevertheless, this cultural involvement has also been coupled with strong institutional constraints to the role of the Port Authority, as well as the 'need to seek for a balance' among different interests (interview, policy maker 5, June 2018). In Italy, port authorities are public institutions who directly respond to the Ministry of Sustainable Infrastructure and Mobility (formerly, Ministry of Infrastructure and Transports). Their role and tasks are thoroughly regulated by the law, thus limiting their potential involvement in any activity – including social and cultural activity – beyond their scope. Their financial autonomy and organisational and administrative capacity are also limited and mediated by the state. Genoa's old harbour is managed by the company Porto Antico Spa, also responsible for cultural programming in the area.

Similarly, in Spain, port decision making is centralised at the state level. APV is part of the state administration and appears to have historically been detached from the city's cultural life. Consorcio 2007, the company established for the delivery of the America's Cup, conveyed into La Marina de València, a permanent management body for the Marina Real Juan Carlos I. La Marina de València also acts as a permanent culture company in the area and as a mediator between APV (state level) and the City Council (city level, Table 6.2).

It is important to note that the establishment of La Marina de València is a relatively recent development and that the leisure port has been underutilised for about ten years after the America's Cup 2007. In addition, the role of APV in the city's life might have even been contracting in recent years due to factors such as the impacts of port expansion on Natzaret and La Punta and the resulting port-city conflict:

Table 6.2 Port and cultural governance arrangements across the four case-study cities.

	Hull	*Rotterdam*	*Genoa*	*Valencia*
Port authority status	Private	City/State	State	State
Harbour management company	n/a	n/a	Porto Antico Spa (public/ private)	La Marina de València (public)
Culture companies (harbour areas)	Absolutely Cultured Ltd (formerly, Hull 2017 Ltd)	Rotterdam Festival	Porto Antico Spa	La Marina de València (formerly. Consorcio 2007)

[Valencia's] port has been socially delegitimised because of several administrative problems, the crisis . . . all the conflict related to the destruction of
La Punta, which is not even going to be used as an area for port activity.
Therefore, I think that the Port Authority has withdrawn a bit from the
public sphere and has come back to its economic, commercial and administrative functions.

(interview, expert 13, May 2018 author's translation)

Nevertheless, it is worth noting a recent involvement of APV in cultural activity, as discussed later in this chapter, which appears to signal a potential shift
from the institution's established landlord position.

A more or less established role of the port authority in promoting culture is
visible in many other port cities. Such a role was not necessarily undermined
by COVID-19. For example, in 2020, Hamburg Port Authority opened core
port areas to the public, hosting cultural events within the port estate: 81 events
attracted 33,000 visitors (Hamburg Port Authority, 2021). The Port Authority
of New York and New Jersey, who published a study on the role of the arts in
local development as early as the 1980s (Port Authority of New York and New
Jersey and Cultural Assistance Center, 1983), also supports cultural activity, in
particular in the World Trade Center campus, which is owned and run by the
Port Authority and where activities were resumed in 2021. 'Arts and culture' is
one of the three community investment pillars, together with 'sports and recreation' and 'education', of PortsToronto, who supports events such as *Beaches
International Jazz Festival* or *Redpath Waterfront Festival* (both of which took
place in 2020 and 2021, either virtually or in a socially distanced format) and
the Waterfront Neighbourhood Centre's Youth Arts Programme and Community Connect Garden.

From the experience of the case-study cities, it appears possible to identify
a number of factors that influence the cultural role of port authorities. Firstly,

leadership and the role of top officials in advocating a greater cultural involvement are key factors, as in the case of the former President of Genoa's Port Authority Giuliano Gallanti. The cultural sensibility of these figures and their interest in backing the role of port authorities as 'patrons' for arts and culture appear to be crucial. Secondly, an established tradition of involvement in culture and in supporting the arts, as in the case of Rotterdam, shapes the mentality of port authorities and thus their attitude towards culture. In this case, it is more likely that port policy makers have a broader understanding of the role of culture in port competitiveness and place making, as the experience of Rotterdam suggests. It is worth stressing that the attitude and capability of port authorities to engage with culture may be rather different where port authorities are centralised (e.g. in Valencia and Genoa) or more embedded into the city (Rotterdam and Hull). The deterritorialisation of ports raises therefore the need for a 'mediator', for example a purposely designed organisation acting as a bridge between state-run port authorities and the city, as in the case of Porto Antico Spa or La Marina de València. Interestingly, in both cases, these organisations were initially established as temporary delivery vehicles for mega events, and subsequently became permanent as part of the legacy of these events. Finally, an important element is the relatively recent interest in culture displayed by port authorities with a traditional landlord position, as in the case of Hull and Valencia. This appears to be arising from a greater awareness amongst port officials of the potential of cultural events in building consensus around port activity and in supporting port competitiveness. Nonetheless, a role in this change may be played by other factors, such as the growing relevance of issues related to culture-led regeneration at the port-city interface within institutional learning and knowledge sharing networks, such as the Association for the Collaboration Between Ports and Cities (RETE).[1]

Ports and port culture

Whether acting predominantly as landlords or developers, port authorities appear in most cases interested in promoting port and maritime culture, with particular emphasis on contemporary ports and maritime activities. As observed by Van Hooydonk (2007), the effective management of the 'soft values' of ports may help restore public support around their activities. Among these soft values, Van Hooydonk (ibid., pp. 19–20) includes: organising cultural events, port storytelling (e.g. through port-themed museums), managing maritime heritage, reinstating the maritime feel, involving port authorities in providing port-related cultural offerings.

While, on the one hand, this interest is a strategy to ensure ports' 'licence to operate' by gaining public support around port activities, on the other hand, the tendency of port actors to embrace culture is enriching local cultural offers with port-related cultural opportunities and activities. An example is the recurrent establishment of port centres, intended as visitor centres, info points and exhibition spaces to communicate the history and activity of ports to the general public. The aim of these initiatives is to maximise the engagement of local community with ports and maritime activities, and to fuel the interest of younger generations in maritime-related occupations and careers. The Association Internationale Villes et Ports (AIVP) defines port centres as 'an interface with a playful atmosphere between the city, the port and the inhabitants, where the port can communicate its missions, projects and associated careers' (AIVP, 2020). Facilities of this kind have been established, in particular in the last decade, in many port cities, such as Aarhus, Antwerp, Dunkirk, Le Havre, Livorno, Montreal, Vancouver. In Rotterdam, FutureLand is a visitor centre and exhibition space at Maasvlakte, opened in 2009 with the aim of showcasing the construction of a modern container terminal. Despite its relatively difficult accessibility, since the venue is located approximately 50 kilometres from the city centre and is surrounded by automatised terminals, FutureLand has generated a stable presence of people in the area (interview, port actor 3, April 2018). The facility is visited by approximately 100,000 people each year and reached its millionth visitor in 2019 (Port of Rotterdam Authority, 2019). As part of its cultural offer, the visitor centre also provides bus and ferry tours of the working port.

Genoa's Port Center is an exhibition space and info point about the history, development and current activity of the port. It was established in 2009 by the Province of Genoa and is located at Magazzini del Cotone. After a temporary closure, the facility was reopened in late 2018. At the time of writing, Genoa's Port Center is owned by the Metropolitan City of Genoa[2] and is run by Porto Antico Spa in partnership with the Port Authority. Although operated by private companies, boat tours of the port are available as part of the local maritime cultural and tourist offer. Boats sail from a central waterfront location – opposite the headquarters of the Port Authority – and coast part of the commercial and industrial port to reach Pegli. Visitors have the chance to see, albeit from afar, working port areas that are inaccessible by land due to safety and security reasons, and that are in part invisible. Such initiatives to encourage residents and visitors to engage with maritime culture and the activity of the port may also promote a 'cultural change' in terms of attitudes towards the port and its role: port development may not necessarily be seen as in opposition to the 'cultural' and 'tourist city' (interview, expert 11, June 2018) as discussed later in the chapter.

Ephemeral, whether occasional or regular, port-centred cultural events are also a means to convey port culture to broader audiences. In Rotterdam, the Wereldhavendagen (World Port Days), initially envisioned in the late 1970s as an open day to showcase the port, became a 3-day festival organised by the Port Authority in partnership with the City Council and a range of local stakeholders. The Wereldhavendagen are a major tool 'to counter the negative effects' of port activity 'and make the citizen "smell and bound" with the port again' (Van Tuijl & Van den Berg, 2016, p. 5) and also to encourage young people to work in the port (interview, event team member 3, May 2018). The event includes a range of activities, such as maritime-related shows along the river, lectures and seminars about the activity of the port, excursions and tours designed to let visitors explore certain working port areas but also seminatural environments that have been transformed as a result of port development (e.g. Landtong Rozenburg, Maasvlakte), education programmes such as the World Port Hackathon (an event about ports and big data, which involves local education institutions).

Port Day Genova e Savona is a 3-day event similar to Rotterdam's Wereldhavendagen, albeit smaller in scale. The Port Day Genova e Savona is delivered by the Port Authority controlling the ports of Genoa and Savona, in partnership with Capitaneria di Porto (harbourmaster), Assoporti[3] and other organisations, as part of the Italian Port Days. The national programme – which involves for instance the ports of Ancona, Civitavecchia Livorno, Naples, Rome Trieste, Venice – is an interesting example of how port authorities can build nationwide cultural synergies. In 2019, 283 visitors attended the Genoese event (Ports of Genoa, 2019), which has latterly been delivered in a blended format combining in-person and online activities. The initiative includes conferences and public lectures about port activity or coastal environments, exhibitions, tours of the port estate and of maritime heritage assets, education programmes and events involving secondary school students or children.

These events should not be confused with maritime festivals broadly defined, for example festivals celebrating aspects of maritime history or heritage, or generalist events held in historic harbour areas. On the one hand, maritime festivals take place in many port and coastal cities, and may contribute to fuelling a certain interest among the public in maritime or naval history. On the other hand, however, port festivals and events such as Rotterdam's Wereldhavendagen or the Italian Port Days engage directly with the activities undertaken in modern commercial and industrial ports and with aspects of education, skills development, economic role and environmental impacts of port activity. These events therefore promote port culture and attempt to stimulate the interest of the local community in what the port actually does.

The role of port authorities in mega events

The visibility associated with large-scale events is another factor that can play in favour of port actors. There is little awareness of the impact of transformative cultural or sporting events on established cultural relations among key port and city actors. The case-study cities display different patterns and outcomes of the cultural involvement of port actors in mega events.

The case of Hull helps illustrate some of the issues that these events raise in the relations between port and city actors. The UK City of Culture 2017 shows how mega events may generate political pressure on key port actors to take part. Especially in times of austerity and shrinking resources for cultural activity, it is not a viable option for such key actors to avoid involvement in the planning and delivery of events that are framed as potentially transformative, once-in-a-generation opportunities for the local community. In Hull, ABP and port companies such as Siemens felt that they *had* to engage with such an important event for the city (interview, expert 2, January 2018). ABP worked with Hull 2017 Ltd, the City Council and port companies on a range of cultural projects and ancillary actions. Under the umbrella of the UK City of Culture 2017, ABP funded and delivered the successful *In-Port Stories*, a pop-up exhibition of photographs, which was organised in cooperation with the local heritage organisation The History Troupe. In addition, ABP donated historic port records to Hull History Centre on the occasion of the event, including accounts of dock development and the history of the Humber, railway plans and navigation maps (ABP, 2017). UK City of Culture banners were allowed in the port estate, in order to reach people travelling by ferry from Rotterdam and Zeebrugge (ABP, 2016). Finally, in 2016, ABP also worked with the City Council to create a public art trail in the Public Right of Way around the perimeter of Siemens facility at Alexandra Dock (Green Port Hull, 2016).

Port companies also played a role in the event. British Petroleum delivered the *BP Cultural Visions Lecture series*, a number of public lectures on topics related to Hull 2017's cultural programming. Siemens Plc Communications Director noted that it was 'natural' for the company to support the event considering its 'significant presence' in the city (Siemens, 2016). ABP's agreement with Siemens about the construction of the wind turbine manufacturing facility at Alexandra Dock included a project to save the Dead Bod mural (interview, port actor 2, February 2018). The mural, representing a dead bird, was allegedly painted in the 1960s on the side of a shed at Alexandra Dock and became a landmark for local fishermen and sailors. The shed was scheduled to be demolished to clear the area for the construction of Siemens' plant. After a local campaign to save the mural, the Dead Bod was removed from its original location, restored and put on public display at Humber Street Gallery in 2017. Another notable example is *Blade*, an art installation part of Hull 2017's *Look Up* programme, consisting of a wind turbine blade manufactured in Hull being displayed in Queen Victoria Square (Figure 6.1). It has been estimated that 1.1 million people saw the installation, while 420,000 interacted with it, before it was moved to the entrance of Siemens Gamesa's facility at Alexandra Dock (Green Port Hull, 2017).

Arguably, the UK City of Culture 2017 stimulated ABP's interest in a greater cultural involvement. However, the company's executive officials were disappointed by the fact that this involvement did not develop much further (interview, port actor 2, February 2018). There was little cooperation between Hull 2017 Ltd and ABP (interview, policy maker 1, February 2018; interview, event team member 1, January 2018; interview, port actor 2, February 2018), while the latter would probably have been keen on playing a greater role in the event. In turn, the City Council did not intervene directly to involve ABP, in line with the aim to minimise its political influence over the event.

In Rotterdam, as many cultural events in the city have been related to 'water', it was expected from the Port Authority to play a role in the delivery of mega events (interview, expert 6, April 2018). Nonetheless, political pressure

Figure 6.1 Blade in Queen Victoria Square in January 2017.

on port actors is perhaps more visible in the case of waterfront redevelopment. Such schemes act as megaprojects and have a degree of visibility and interest at the local level that may be comparable to that of a large-scale event. In this case, the Port Authority may take part as a result of a specific request from the City Council (interview, event team member 2, April 2018). For example, the Port Authority was politically pressured to contribute to the development of the RDM Campus (interview, expert 3, April 2018). In the case of the European Capital of Culture 2001, in line with its established tradition of supporting culture and the arts, Rotterdam Port Authority took part in a range of initiatives, for example an event organised in partnership with New York Port Authority to celebrate migration and Dutch-American connections. It is also worth considering the involvement of the Port Authority in the smaller-scale cultural events that have been delivered after the European Capital of Culture 2001. As suggested earlier, this involvement can be interpreted as a strategy to generate interest and consensus around port activity. An example is the already mentioned Port of Rotterdam North Sea Jazz Festival, for which the Port Authority is the title sponsor.

In Genoa, the 1992 Specialist Expo was managed by Colombo '92, a partnership among the Regional, County and City Councils, Consorzio Autonomo del Porto (Port Autonomous Consortium, the former Genoa Port Authority) and the Chamber of Commerce. After some initial administrative difficulties affecting the immediate legacy of the event, the redeveloped portion of the harbour was leased to Porto Antico Spa – of which Consorzio Autonomo del Porto held 10% of the shares – from 1995 to 2050 (Mastropietro, 2007, p. 177). In the case of the European Capital of Culture 2004, the Port Authority was a partner of Genova 2004 Srl. In addition, the administrative director of the Port Authority sat on the board of the culture company (interview, event team member 5, June 2018). Despite the fact that the partnership did not present any major difficulties, some event organisers felt that the Port Authority could have contributed more (interview, event team member 4, June 2018). Nevertheless, the contribution of the Port Authority should be pondered considering the fact that the joint effort with the City Council in the reconversion of Porto Antico had already been completed. Thus, the event was predominantly managed by the City Council as the concessionaire of the state-owned former port land (interview, expert 12, June 2018). After Genoa's mega-event era, the Port Authority has been working with the City Council on a range of cultural projects and events. An example is Museo delle Migrazioni (Museum of Migrations) for which the Port Authority produced a database about migrants who had left Italy from the port of Genoa (interview, event team member 5, June 2018). The Port Authority has also contributed to the organisation of the traditional Regata delle Repubbliche Marinare (interview, policy maker 4, June 2018) and to the city's regular cultural programming (interview, policy maker 6, June 2018).

In Valencia, APV's involvement in international sporting events should be examined considering its role within coalitions of interest including the City Council, the Regional Council and private event promoters, namely the Société Nautique de Genève and Formula One Group. This meant that there was good collaboration among the actors involved in the promotion of these events as there was a shared vision of the role of these events in urban development, although such a vision was not necessarily supported by the local community (interview, policy maker 8, June 2018). APV worked closely with the City Council in the transformation of the inner harbour and its separation from the working port. The Port Authority opened part of the port estate for the celebration of the America's Cup and the Formula One European Grand Prix, despite the fact that, as discussed in Chapter 5, this raised a range of issues including disruptions for port activity. However, the contribution of the Port Authority was limited, especially due to the very nature of the events held in the city. It is nonetheless worth noting that APV has recently been involved in cultural events aimed at showcasing the history of the port. In the last few years, APV has promoted, also in partnership with other local institutions, ephemeral exhibitions about the history and development of the port (see e.g. Valencia-port, 2018a, 2018b), which involved the use of maritime heritage assets.

As in the case of the cultural role of port authorities, event-led regeneration on the waterfront appears to be influenced by a range of political factors. The most prominent is, again, leadership, as single senior officials have been crucial for constructive relationships, in particular in those cases where they moved from the Port Authority to the City Council or vice versa. For example, Matt Jukes was Hull's Port Director from 2008–2013 and then CEO of Hull City Council immediately after that. Giuliano Gallanti was the Director of Genoa's Port Authority from 1997–2001 and was particularly committed to promoting port-city relationships. Prior to becoming Valencia's Port Director in 2015, Aurelio Martínez Estévez was Councillor for Economics and Finance of the Generalitat Valenciana in 1993–1995, mayoral candidate in the 1995 Local Elections, Director of the Department of Economics of the University of Valencia and President of the Instituto de Crédito Oficial from 2004–2009. The political orientation of institutional actors and their relationships with the central government have also proved to be key in Genoa and Valencia, while this appears to be less important a variable in Hull and Rotterdam. This aspect could be a characteristic feature of Mediterranean port cities, as it is highlighted in other cases. For example, Andres (2011) reports that established political conflicts in Marseille were behind tensions between the city and the state, and contributed to the fragility of the partnership behind the ECoC 2013.

Port cities and cities of culture: competing views?

Maritime port cities owe their very existence to the presence of a port. Despite experiencing deindustrialisation and restructuring since the 1970s, many of these cities are still thriving maritime hubs. Nonetheless, the exceptionalism of port cities may be a factor that relegates them into a separate league when it comes to interurban competition, even in the case of cities hosting dynamic and strategic ports. The rise of culture- and event-led regeneration as a response to port and socio-economic restructuring in the last decades of the 20th century implied that port cities as diverse as Barcelona, Glasgow, Liverpool or Rotterdam are now branded as *cities of culture* alongside their established role as *port cities*. This means that urban policies and planning may display two, possibly competing, urban imaginaries (the 'port city' and the 'city of culture'), sometimes failing to fully combine these visions. As noted by Kowalewski (2018, p. 3), the clash between industrial and tourist port activities has been an aspect of port-city relationships since the late 18th century, as the city's maritime identity has increasingly been associated with leisure rather than work. A similar phenomenon is visible in the case of coastal towns and cities, coastal resorts or fishing towns, which are being rebranded as cultural products (see e.g. Ward, 2018). The growing competition among cities that characterises the contemporary global capitalist economy has led port cities to compete with non-port cities in a range of areas, most notably cultural consumption. As effectively portrayed by Warsewa (2017, p. 155), '[t]hose who in former times had been pilgrims, merchants, immigrants, emigrants, soldiers or seafarers in port cities, are today festival- and culturegoers, commuters, migrants, businesspeople, students, Ryan Air customers, football fans, congress-attenders and science nomads in every town'.

It is therefore worth exploring the tension between these two urban imaginaries, as well as the actual role of cultural imaginaries behind the rhetoric of culture- and event-led regeneration. In the following pages, the link between strategic goals related to the development of the port and of the local cultural or tourist economy is commented, focusing on the relative importance of these aspects within visions of urban and economic development. In addition, the meaning of the exceptionalism of maritime port cities within interurban competition is examined more in depth. What does it mean for a maritime port city to compete with a non-port city to attract cultural consumers? How do policy makers manage port city culture within interurban competition? What emerges from the experience of the case-study cities is that there may be some tension between these urban imaginaries, yet there is a growing interest to blend them. However, policy makers may be inclined to downplay the maritime exceptionalism of their cities, especially where this is perceived as a competitive disadvantage.

Development strategies in port cities of culture and events

Both the development of the port and of a dynamic cultural and tourist economy are cornerstones of development strategies in maritime port cities that have hosted mega events or that have been attempting to achieve culture-led regeneration. The role of these strategic priorities and their interconnection, or lack thereof, is visible in local planning documents.

In Hull, Green Port Hull and the UK City of Culture 2017 have been the two stories shaping policy discourses in the last decade. These two visions appear to have a comparable relevance within the 2013 City Plan, which aims at making Hull a hub for the development of renewable energies *and* a world-class visitor destination. The development of the local maritime cluster is pivotal to the former aim, while the UK City of Culture was perceived as a catalyst for the latter. Notwithstanding the visibility of the UK City of Culture, the port and renewable energy clusters are nonetheless perceived as dominant in terms of their contribution to the local economy. For example, despite recognising the role of the UKCoC as a catalyst for economic development, the Humber LEP's Strategic Economic Plan 2014–2020 (Humber Local Enterprise Partnership, 2014) placed renewable energy, rather than culture, at the heart of its economic strategy. The smooth delivery of the UK City of Culture did contribute to strengthening port-city relationships, yet the event was not necessarily considered as 'a game changer' by the totality of local economic stakeholders, as Siemens' investment was perceived as 'more important' (interview, event team member 1, January 2018). In other words, the transformative role of the UK City of Culture, which was widely anticipated in terms of socio-economic regeneration (e.g. the once-in-a-lifetime-opportunity discourse) and was acknowledged in the City Plan, did not appear to materialise with the same magnitude in local economic development strategies.

In Rotterdam, urban policy shows an established awareness of the role of culture as a powerful place-making device in the context of urban regeneration.

Cultural events and facilities have been playing a pivotal role in promoting and 'humanising' waterfront redevelopment. For example, the European Capital of Culture 2001 itself helped celebrate the redevelopment of Kop van Zuid. Culture is perceived as a means to enhance Rotterdam's attractiveness and, contingently, its competitiveness as a port. In comparison with Hull, there is no evident juxtaposition between port and culture-led development strategies, as culture is not framed in urban policy as an independent strategy, possibly in competition with other urban imaginaries, yet more as a component of spatial and economic development strategies. For example, Stadsvisie 2030 (Gemeente Rotterdam, 2007) aims at promoting Rotterdam as an 'international city on the river', combining an 'excellent port', the gradual transformation of port areas into urban areas (with port activities expected to gradually move to Maasvlakte), and an attractive city centre. It is important to note that as heavy port activities move out, businesses operating in the broader maritime cluster would locate in these waterfront areas. The City Council aims at building a strong local economy by promoting knowledge and innovation, in particular in the maritime cluster, tourism and leisure. Making Rotterdam an attractive city is understood as linked with fostering an attractive business climate, which in turn would generate employment. The pillars of the strategy are therefore the development of the port, of promising economic sectors, of popular residential areas and of the modern city centre on the river. The aforementioned case of Makers District is a good example of how this overall strategy works on the ground. The spatial vision for the redevelopment of the M4H area portrays the future of this part of Rotterdam as that of a mixed-use area combining innovative light industrial activities, housing, cultural and creative activities. The innovative and edgy character of the area is sought to be fostered by the combination of these, to some extent equally important functions.

In Genoa, one could argue that mega events and event-led regeneration are seen by policy makers as a thing of the past. These events did help diversify the local economy and promote the city as a cultural and heritage tourism destination. Despite being widely acknowledged as a crucial factor in the transformation of Porto Antico, these events are no longer perceived as potential catalysts for further redevelopments in the area. Although current spatial plans and visions at the port-city interface, such as Renzo Piano's Blueprint, include cultural activities and facilities, there is no clear culture-led regeneration vision behind them. At the local planning level, as in the case of Hull, port development and culture coexist as standalone strategic lines. The current local plan (called Piano Urbanistico Comunale, see Comune di Genova, 2015), which includes strategic development objectives, aims at making Genoa a polycentric city, whose development trajectory is founded on port/industry, R&D, tourism and culture. Genoa should be an attractive location for businesses in sectors that can replace traditional heavy industry, such as innovation and technology, creative industries, cultural activity and tourism. The plan reflects the idea that mega events have played a crucial role in the recent past, yet it focuses more on aspects of sustainable cultural and tourism development. Nonetheless, the rebuilding of the relationships between the city and the sea, which was the rationale for the transformation of Porto Antico, remains a strategic priority. The 'blue line' of urban waterfronts is still undergoing transformation through a combination of large-scale schemes (such as the already mentioned redevelopment of the eastern section of the port) and small-scale interventions aimed at ensuring quality and connecting with local specificities. Transformation at the port-city interface is agreed with the Port Authority, through the definition of areas where shared planning contents apply and are included in both the local plan and the port plan.

In Valencia, the extraterritoriality of the Port Authority as part of the state administration generated a traditional 'dichotomy' in local planning (interview, expert 13, May 2018, author's translation). This is arguably the main reason behind the lack of an integrated, holistic vision encompassing port and culture-led urban development. The former followed its growth trajectory, while the latter made occasional use of the port to market the city internationally. However, event-led regeneration in Valencia set the scene for the Special Plan for the Marina Real Juan Carlos I (interview, city planner 5, May 2018), which was launched in 2014 with the aim of managing the Marina as a leisure hub and consolidating its role of new centrality. The regional strategy Comunitat Valenciana 2030 (Generalitat Valenciana, 2012) aims at consolidating the region's role as the southern gate of Europe, by strengthening the local rail network and promoting the Mediterranean Railway Corridor, to support the development of the port. The document makes use of the discourse of 'diversification' and emphasises the economic role of cultural industries and the cultural cluster in Valencia's city centre. Strengthening the local and regional cultural offer is seen as a means to attract talents and inward investment. However, this strategy appears rather different from the idea of making Valencia a cultural pole at the European and global level, hosting global events of the 21st century that permeated the 1990s strategic plan (Ajuntament de València, 1997). Nonetheless, what is visible in both strategic documents is that the fast-growing port is not a central element in the city's spatial and economic development strategies. Nevertheless, as seen in the case of Parque de Desembocadura and as in the case of Genoa, the City Council and the Port Authority do engage in planning discussions about the transformation of the port-city interface, which benefit from the provision of a range of planning tools disciplined by national and regional regulatory frameworks.

The four case-study cities display different approaches to culture and events in relation to local development, as well as different extents of integration between port development and culture as strategic priorities. What generally emerges from their experience is that even in those cities where culture and events became at some point prominent, for example as an alternative policy to compensate for port restructuring at the turn of the millennium or as a means to seek a competitive advantage, the maritime economy now seems to be regaining its strategic role. Recent strategic documents also show, as discussed in Chapter 4, how in maritime port cities where mega events have been held, policy makers are generally shifting their attention to other aspects, such as sustainable cultural urban policies levering on local specificities or creative industries. The differences in the approaches adopted in the case-study cities do reflect local political settings at the port-city interface. For example, Genoa and Valencia show how the nature of statutory planning frameworks is vital for city councils and state-controlled port authorities to be able to engage in discussions about the city's development trajectories. Conversely, Rotterdam shows how where port authorities are highly embedded locally, more sophisticated approaches can be developed in order to build synergies between the development of the local maritime cluster and cultural urban policy.

Port and culture as competing policy discourses

The tendency of port authorities to engage with cultural activity as an indirect means to promote port competitiveness does not necessarily appear to be paralleled by a greater interest in port activity from the side of urban actors. When it comes to port activity and the port-related image of cities, the attitude of city policy makers can be rather different from the – whether or not instrumental – interest displayed by port actors in the city's cultural affairs. The key argument is that, in some cases, policy makers tried or have been trying to refashion the port city image – or certain aspects of the city's maritime-related image, such as dominant narratives of local port city cultures focused on specific activities – in the attempt of transforming their cities into 'cities of culture' to pursue urban regeneration and economic development.

This is primarily connected with a political intention to overcome established negative perceptions associated with port activity, as a means to increase the city's attractiveness. In the late 20th century, deindustrialising and declining European port cities have been stigmatised as problem places in relation to socio-economic decline, unemployment, crime, pollution, as in the case of many declining industrial cities in Europe and North America.[4] In addition, the neglect of the port-related image is sometimes linked to the willingness to leave behind painful or controversial aspects of local maritime histories, or dissonant heritage (Tunbridge & Ashworth, 1996), such as in the case of fishing in Hull or slavery in Liverpool. It is important to note that the perception of the port city image as 'problematic' is, or has been, a particular feature of maritime port cities in Europe. For example, the port city image in Asia often tends to be associated to a greater extent with the city's maritime and economic power, such as in the case of Singapore or Shanghai. Therefore, in these cities, policy makers may tend to embrace and praise the port city image as a key component of their branding strategies, rather than downplaying it.

The case-study cities of the book provide examples of this ambivalent attitude in their culture- and event-led regeneration strategies as well. In Hull, in particular in the 1980s and 1990s, fishing narratives were marginalised, in what could be described as an attempt to 'sweep fishing under the carpet' (interview, expert 1, January 2018). The City Council tried to get rid of something that was perceived as a negative aspect of the city's maritime heritage. As a matter of fact, fishing was only one aspect of Hull's rich maritime history and heritage, together with, for example, maritime trade, shipbuilding, coal shipping and food handling. However, in the 20th century and until the 1970s, distant-water trawler fishing and its ancillary industries used to employ a large number of local workers. Such fishing practices also involved considerable risks (see e.g. Schilling, 1966): many fishermen and sailors lost their lives at sea due to the dangers of distant-water fishing. Arguably, this has been among the reasons behind a tendency of policy makers to not emphasise fishing. For example, in 2005, Hull City Council preferred to focus on the organisation of Wilberforce 2007, rather than investing in the celebration of SeaBritain (interview, expert 1, January 2018).[5] The 2013 bid for the UK City of Culture made little reference to the city's fishing past. Yet, despite this initial choice, fishing history and heritage became increasingly important in the final programme. For example, fishing was a key theme in the opening event *Made in Hull* and contributed to connecting people with the event itself.

Rotterdam has long been known as '*de havenstad*' (*the* port city, interview, expert 3, April 2018) and no one would question the city's maritime identity and its role as strategic port in Europe. However, in the early 2000s, the City Council did not appear keen on mobilising the port city image (interview, event team member 2, April 2018). As commented by two informants:

> [*Culture-led regeneration*] is a very easy way to change [the] image of cities with a workers' history, with the port legacy, which for the locals isn't very pleasant. I was always very surprised . . . [by] how negatively they [*policy makers*] see [the] port, how negatively they want to get rid of the port feeling from their city. At least my impression was that. I [have been studying] Shanghai [for] a long time, but [there] they never really [had] a negative feeling of [the] port.
>
> (interview, expert 6, April 2018)

> [A]t least in the whole 20th century, I think, everybody who talks about Rotterdam refers to the port. This interest is undiminished still, I think. And also, those Wereldhavendagen, the World Port Days, I think they are very popular. But the funny thing is that most cultural policy makers always have this mantra of 'we've got to get rid of this port city name, of this port city image. We've got to get culture in [until] it becomes a cultural city, instead of a port city'. They don't have the vision, I think, many of them. Maybe that's changed, [maybe they now] have a vision of culture that integrates the port, in a way, and the feeling of the port, which is what artists easily do. [Artists] don't see this opposition between the port and culture. They are interested in the city because of the port. So, it's a sort of inspiration, but policy makers . . . at least they used to see these as opposite things. So, 'let's get rid of the port image, let's try to be a cultural city'.
>
> (interview, expert 7, April 2018)

This shows how, at least until the beginning of the 21st century, the imaginaries of the 'port city' and the 'city of culture' have to some extent been in competition, while many city policy makers have been willing to get rid of the port city image. Rotterdam has long been perceived as a workers' city, polluted and dangerous, overshadowed by its cosmopolitan neighbour Amsterdam. Thus, a question can be raised about whether policy makers wished Rotterdam to be more ordinary a city, cleared by the 'disadvantage' of being a port city. As noted by a local planner: 'more people live here, more people are proud of it . . . like a normal city, you can say' (interview, city planner 3, April 2018). Of course, this idea of a *normal city* must be interpreted in the context of an informal discussion. However, this expression shows how the port city nature may actually be understood by policy makers and planners in relation to assumptions of disadvantage in comparison with non-port cities. It assumes that attractiveness and civic pride is linked with normalcy, with being ordinary, which is what a maritime port city is not. Such perceived maritime-specific disadvantage is the outcome of the negative externalities of port activities – for example pollution – and the socio-economic impacts of their restructuring (e.g. unemployment and crime). Arguably, these assumptions are the driving force behind attempts to refashion the image of port cities.

The competition between these two urban imaginaries, with the associated attempt to get rid of the port image, has been a well-established theme in policy making in Genoa. This tension appears nonetheless different in comparison with the case of Rotterdam. In particular in the 1980s, although its status of industrial port city was being questioned, a certain extent of resistance and rejection of the idea of Genoa as a cultural city used to permeate political discourses. As observed by an informant:

> We have to consider that [Genoa was] an industrial city, a port city, a very left-wing city. And still in the late 80s . . . a famous [*politician*] ended a rally in Piazza de Ferrari [*Genoa's main square*] by saying 'we don't want the city of waitpersons', meaning 'we don't want the tourist city'. . . . Why? Because the tourist city was seen as an enemy of the industrial city. . . . [A]s early as the 60s, some were speaking of the tourist city, but they had been quite marginalised because in the end it was the industrial city that won, the working city, the blue-collar city, and so on. And who was speaking of tourism was seen as someone who wished the harm of workers, of the working class, a reactionary, a conservative, and so on. Then, in the end, they realised that more and more factories were closing down, moving, delocalising, that the state-owned industry was collapsing and, slowly, they realised that . . . not the tourist city, but the diversified city – how it was called in many policy documents during the Pericu administration, the 'diversified city' – was an almost natural evolution. Then, in the end, this model went on without great tension within the Left.
>
> (interview, expert 10, June 2018, author's translation)

Notwithstanding this initial ideological opposition, Genoa's mega-event policy in the 1990s and 2000s appears to have had a considerable impact in reshaping the city's image as a city of culture. As suggested by a member of the ECoC 2004 company:

> [If] 40 years ago, 50 years ago you had asked a Genoese to identify Genoa, they would probably have thought about the docks, the lighthouse, the ships unloading [goods] . . . Nowadays, probably they would think more about Via Garibaldi, the Palaces of Strada Nuova, Rubens' paintings, Palazzo Ducale . . . If I may venture into a chromatic guess, if 50 years ago you had asked a Genoese 'what colour do you see Genoa?' they would have said 'grey'. Now, they would probably say 'red'.[6]
>
> (interview, event team member 4, June 2018, author's translation)

In the case of Genoa, as in that of Rotterdam, the current relation between these different visions of the city, as well as the attitude of policy makers towards the port city image, are best explored by considering aspects of commodification of maritime culture and heritage. As shown in Chapter 7, the relationship with the port and the sea mobilised by culture- and event-led regeneration has become a critical selling point for these schemes.

In the case of Valencia, no substantial tension is visible between urban imageries as a Mediterranean port and a tourist destination. However, these two sides of Valencia's image are little connected, either. Since the mid-1990s, Valencia's selling points have been its historic centre and sandy beaches and later its grand contemporary architecture, rather than its maritime heritage and identity. The redeveloped inner harbour was arguably conceived as a place for cultural consumption at the water's edge, with little connection with local meanings. The fact that Valencia's economy has traditionally been less dependent on the port in comparison with other port cities, is a factor behind this lack of tension, yet little connection, between maritime and cultural imageries: there is no port-related industrial stigma for policy makers to depart from, in contrast with cities such as Rotterdam, Genoa, Liverpool or Marseille.

Lessons from the governance of port cities of culture and events

Despite the differences in their established positions, port authorities appear to be more interested in engaging with the city's cultural life. On the one hand, this merely shows a greater awareness among port actors of the potential of culture to strengthen public support around port activity and to contribute to port competitiveness. On the other hand, this also suggests a reshaping of port-city relationships around different conditions, values and meanings.

European port cities of culture display the coexistence of two different imaginaries, respectively related to maritime industry and trade and to culture and tourism. Maritime activity appears to play a dominant economic role, while cultural activity is perceived more as a catalyst. Although there are signs of a different attitude of port authorities and companies towards culture and the city, this is not necessarily reflected in the way in which local policy makers perceive the port. These two imaginaries may still be competing city branding narratives, as city policy makers may be attempting to overlook or get rid of the – negative aspects of – maritime history and identity. As noted by Van Hooydonk (2007, p. 85), many European port cities had to fight a 'heroic battle' to retain their maritime character despite the migration and restructuring of ports. Perhaps, in some cases, a new 'battle' is yet to be fought against the desire of port cities to be 'ordinary' and to compete with non-port cities on the same grounds, without the 'disadvantages' arising from their maritime exceptionalism.

Notes

1 RETE is a network of port and city officials, port planners and academics promoting the cooperation between cities and ports and investigating the port-city interface. See http://retedigital.com/en/.
2 The Metropolitan City of Genoa replaced the former Province of Genoa – in accordance with the national Law 56/2014, which reformed Italian local authorities – and operates as an intermediate level of government between local councils and Liguria Regional Council.
3 Assoporti is the association of the Autorità di Sistema Portuale (AdSP, the reformed port authorities established through the so-called Legge Delrio). See: www.assoporti.it/it/associazione/.
4 For a discussion of the role of mega events in stigmatised maritime port cities, see Tommarchi and Bianchini (2022).
5 Wilberforce 2007, part of the national programme Remembering 1807, celebrated the 200th anniversary of the abolition of the slave trade in Britain with a year-round cultural programme. SeaBritain was a nation-wide festival about the country's relationships with the sea, which was celebrated in 2005 on the 200th anniversary of the Battle of Trafalgar.
6 Red was the colour used in official marketing material to brand the European Capital Culture 2004.

Bibliography

ABP (2016) ABP announces City of Culture partnership at gateway to Europe. *ABP*, 21st June. Available at: www.abports.co.uk/newsarticle/331/ [Accessed 23/10/2017].
ABP (2017) Hull history centre takes on largest archive project ever thanks to ABP. *ABP*, 22nd June. Available at: www.abports.co.uk/newsarticle/457/ [Accessed 23/10/2017].
AIVP (2020) What is a port center. *AIVP*. Available at: www.aivp.org/en/acting-sustainably/port-center-by-aivp/what-is-the-port-center/ [Accessed 27/08/2021].
Ajuntament de València (1997) *Plan Estrategico Valencia 2015*. Valencia: Ajuntament de València.
Anderson, B., & Holden, A. (2008) Affective urbanism and the event of hope. *Space and Culture*, 11(2), 142–159.
Andres, L. (2011) Marseille 2013 or the final round of a long and complex regeneration strategy? *Town Planning Review*, 82(1), 61–76.

Comune di Genova (2015) Piano Urbanistico Comunale Vigente. *Comune di Genova.* Available at: www.comune.genova.it/servizi/puc [Accessed 03/09/2021].

Cox, K. R. (1993) The local and the global in the new urban politics: A critical view. *Environment and Planning D. Society and Space*, 11, 433–448.

DeltaPORT Donatiefonds (2020) *Wat Is Het DeltaPORT Donatiefonds.* Available at: www.deltaportdonatiefonds.nl/ [Accessed 11/05/2020].

Dooms, M., Verbeken, A., & Haezendonck, E. (2013) Stakeholder management and path dependence in large-scale transport infrastructure development: The port of Antwerp case (1960–2010). *Journal of Transport Geography*, 27, 14–25.

Gemeente Rotterdam (2007) *Stadsvisie Rotterdam. Ruimtelijke Ontwikkelingsstrategie 2030.* Rotterdam: Gemeente Rotterdam.

Generalitat Valenciana (2012) *Comunitat Valenciana 2030. Síntesis de la Estrategia Territorial.* Valencia: Generalitat Valenciana.

Green Port Hull (2016) ABP and Hull City Council unveil artwork installations on Alexandra Dock footpath. *Green Port Hull*, 19th May. Available at: https://greenporthull.co.uk/news/abp-and-hull-city-council-unveil-artwork-installations-on-alexandra-dock-fo [Accessed 23/10/2017].

Green Port Hull (2017) Permanent location planned for Siemens Gamesa blade that became City of Culture sensation. *Green Port Hull*, 8th September. Available at: https://greenporthull.co.uk/news/permanent-location-planned-for-siemens-gamesa-blade-that-became-city-of-cul [Accessed 31/11/2017].

Hamburg Port Authority (2021) *Culture Is Calling at the Port of Hamburg. ESPO Award 2021 on Social Integration of Ports.* Available at: www.hamburg-port-authority.de/fileadmin/user_upload/20210617_Impressionen.pdf [Accessed 27/08/2021].

Humber Local Enterprise Partnership (2014) *Strategic Economic Plan 2014–2020.* Available at: www.humberlep.org/wp-content/uploads/2014/11/StrategicEconomicPlan.pdf [Accessed 24/09/2019].

Jacobs, W. (2007) *Political Economy of Port Competition: Institutional Analyses of Rotterdam, Southern California and Dubai.* Nijmegen: Academic Press Europe.

Kowalewski, M. (2018) Images and spaces of port cities in transition. *Space and Culture*, 24(1), 53–65.

Mastropietro, E. (2007) I grandi eventi come occasione di riqualificazione e valorizzazione urbana. Il caso di Genova. *ACME – Annali Della Facoltà di Lettere e Filosofia dell'Università degli Studi di Milano*, 60(1), 207.

Notteboom, T., De Langen, P., & Jacobs, W. (2013) Institutional plasticity and path dependence in seaports: Interactions between institutions, port governance reforms and port authority routines. *Journal of Transport Geography*, 27, 26–35.

Port Authority of New York and New Jersey and Cultural Assistance Center (1983) *The Arts As an Industry: Their Economic Importance to the New York-New Jersey Metropolitan Region.* New York: The Port Authority of New York and New Jersey.

Port of Rotterdam Authority (2019) Ten years of FutureLand. *Port of Rotterdam*, 23rd May. Available at: www.portofrotterdam.com/en/news-and-press-releases/ten-years-of-futureland [Accessed 15/08/2019].

Ports of Genoa (2019) Port Day 2019 – Programma di Genova. *Ports of Genoa.* Available at: www.portsofgenoa.com/it/component/publiccompetitions/document/423html?view=document&id=423:port-day-2019-genova&Itemid=221 [Accessed 17/09/2019].

Schilling, R. S. F. (1966) Trawler fishing: An extreme occupation. *Proceedings of the Royal Society of Medicine*, 39, 405–410.

Siemens (2016) Siemens named as Hull UK City of Culture 2017 Major Partner. *Siemens*, 22nd September. Available at: www.siemens.co.uk/en/news_press/index/news_archive/2016/siemens-named-as-hull-uk-city-of-culture-2017-major-partner.htm [Accessed 02/08/2019].

Tommarchi, E., & Bianchini, F. (2022) A heritage-inspired cultural mega event in a stigmatised city: Hull UK City of Culture 2017. *European Planning Studies*, 30(3), 478–498.

Tommarchi, E., Hansen, L. E., & Bianchini, F. (2018) Problematising the question of participation in Capitals of Culture. *Participations*, 15(2), 154–169.

Tunbridge, J. E., & Ashworth, G. J. (1996) *Dissonant Heritage: The Management of the Past as a Resource in Conflict*. Chichester: John Wiley & Sons.

Valenciaport (2018a) Valenciaport lleva a la Universitat Politècnica de València la exposición de planos que repasa la historia gráfica del puerto. *Valenciaport*, 26th February. Available at: www.valenciaport.com/valenciaport-lleva-a-la-universitat-politecnica-de-valencia-laexposicion-de-planos-que-repasa-la-historia-grafica-del-puerto/ [Accessed 04/10/2018].

Valenciaport (2018b) El Edificio del Reloj acoge una muestra de todos los edificios emblemáticos de la dársena histórica del Puerto de Valencia. *Valenciaport*, 28th March. Available at: www.valenciaport.com/el-edificio-del-reloj-acoge-una-muestra-de-todos-losedificios-emblematicos-de-la-darsena-historica-del-puerto-de-valencia/ [Accessed 04/10/2018].

Van der Lugt, L. M., & De Langen, P. W. (2007) Port authority strategy: Beyond the landlord: A conceptual approach. *International Association for Maritime Economics (IAME) Conference*, Athens, 4–6 July.

Van der Lugt, L. M., De Langen, P. W., & Hagdorn, L. (2015) Beyond the landlord: World-wide empirical analysis of port authority strategies. *International Journal of Shipping and Transport Logistics*, 7(5), 570–596.

Van der Lugt, L. M., De Langen, P. W., & Hagdorne, L. (2017) Strategic beliefs of port authorities. *Transport Reviews*, 37(4), 412–441.

Van Hooydonk, E. (2007) *Soft Values of Seaports: A Strategy for the Restoration of Public Support of Seaports*. Antwerp: Garant.

Van Tuijl, E., & Van den Berg, L. (2016) Annual city festivals as tools for sustainable competitiveness: The world port days Rotterdam. *Economies*, 4(11), 1–13.

Van Ulzen, P. (2007) *Imagine a Metropolis. Rotterdam's Creative Class 1970–2000*. Rotterdam: 010 Publishers.

Vries, I. (2014) From shipyard to brainyard: The redevelopment of RDM as an example of a contemporary port-city relationship. In Alix, Y., Delsalle, B., & Comtois, C. (eds.) *Port-City Governance*. Paris: Editions EMS, 107–126.

Ward, J. (2018) Down by the sea: Visual arts, artists and coastal regeneration. *International Journal of Cultural Policy*, 24(1), 121–138.

Warsewa, G. (2017) The transformation of port cities: Local culture and the post-industrial Maritime city. *WIT Transactions on The Built Environment*, 170, 149–159.

7 Event-led regeneration and symbolic port-city links

The discussion of event-led regeneration in the context of port-city relationships would not be complete without an analysis of the symbolic facets of their mutual connection. Event-led regeneration in port cities may encompass profound transformation of inner harbour areas and waterfronts, affecting social and political relations, cultural values, local and external perceptions of the city and, in particular, civic pride, which has traditionally been a distinctive feature of port cities (Van Hooydonk, 2007, p. 85). In this chapter, the socio-cultural aspects of mega events and their connection with port-city relationships are explored, by discussing issues of authenticity and maritime culture within these events and their legacy. The chapter also shows how actually existing symbolic port-city links influence the legacy of mega events and their impacts on the evolution of port-city relationships. Mega events and event-led regeneration often appear to be focusing more on exploiting the symbolic character of water than on celebrating the maritime nature of port cities, to the detriment of maritime distinctiveness and authenticity. Unintended consequences such as spatial disparities or forms of counter-gentrification or the failure of culture- and event-led regeneration processes are possible where actually existing port-city relationships – in particular established socio-cultural links – are overridden.

The cultural demaritimisation and remaritimisation of port cities

In some port cities, the gradual diversification of local economies initiated to respond to deindustrialisation and port restructuring in the last decades of the 20th century has to some extent questioned the role of port activity itself. In others, established or even new maritime practices are gaining economic relevance over other sectors of the local economy. In disciplines such as transport economics, the concepts of demaritimisation and remaritimisation of port cities are sometimes deployed to describe these economic trends. For example, Musso and Bennacchio (2002) use the term 'demaritimisation' to describe the shrinking role of port and maritime activities within local economies, counterbalanced by a greater importance of other economic activities, as a component of the weakening ties between ports and cities. Conversely, the authors use the

DOI: 10.4324/9781003165811-7

term 'remaritimisation' to describe the opposite process of increasing economic relevance of maritime activities.

As suggested by Musso and Ghiara (2009, p. 63), the term 'demaritimisation' is not unambiguous and may also be understood from a cultural perspective. The growing separation between ports and cities that has been commented in the literature has impacted on the social and cultural aspects of their relations as well. As observed by Van Hooydonk (2007, p. 42), port migration has weakened the 'psychological ties' between city dwellers and the port and has been transforming the latter into 'dehumanising islands drifting away from society'. Recent trends of building new port terminals in entirely new locations pose new risks to port cities in terms of loss of their maritime feel, as 'docks and rivers may become lifeless pools of water, quays may be rendered meaningless, port heritage may be demolished mercilessly' (Van Hooydonk, 2009, p. 19). These processes, together with the automatisation and securitisation of modern ports, have led to the loss of traditional practices shaping urban ports and their cities.

It is therefore possible to borrow the concepts of demaritimisation and remaritimisation from port studies and to stretch them to comment on the cultural and symbolic dimension of the evolution of port-city relationships.[1] *Cultural demaritimisation* may be defined as a gradual loss of those aspects that constitute local maritime cultures. Such elements may include maritime tangible and intangible heritage, residents' awareness of local maritime history and interest in port activity, emotional ties with the port and the sea. Without using the term 'cultural demaritimisation', Van Hooydonk (2009, p. 19) provides an effective description of this process: '[w]ithout port activities and sea vessels calling, a port city will lose its vitality, its charm and its atmosphere as its genius loci inevitably evaporates'. However, it is important to note that this loss of maritime culture is not necessarily an inevitable consequence of structural processes upon which local policy makers have no control. Rather, it may be the – intended or unintended – outcome of local urban or cultural policies aiming at refashioning the city's identity and image in order to move away from 'undesirable' port- or maritime-related narratives. The attempts of city policy makers to downplay the city's port image in the context of interurban competition, as discussed in Chapter 6, can be read as forms of cultural demaritimisation, which ultimately foster a symbolic port-city separation. This might play against other maritime-related narratives and meanings that are overshadowed by more prominent ones, for example as in the case of Hull's fishing past or Genoa and Glasgow's accounts as a working-class city.

Port cities may also display a retightening of their cultural ties with the port and an increased emphasis on maritime culture and heritage, which may be described as *cultural remaritimisation*. This process may be fuelled by attempts to restore and mobilise maritime heritage assets within urban regeneration schemes, raise awareness of local maritime history and heritage, or rediscover less well-known narratives of the city's maritime identity. Nonetheless, such a process may not necessarily build on aspects of the local port city culture and may introduce new, unauthentic elements. For example, Johnsen (2009,

p. 115) argues that local and regional authorities have used maritime festivals in Southern Norway to 'invent' traditions (as generally described by Hobsbawm & Ranger, 2012), by orienting heritage narratives in order to promote economic growth in a context of competition with other local communities. Another example is the use of marinas in culture-led waterfront redevelopment schemes, which may introduce or emphasise sailing for reasons of economic development where this is at odds with local maritime traditions (Table 7.1).

Cultural demaritimisation and remaritimisation may be interpreted as maritime-specific processes of deterritorialisation and reterritorialisation, as understood by Tomlinson (1999) as a disconnection between place and culture. Nevertheless, it would be simplistic to interpret these processes as dichotomic, as maritime-related aspects of local identities are not merely retained/lost or confirmed/transformed. Such processes need to be further problematised considering how they engage with, interpret and contribute to shaping port city imaginaries in relation to local meanings (see e.g. Atkinson, 2007).

In many European maritime port cities, processes of cultural demaritimisation or remaritimisation appear to be fuelled by a number of factors. Firstly, the restructuring of contemporary commercial and industrial ports is a major driver, in particular considering that it prevents residents from seeing and experiencing the port in their daily lives. Secondly, policy discourses and planning strategies attempting to get rid of the port city image may encourage these processes, with the aim of transforming port cities into 'ordinary cities' and removing those aspects that policy makers perceive as a disadvantage within interurban competition. Thirdly, standardisation and loss of authenticity in port

Table 7.1 Forms of cultural demaritimisation and remaritimisation of port cities.

	Generative mechanisms	*Rationale/driving forces*	*Impacts*
Cultural demaritimisation	Deliberate policy	• Overcoming stigmatisation • Generating a competitive advantage in interurban competition	• Loss of traditional maritime practices, heritage assets, port cityscapes • Introduction of non-maritime-related cultural functions and facilities in port cityscapes
	Structural processes	• Physical/functional port-city separation • (Non-maritime-related) cultural consumption	
Cultural remaritimisation	Deliberate policy	• Economic diversification • Rebranding • Economic growth through the tourist sector	• Restoration of maritime heritage assets/narratives • Introduction of maritime-related cultural functions and facilities • Creation of new (possibly inauthentic) port and maritime meanings
	Structural processes	• Maritime-related cultural consumption • Touristification (e.g. cruise tourism)	

cities may be an outcome of waterfront redevelopment strategies, especially in relation to the commodification and spectacularisation of maritime cultures and port cityscapes. Spectacularisation is intended here as the celebration of aspects of local cultures and heritage through spectacular events or art installations, or simply the attempt to visually present urban spaces or heritage assets in spectacular ways, for example through the use of viewpoints and visual perspectives in regeneration schemes.

Processes that can be associated with cultural demaritimisation and remaritimisation have been operating in different timeframes across the case-study cities of the book. For example, Hull's 'trawlertown' in Hessle Road, where many fishermen and sailors working on distant-water fishing trawlers used to live with their families and which was perceived as 'a world in itself' (as reported by Horobin, 1957, p. 343), gradually disappeared after the 1970s, as fish trade moved away from St. Andrew's Dock. This process disrupted traditional ties and rhythms and caused the dispersal of Hessle Road's fishing community (Byrne, 2015, 2016). As a result, part of St. Andrew's Dock was redeveloped and transformed into a retail area with no distinctive character (Atkinson et al., 2002, p. 31). Despite the fact that Rotterdam is still referred to as *de havenstad*, the actual impact of the port on residents' daily lives should be problematised. As the working port moved westwards, and security measures tightened, Rotterdammers have gradually been losing track of current port activity and maritime practices (Van Tuijl & Van den Berg, 2016, p. 5). At the same time, as explored later, attempts to recover the city's relationship with the river have introduced new imaginaries and practices in relation to the waterfront. In Genoa, despite the gradual migration of the working port, a lesser extent of demaritimisation is observable. This can be explained by considering the physical proximity of the port – in particular the old harbour – to the city, and the traditional tighter relationships between these two entities in comparison with other port cities. The redevelopment of Porto Antico helped retain the port feeling in the heart of Genoa, notwithstanding mild issues of loss of authenticity and standardisation, which are examined in this chapter. In Valencia, on the one hand, the development of the commercial (container) port has redefined local maritime practices and has changed established port-city relationships. On the other hand, as part of the political project of the Conservative local government in office since the early 1990s, a new maritime feeling was sought as a key selling point to market the city internationally.

Similar patterns are visible in port cities across the world. As seen in Chapter 5, in Rio de Janeiro, event-led regeneration contributed to the redevelopment of a derelict port area at Gamboa. The area was transformed into a new urban centrality through a culture-led regeneration model, boosted by the Olympics, which encompassed a flagship cultural facility, the Museum of Tomorrow designed by Santiago Calatrava. Nonetheless, little reference to the former port cityscape is now visible in the area, as this intervention was largely based on a 'port out, city in' logic that was mirrored in the symbolic dimension of the project. As the opposite experience of Genoa and Valencia suggests, these processes are closely linked with symbolic port-city relationships resulting from local geographical settings. For example, due to the peculiar geography of Singapore, ships entering or leaving the port are easily visible from many parts of the city-state. As a result, residents and visitors still enjoy a marked maritime feeling despite port migration and the fact that the transformation of many waterfront areas aimed at creating an attractive 'downtown' atmosphere to the detriment of local identity (Chang & Huang, 2011).

Due to their transformative potential, culture- and event-led regeneration can produce significant impacts on ongoing processes of cultural demaritimisation or remaritimisation. Cultural and sporting events and mega events in port cities play a role in framing the maritime identity of these cities, for example by mobilising port cityscapes. The symbolic impact of these events on the port-city interface needs to be taken into account by considering that socio-cultural port-city relationships tend to be more distant, as the port no longer affects the daily lives of port city dwellers as it used to do in the past. Wherever event-led regeneration aims at engaging with local maritime cultures, it may contribute to fostering such processes in more or less subtle ways, for example by 'imposing' new maritime imaginaries, by constructing place authenticity to meet visitors' expectations or by overlooking existing local maritime narratives and practices. The chapter explores aspects of commodification of maritime cultures, the role of water and maritime cultures in city branding, the particular case of emerging maritime cultural districts across European port cities, to provide insights on how processes of cultural demaritimisation and remaritimisation work on the ground.

Commodification of port city culture and port cityscapes

Critics of culture- and event-led regeneration point at the tendency of these processes to commodify culture, heritage, local specificities and public space (see e.g. Evans, 2003; García, 2004; Binns, 2005; Miles, 2005). This process of commodification operates on two dimensions. On the one hand, it may deliberately contribute to generating unauthentic culture (Zukin, 2006 [1995]), with the aim of increasing audience and visitor figures. On the other hand, culture- and event-led regeneration schemes may tend to replicate similar urban environments across cities (Evans, 2003; Richards & Wilson, 2006), which are hybridised in relation to 'local and vernacular clichés' (Muñoz, 2006, p. 180). In the case of port cities, these spaces are shaped by taking into account external expectations around contemporary urban waterfronts. These processes operate at the detriment of authenticity. Authenticity can be sanitised, to be more easily saleable (Povey & Van Wyk, 2010), or staged (MacCannell, 1976) by those providing tourist experiences, with the aim of fulfilling visitors' expectations about a place. This is also coupled with an existential authenticity, which is framed by visitors themselves according to their personal feelings and values (Wang, 1999; Richards, 2007). Through time, a contrived or inauthentic cultural product may nonetheless be perceived as authentic in a process defined as emergent authenticity (Cohen, 1988, p. 379, in Johnsen, 2009, p. 123), which may be facilitated by cultural or sporting events.

These different dimensions of authenticity and commodification are closely related to internal and external perceptions of cities and to urban and cultural policies, especially as regards the stigmatisation of places. Territorial stigmatisation emerges from historical events or certain characteristics that are considered 'particular' of a place in relation to the contextual norms of a specific time, such as the perception of Las Vegas as a 'sinful city' (Foster, 2018), or may be linked to urban disadvantage (Wacquant, 2007, 2008; Wacquant et al., 2014). Although stigmatisation is not a permanent phenomenon, negative perceptions of places and their social impacts may endure in time and are not necessarily eradicated through urban renewal (Gourlay, 2007). Many European port cities have been stigmatised because of their exceptionalism and socio-economic context. Cultural and urban policies have been trying to subvert these preconceptions by generating positive narratives of port cities. Examples are the negative perceptions about Hull as a declining fishing town against positive narratives related to the UK City of Culture 2017 and the development of renewable energies (Tommarchi & Bianchini, 2022), or the accounts of Rotterdam as a port workers' city being challenged by its renewed international image and ultramodern architecture. Event-led regeneration also acts on preconceptions of urban port areas, as in the case of Genoa's Darsena Comunale, where cultural functions such as the Maritime Museum built for the European Capital of Culture 2004 helped challenge perceptions of the area associated with crime. Of course, this is not a European-specific phenomenon. For example, the development of Porto Maravilha in Rio de Janeiro, can be read as a similar process of 'territorial de-stigmatisation' of the area (Broudehoux & Carvalhaes, 2017), which nonetheless led to concerns among residents about the 'whitening' and 'sanitising' of the area to maximise cultural consumption (ibid., p. 502).

In port cities, the relation between commodification and authenticity is also linked with processes of cultural demaritimisation or remaritimisation. Culture- and event-led regeneration may directly contribute to these processes as a result of transformation, or in some cases destruction, of authentic maritime heritage and port cityscapes through the creation of standardised and sanitised urban environments. On the one hand, standardisation and sanitisation provide visitors with 'familiar' urban environments and 'safe' tourist experiences, eventually increasing the city's attractiveness. On the other hand, they generate a 'sense of déjà vu' across seemingly exchangeable redeveloped waterfronts and docklands (Van Hooydonk, 2009, p. 19). Artists and a range of creative professionals have traditionally been interested in urban port areas, such as in Rotterdam (interview, expert 7, April 2018), because of their maritime feeling. The edgy appearance and feel of urban port areas is an asset to market redeveloped waterfronts to these specific 'audiences'. However, the attempt to standardise and sanitise waterfronts with the aim of attracting a broader range of generalist visitors and cultural consumers risks repelling certain cultural producers – both as a result of gentrification (Lorente, 2002, p. 100) and of a changing port cityscape – and specialist consumers. Artists, creatives and specialist visitors may no longer be interested in highly commodified – and visited – waterfronts displaying a contrived edgy character. These issues raise questions as to whether the maritime character of European port cities is really valued or just commodified through culture- and event-led regeneration. For example, Kowalewski (2018, p. 3) observes that elements of the traditional image of port cities have been mobilised to build an artificial imaginary of the port city which is being commodified for marketing purposes.

Maritime culture and heritage are key elements in the identity of the four case-study cities. Nonetheless, these cities show rather different approaches to them – influenced by national settings and local specificities – spanning in a continuum from the search for authenticity to the privatisation of public space and the commodification of maritime cultures. Mega events also contributed to fuelling distorted narratives of local maritime cultures and heritage for branding purposes. In the case of Hull, physical regeneration directly or contingently linked with the UK City of Culture 2017 was not particularly maritime specific. The Stage @The Dock is an exception, albeit it does not display a particular maritime character beyond its location at the connection between the River Hull and the Humber Estuary. Despite the risks of retail gentrification, the Fruit Market area has kept part of its original character. This was the result of specific policies to control gentrification and standardisation, which were possible since Hull City Council acted as Lead Development Partner (interview, city planner 1, February 2018). Hull's distinctive waterfront environments were also retained. Even though the restoration of the Dead Bod is an interesting example in terms of the cultural role that port authorities and actors can play, it raises questions in relation to commodification, staged authenticity and the social impacts of certain cultural projects in the peculiar settings of European port cities. Although this project prevented the Dead Bod from being destroyed, the fact that the mural is now a piece of public art and a symbol of the regeneration of the area suggests that its audience might have changed from those recognising themselves as connected with the city's fishing past.

Rotterdam is distinctive among the case-study cities as cultural and sporting events have not acted as the main catalyst for urban regeneration and waterfront redevelopment. Waterfront redevelopment schemes had been delivered as early as the 1970s and are still being implemented, without any major events to act as a catalyst for transformation as in the case of the 1992 Olympics in Barcelona or the 1992 Specialist Expo in Genoa. Rather, events such as the European Capital of Culture 2001 were used as a means to celebrate and possibly spectacularise these redevelopments. A distinctive feature of waterfront redevelopment schemes in Rotterdam is that they clearly drew from similar projects delivered in US cities such as Baltimore. The 'tragedy' of this American inspiration (Hajer, 1993, pp. 62–64), epitomised by the 'mini-Manhattanesque vision' of Kop van Zuid (Tzonis, 1993), provided the city with contemporary architecture and a marked post-industrial and international look, which nonetheless reframed its authenticity. In their study of resident perceptions of flagship waterfront redevelopment projects, Doucet et al. (2011) show that, overall, residents responded positively to the redevelopment of Kop van Zuid, albeit support tend to diminish with age. A number of street surveys with residents and visitors conducted as part of the research behind the book highlighted that some residents in their 60s and 70s, in line with Doucet et al.'s results, perceived redeveloped waterfront areas such as Kop van Zuid as 'unpleasant', disrespectful of local identity and designed to target tourists and young people. Surveyed tourists appeared to appreciate the city's contemporary architecture, but when asked if they believed that these redevelopments were in line with Rotterdam's maritime identity, some of them pointed out that the presence of skyscrapers does not encourage visitors to think about the port. Although the goal of the aforementioned street surveys was not to perform a comprehensive analysis of resident perceptions of the redevelopment, these views suggest that the search for an attractive, international urban environment on the waterfront might be operating at the detriment of the city's symbolic connection with its port.

In Genoa the gradual redevelopment of Porto Antico through a range of planning tools and mega events, is perceived as a success among local policy makers and experts. This success, is also perceived to be linked with the restoration of the city's traditional connection with the sea and the rediscovery of its maritime identity:

> [19]92 demonstrated that this transformation was possible. . . . Genoa that got back its view of the port . . . Genoa that restarted from those aspects of its identity. . . . A city linked to the sea that nonetheless lost its view of the sea. This is the paradox. . . . This is one of the elements of success, I think (also of Piano's design), which was centred on the most specific elements, the DNA of the city actually, moving towards a new phase, but building on the past. For example, the rediscovery of port cityscapes is really important, a really powerful thing. Because the city had lost this aspect of its identity.
> (interview, expert 10, June 2018, author's translation)

Interestingly, the policy concept of 'waterfront' appears to be deeply connected with culture and leisure. The word 'waterfront' – in English, not its Italian translation – is commonly used by local policy makers to refer to the redeveloped Porto Antico and the project of redevelopment of a larger section of the city's seafront for leisure purposes (as emerged in many interviews with local informants – policy maker 5, June 2018; port actor 4, June 2018; expert 11, June 2018; port actor 7, June 2018). Thus, the idea of 'waterfront' as it is framed locally does not include seafront areas devoted to industrial or commercial activities. This is an example of how the physical separation of the working port from the city impacts on the imaginaries of the city's relationships with the sea.

In the case of Genoa, local informants – and a few residents interviewed in the area – did not perceive Porto Antico as a particularly standardised or commodified space. This characteristic of the redeveloped old harbour can be interpreted as a result of different processes. Arguably, the 2007–8 economic and financial crisis played a role in slowing down real estate development after the European Capital of Culture 2004 (interview, expert 9, May 2018). A certain extent of homogenisation is nonetheless visible. For example, national restaurant and food chains such as Rossopomodoro and Eataly opened branches in Porto Antico, together with global chains such as Burger King and, a few meters off the harbour, McDonald's. As noted by one informant:

> Yes, some of this commercial homogenisation, some of this homogenisation of consumption, some of these tourists who do there [*in Porto Antico*] what they do anywhere else, some of this touristification which we were not accustomed to [is visible] . . . There are some of these elements, I think.
> (interview, expert 10, June 2018, author's translation)

However, the case of Genoa shows attempts to pursue authenticity and avoid a radical standardisation of Porto Antico, through the promotion of material assets – for example buildings and cranes – and immaterial aspects of local maritime heritage. Such a strategy also attempted to avoid a pervasive presence of retail activities. As mentioned, Magazzini del Cotone (Figure 7.1) were redeveloped into a conference centre and a library. This choice presented some risks because commercial functions are more likely to be successful, as the Maremagnum shopping centre in Barcelona's Port Vell demonstrates. In fact, Magazzini del Cotone were not immediately successful in terms of use and revenues.

Figure 7.1 Historic port cranes in front of Magazzini del Cotone.

Nevertheless, this willingness of retaining the maritime character of Porto Antico was arguably related to the commodification of space itself. Event-led regeneration levered on the area's maritime character also because this aspect was considered to be more easily saleable:

> I think these transformations focus on maritime culture, on Genoa's history as a maritime city and so on, because they are the most distinctive and thus commodifiable [aspects]. . . . They do so in the logic, let's say, [of] 'we are going to sell this better.'
>
> (interview, expert 12, June 2018, author's translation)

In the case of Valencia, the standardisation and sanitisation of the inner harbour and waterfront areas were part of the Conservative local government's political project to transform Valencia into a top tourist destination. This is the main reason why the redeveloped inner harbour displays a strong post-modern appearance. To different extents, redevelopment schemes of this kind across Spain, such as Barcelona's Parc del Fòrum, Port Vell and Port Olímpic and Málaga's inner harbour, show similar features (Figure 7.2).

(a)　　　　　　　　　　　　　(b)

(c)　　　　　　　　　　　　　(d)

Figure 7.2 Redeveloped waterfronts across Spain: Marina Real Juan Carlos I in Valencia (top left and right), Muelle 1 in Málaga (bottom left), Parc del Fòrum in Barcelona (bottom right).

Valencia is nonetheless an example of how mega events and megaprojects have contributed to consuming local cultural potential and overshadowing existing assets (Carrasco & Pitarch-Garrido, 2017, p. 725). For example, the team bases built on the harbourside for the America's Cup – which were not dismantled after the event – had a considerable impact on the port cityscape and concealed maritime heritage assets (interview, policy maker 8, June 2018; Figure 7.3).

An instrumental view of culture as a means to pursue urban and economic development arguably damaged the historic port and its heritage assets:

> In the case of Spain, and Valencia is an extreme example, culture has become an empty container, that is to say an excuse, a form of legitimisation for urban transformations linked to real estate interests and, eventually, corruption, as it is being demonstrated. . . . [I]t creates theme-park spaces, in some ways. . . . In the case of Valencia, I think it was clear in the redevelopment of the old harbour in the area of the marina . . . [that this area] was disfigured, I think. If not permanently, [its redevelopment] disfigured its historic heritage, that of a mercantile, a fishing port. It shifted towards an area oriented to external projection, branding, business.
>
> (interview, expert 14, May 2018, author's translation)

Figure 7.3 America's Cup team bases in 2018.

Since 2015, a different model of culture and regeneration has been pursued, based on a departure from the concept of urban spectacle and the idea of Valencia as a venue for hosting international events (interview, expert 13, May 2018). The end of Valencia's mega-event era and the related political project also meant that, despite the discussed issues of gentrification and touristification, the nearby El Cabanyal-El Canyamelar retained at least part of its distinctiveness and maritime character, which counterbalances the marked post-modern appearance of the redeveloped harbour (interview, policy maker 8, June 2018).

In the light of this erosion of authenticity and maritime heritage, the idea that mega events have contributed to give port areas 'back' to the local community should be problematised. Undoubtedly, a certain extent of reconnection – albeit not fully achieved – in terms of accessibility of inner harbours and waterfront areas appears unquestionable. Yet, instead of contributing to port-city reconnection from the side of maritime culture and heritage, mega events – as part of a broader and longer-term regeneration strategy – appear to have contributed to a certain degree of cultural demaritimisation and remaritimisation around new, artificial prerequisites. Of course, this is far from being a Valencia-specific phenomenon:

> most of these cities, port cities, especially in Europe but I think all around the globe, have undergone transformation processes that somehow have partially erased this memory, developing models that look quite similar to each other. Especially since the 90s, we have all the leisure/tourism-oriented redeveloped waterfronts, most of them having the same kind of amenities, shopping malls, casinos, a couple of hotels, maybe two museums, that on the one hand pretended the opening of these areas, but on the other hand, I think, have caused the very opposite.
>
> (interview, event team member 6, June 2018)

Similar accounts can be found in other port cities where mega events were deployed to assist urban regeneration. For instance, waterfront redevelopment in Marseille, linked to the ECoC 2013, was based on a marked reframing of the city's skyline, which was eventually hampered by the 2008 crisis (Andres, 2011). Similarly, in Liverpool, where the ECoC 2008 contributed to boosting urban regeneration and waterfront redevelopment, policy makers have been pursuing a profound transformation of the port cityscape, which has recently led to the city being stripped of its World Heritage status (BBC, 2021). In the case of Rio de Janeiro's Porto Maravilha, as noted by Broudehoux and Carvalhaes (2017), many former industrial and office buildings in the area were demolished and replaced by office towers, while flagship cultural facilities such as Calatrava's Museum of Tomorrow contributed to promoting an instrumental, globalised vision of culture that has little to do with the maritime character of the area.

In the context of an increased attractiveness of former or working urban port areas and the attempt to call port and maritime practices back into the city's daily life, a key question emerges. Are ports themselves becoming tourist attractions? This question appears of particular interest against the traditional perception of port cities as both attractive and repulsive places, deprived, polluted and dangerous, yet open to the world. For example, as suggested by Hein (2018, pp. 924–925) in the case of petroleum landscapes in the Netherlands, modern industrial and port facilities could become heritage themselves: '[a]fter all, traditional windmills and canals were also originally engineering devices and have now become part of the national imagination and a tourist attraction'. A potential tourist appeal of working port areas raises a series of issues, including planning and mobility issues, since many modern ports are now located several kilometres away from city centres. Reliable figures for port visitors appear difficult to obtain. While port centres do provide visitor figures – although these facilities are not present in every port and may be visited by a niche public – it is virtually impossible to discern the number of 'port tourists' from that of other visitors in those working port areas that are still in central city locations, as in the case of Genoa and Valencia. Nevertheless, the extent to which port areas are perceived as potential tourist magnets may be indirectly explored considering the range of policies and activities aimed at selling ports to visitors through the spectacularisation of port cityscapes, for example through spectacular events or art installations or simply through the creation of impressive visual perspectives on heritage assets.

All the case-study cities display attempts to spectacularise urban port areas. In many cases, this spectacularisation focuses on clean and saleable port facilities and practices. Culture- and event-led redevelopments as well as flagship cultural events aim to showcase and celebrate light activities and clean aspects of the city's maritime attitude. Where working port areas are accessible or visible, this strategy is coupled with sanitisation, through which 'ugly', 'dirty' and unpleasant elements of ports are overlooked or concealed.

In Hull, waterfront redevelopment in the 1980s and 1990s introduced panoramic viewpoints on the Humber Estuary and contributed to valuing maritime heritage assets around the marina. Attempts to spectacularise Hull's maritime heritage and relationship with the sea included public realm improvements in Humber Street and around the marina, UKCoC banners being displayed at the marina (during and after the event), projections on maritime heritage buildings such as the Maritime Museum during the opening event *Made in Hull*, the use of waterfront spaces for spectacular events, such as *Flood²* at Victoria Dock and the fireworks at the opening event. In the case of Hull, spectacularisation needs to be problematised beyond the established criticisms around the discourse of urban spectacle. Panoramic viewpoints, walkways on the waterfront and around the marina, and the recent efforts to spectacularise maritime functions and heritage have arguably contributed to making Hull's maritime assets more accessible. For example, public realm improvements in Humber Dock Street and the redevelopment of the nearby Fruit Market area encouraged residents and visitors to use the dockside and to look at sailboats and maritime heritage assets. Similarly, many cultural events within the UKCoC programme and after

2017 made use of physical heritage assets, also through their spectacularisation, to tell local stories and to encourage residents and visitors to engage with less well-known heritage (interview, policy maker 1, February 2018; interview, city planner 1, February 2018; interview, event team member 1, January 2018). The projections during the opening event *Made in Hull*, for example, showed images about the city's fishing past, which helped the local community connect with the event. *Urban Legends: Northern Lights*, an ephemeral event delivered by the legacy company Absolutely Cultured Ltd in 2018, involved kinetic art trails in less well-known areas of the city (Tommarchi & Bianchini, 2020, p. 246). The historic Guildhall was also mobilised by the successful theatre play *The Last Testament of Lillian Bilocca*, which celebrated activism to improve fishermen's working conditions after the 1968 Triple Trawler Disaster and made use of some of the spaces where the narrated events took place.

While being an example of an industrial port city since the 1990s, Rotterdam has become a popular visitor destination in the last couple of decades. Tourists visit Rotterdam in particular because of its architecture. However, port-related tourist activities and facilities, such as boat tours of the port, the FutureLand visitor centre and the Wereldhavendagen, appear to be increasingly popular as well. Thus, in contrast with the recent past, the port itself now appears to attract tourist, rather than contributing to a negative image of the city, shifting from a transport and economic infrastructure generating negative externalities to an asset for cultural tourism (interview, expert 6, April 2018). Arguably, the spectacularisation of the riverfront and of former port areas has been playing a role in this. Waterfront redevelopment in Rotterdam celebrated the reconstruction of the city after the Second World War and has contributed to spectacularising urban development and the city's relationship with the river and the port. Apart from the already mentioned role of iconic architecture, these schemes made it possible to watch cruise liners, small container ships and other vessels sail along the river in the heart of the city. Panoramic walkways on the waterfront allow residents and visitors to watch cruise liners dock at and set sail from Wilhelminapier and to look at the skyline of Kop van Zuid.[3] In addition, harbours such as Leuvehaven or Veerhaven now host a large number of sailboats, some of them of historic value and part of the former outdoor Harbour Museum (Figure 7.4). The former Holland America Line's terminal is now a panoramic viewpoint on the river (Figure 7.5). The city's maritime attitude is also celebrated in a more symbolic way. Images of the ports and of ships sailing along the river are displayed, sometimes in real time, on a large screen at Rotterdam Central Station (Figure 7.6). Originally, the idea came from the artist collective Kunst en Vaarwerk (Art and Boating, interview, expert 7, April 2018) and the screen was conceived as a billboard showing images of the port. The screen has shifted from a 'cliché' to something that residents 'can be proud of' (interview, city planner 3, April 2018) and appears effective in making visitors engage with Rotterdam's maritime nature since their very arrival.

Cultural and sporting events have been displaying the same strategy of spectacularisation of the riverfront and the city's ties with the port. For example, the little physical transformation related to the ECoC 2001 concentrated in

Figure 7.4 Sailboats, cranes and lighthouse in Leuvehaven.

Figure 7.5 Panoramic viewpoint in front of Hotel New York.

Figure 7.6 Screen at Rotterdam Central Station.

Kop van Zuid, while the Wereldhavendagen include a number of spectacular events in the same area on the river every year.

In Genoa, the event-led redevelopment of Porto Antico has been deploying the spectacularisation of a range of maritime heritage assets and activities. Panoramic viewpoints make it possible to watch cruise and ferry liners entering and exiting the harbour. Yachts and leisure boats are berthed on the waterfront, at a few meters from bars and restaurants. Next to Magazzini del Cotone, Arena del Mare (arena of the sea) is a public area used as an outdoor cultural venue. Although light and clean maritime functions are spectacularised, from Magazzini del Cotone visitors can have a glimpse of the working port as well (Figures 7.7 and 7.8).

This spectacularisation of both light and heavy port functions appears in contrast with the established attitude of hiding working port areas that is visible in other areas of the port–city interface, such as in Prà. To a certain extent, this suggests the possibility of an imminent cultural change in port–city relationships, where mega events have played a role:

> you can see what the attitude towards the commercial port is. I mean, there are specific [design] choices, for example, to visually isolate the port. If one walks along the green space in Prà, where there are these recreational and

Figure 7.7 Panoramic viewpoint at Magazzini del Cotone.

Figure 7.8 Cranes in the working commercial port visible from Magazzini del Cotone's viewpoint.

tourist activities, at some point they will see this barrier, this mountain that hides the port. And the idea is 'the more we hide that bad and ugly thing, the better we feel'. This doesn't happen anymore. Those who go to Magazzini del Cotone at night can see the lights of port activities in the terminal, as something that is part of the beauty of the city. The cultural change is that. And that was certainly generated by the cultural events that took place in the city, because these events create identity.

(interview, expert 11, June 2018, author's translation)

Similarly, boat tours of the port display this feature. As they sail from the Aquarium to Pegli, visitors can see both the redeveloped Porto Antico and part of the working port. This includes the Exxonmobil plant, the commercial and industrial port area in Sampierdarena and the airport, as well as the historic Lanterna lighthouse (Figures 7.9 and 7.10).

An effort to spectacularise light and heavy port functions and infrastructure is also visible in Valencia. As mentioned, the new exit channel separated the leisure harbour from the working commercial port. This created a safe space for recreational boating and sailing. As in the other case-study cities, yacht berths have been spectacularised. However, cruise ships are not clearly visible because of the current location of the cruise terminal. As regards the working port, part of the protection wall that was retained after the redevelopment of

Figure 7.9 Porto Antico as visible from a boat tour of the port.

Figure 7.10 Working port area with the Lanterna in the background, as visible from a boat tour of the port.

the inner harbour is still in place. Nevertheless, Parque Bufa la Nau, next to the south section of the turning bridge designed by Santiago Calatrava as part of Valencia Street Circuit, allows visitors to have a glimpse of the container port. This changing attitude is visible in the case of temporary and permanent Ferris wheels installed in port areas. In 2015, a temporary Ferris wheel – at that time the tallest temporary one in Europe – was installed from March to May (Europa Press, 2015). However, the proposal to install a permanent Ferris wheel in the same area, next to the north section of the unused turning bridge, was rejected in 2020, as a sign of the post-2015 local government's intention to avoid the spectacularisation of culture. The 123-meters-tall proposed Circular View would have been one of the tallest in Europe together with the planned Whey Aye Wheel on Newcastle's Quayside (140m). In the last few years, a temporary Ferris wheel has also been installed in the winter in Genoa's Porto Antico, in the Arena del Mare area (Porto Antico Spa, 2018).

Water and city branding

The location of waterfront redevelopment schemes represents their key selling point. This raises a question as to whether such redevelopments have been promoting maritime cultures or have merely been exploiting proximity to water for branding purposes. Undoubtedly, water is a powerful archetype in urban development. Lynch (1960) identified five physical elements constituting the image of cities: paths, edges, districts, nodes and landmarks. Edges are understood as physical elements acting as boundaries, such as railways, walls and of course waterfronts. Waterfronts themselves have been largely interpreted as places of pleasure in relation to the human fascination with water (Dovey, 2005, p. 23). Maritime features and proximity to water have long been mobilised for urban regeneration, real estate development and city branding purposes (see e.g. Malone, 1996; Norcliffe et al., 1996; Ward, 2011). The search for sanitised and saleable distinctiveness may generate a maritime-kitsch aesthetics in regeneration processes (Atkinson, 2007): although such aesthetics may be positively perceived by residents (as in the case of Hull's Victoria Dock Village, ibid., pp. 531–532), the outcome of these processes may diverge sensibly from local distinctiveness.

The case-study cities display similar tendencies in exploiting the symbolic potential of water for urban development, as well as stronger references to water rather than to ports within event programming. Nevertheless, Hull stands as a particular case. In Hull, as in many other European port cities, water has been mobilised to encourage new ways of relating to the waterfront, for example through marinas, walkways along the waterside, urban amenities. Cultural events such as Freedom Festival engaged with water or with the marine – rather than maritime – nature of the city, sometimes in spectacular and innovative ways.[4] However, other events (for instance Sea Trek in 2001[5] or the Hull and Folk Maritime Festival[6]) and many events in 2017 (such as *Made in Hull* or *The Last Testament of Lillian Bilocca*) did engage with the city's maritime history and heritage. In part, this can be explained by considering the nature of the UKCoC as a cultural festival. Nonetheless, this approach was not necessarily displayed by similar events in other port cities, such as the ECoC in Rotterdam or Genoa.

In Rotterdam, water has traditionally been a central element in event bids and programmes. Within the ECoC 2001 programme, the subtheme Stromende Stad (Flowing City) framed Rotterdam in relation to migration but also to its nature of a city on water. This is also related to the strategic symbolic value of waterfronts, which feature particularly well in the media (interview, expert 5, April 2018). However, some of these events might have been missed opportunities to build a stronger connection with the river. As noted by Pijbes (2016, p. 21):

'In 2004, I was asked for my response to the bid book put together by Rotterdam with the aim of capturing the title of Sports City 2005. There were hundreds of pages, but nowhere could I find a sport that was related to water, let alone the River Maas. No sailing, no water skiing, no swimming, no synchronised diving, none of that. A missed opportunity – when virtually everything connected to the port or the river, in cultural terms as otherwise, has potential and can be successful in Rotterdam. The Submarine Wharf and a wealth of small initiatives at Katendrecht are testament to that.'

'However characteristic they may be, the port and the river rarely feature in cultural policy. . . . If you didn't know better, you might think *this city lies with his back to the river*. What is Rotterdam's Unique Selling Point? The business of a global port and a location on a characteristic river to which Rotterdam owes its origins.'

(ibid., p. 22, italics added).

With the notable exception of the Wereldhavendagen, when cultural and mega event programming have framed Rotterdam in relation to the river, they have done so more with regard to the city's relationship with water as an attractive architectural element rather than in connection with port-city relationships (interview, expert 6, April 2018). Mobilising the archetypical power of water is also connected with securing event themselves:

the strong element we always propose in any documents and suggestions to link Rotterdam with mega events [is] often to say that water is such a special element that it can be made use of. If Rotterdam wants to host the Olympic Games. It's not 'port city', as you mentioned, but it's 'water'.

(interview, expert 6, April 2018)

The case of Genoa is another example of the symbolic power of water and its potential in waterfront redevelopment schemes. The role of water as an architectural element was arguably crucial to the successful redevelopment of Porto Antico. It was also mobilised within mega events, both physically and from a symbolic perspective. Many events were held on the waterfront, while Ponte Parodi was initially envisioned as the focal point of the whole ECoC 2004. The connection of Genoa with the sea was celebrated by the 1992 Specialist Expo and the ECoC. As commented by a local informant:

[s]o, the sea is of course something attractive. As Renzo Piano says, the sea always gives the perception of infinity. He always says 'when I was a child, I used to sit on the quay with my father; I looked at the sea and I could see afar'.

(interview, event team member 5, June 2018, author's translation)

Proximity to water and the mobilisation of its symbolic power may also be a means to counterbalance the impacts of port restructuring and demaritimisation:

proximity to water, just like Renzo Piano teaches us, is a great opportunity and possibility. So, even if the city loses, let's say, its strictly maritime character, about goods handling and so on, other things will be retained.

(interview, policy maker 5, June 2018, author's translation)

In many port cities, deindustrialisation and the restructuring of ports have created the conditions to make urban waters cleaner and more attractive. This was a crucial aspect in the case of Barcelona, where the waterfront redevelopment process triggered by the 1992 Olympics reconnected the city to the sea and contributed to transforming the 'Catalan Manchester' into a global tourist destination. Nevertheless, in Barcelona, the Olympics played a key role in shifting perceptions of the waterfront and urban waters. Derelict industrial areas and informal settlements on the seafront were cleared and replaced with promenades, artificial sandy beaches and leisure and commercial facilities. The city's proximity to the sea is now perceived in aesthetic, rather than functional, terms. The sea is pleasantly associated with leisure and tourism and with a positive image of Barcelona, rather than playing a strictly functional role as a navigable waterway or a dumping ground for industrial and urban development (Figure 7.11).

Cleaning-up programmes were integral part of waterfront redevelopment schemes in Singapore (Chang & Huang, 2011), and arguably contributed to changing public attitudes towards urban waters. In Rio de Janeiro, the problematic cleaning up of Guanabara Bay was a major issue in relation to the Olympics and was mentioned in the media as one of the reasons why the city's bid for the 2004 Olympics was unsuccessful (see e.g. Silvestre, 2017; Boykoff & Mascarenhas, 2016).

Figure 7.11 Waterfront redevelopment in Barcelona, driven by the 1992 Olympic Games.

In Valencia, as in Barcelona, the perception of water changed from something related to industry to an asset for sport and leisure activities (interview, event team member 6, June 2018). However, mega events in Valencia have exploited proximity to water as an element to create a saleable, international and exclusive urban environment, addressed to foreign and wealthy visitors and able to project Valencia globally. As a matter of fact, mega events in Valencia were sporting events, which are of course rather different from cultural events such as the ECoC, and do not necessarily engage with local history or specificity. However, it appears possible to suggest that the America's Cup attempted to encourage a local sailing culture, while it did not engage with local maritime culture and heritage despite having the potential to do so. Although the trophy was displayed in the Veles e Vents building and part of the tinglados hosted an exhibition of replicas of past America's Cup boats, there was little connection with local maritime heritage, shipbuilding or fishing practices. For example, the event did not mobilise the nearby Les Drassanes, a 14th-century shipyard next to the harbour.

Maritime cultural quarters

In port cities, maritime history, heritage and identity are increasingly mobilised as selling points as part of heritage-led regeneration schemes. An example is the emergence of maritime cultural quarters,[7] interpreted as heterogeneous sets of maritime-related cultural assets including cultural facilities such as maritime museums or heritage assets such as historic shipyards, port cranes, ships or boats. These assets are mobilised with the aim of providing a maritime-related cultural offer to residents and visitors and therefore of promoting forms of cultural consumption levering on maritime cultural resources. Considering their maritime character, they should be distinguished from generalist waterfront redevelopment schemes, whether or not culture-led, which albeit tapping on aspects of local port city culture and image nonetheless tend to provide generalist, not maritime-related, functions. Maritime cultural quarters emerge in inner harbours or waterfronts, in particular in heritage-rich urban port areas. In some cases, these environments are connected with the legacy of mega events. Maritime cultural quarters can be examples of heritage-led regeneration in the 'post-mega event' phase, where more sustainable development models are sought.

The case-study cities of the book display either existing, planned or proposed maritime cultural quarters, which are either part of event legacy strategies or have been developed independently from mega events. In the latter case, they indirectly benefitted from the visibility of these events and the increased attractiveness of their cities. Although unrelated to the event, *Hull: Yorkshire's Maritime City* has increasingly been perceived as a legacy project of the UK City of Culture 2017. Arguably, the same interest in maritime-related events and activities that emerged in 2017 has been visible in the case of this project, which in turn maintained momentum around the 'rediscovery' of the city's maritime heritage. The scheme aims at creating a maritime-related cultural offer by restoring and connecting a number of maritime heritage assets. This project is connected with the proposed cruise terminal at Sammy's Point and the ambition to make Hull a world-class visitor destination set in the City Plan. The restoration of maritime heritage assets – together with the redevelopment of Fruit Market, the public realm improvements undertaken in 2015–2016, and the fact that the proposed terminal would be located next to The Deep and the Old Town – may encourage cruise passengers disembarking at Hull to visit the city centre as part of their journey.

Hull City Council is raising £27.4 million for the project, having already secured £13.6 million from the National Lottery Heritage Fund (Hull City Council, 2019; National Lottery Heritage Fund, 2019). The scheme includes the refurbishment of the Maritime Museum and adjacent Dock Office Chambers, the restoration of a dry dock berth at the North End Shipyard for the Arctic Corsair (a 1960s distant-water fishing trawler, which will be moved from its current location at the Museums Quarter) and the restoration of the Spurn Lightship at the marina (Figure 7.12). The project is also an opportunity to 'rebalance' maritime narratives, by taking into account aspects that have been neglected in the UKCoC programme (interview, city planner 1, February 2018), such as shipbuilding.

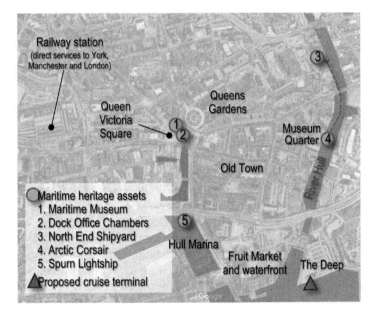

Figure 7.12 Maritime heritage assets involved in the *Hull: Yorkshire's Maritime City* scheme.

Source: Author's elaboration. Imagery ©2019 Google. Map data ©2019 Google. Reprinted with modifications from: Tommarchi, E. (2020) Port Cities, Heritage Cities. A comparative perspective on maritime cultural quarters. *PortusPlus*, 9, 1–18. Available at: www.portusplus.org/index.php/pp/issue/view/9.

In Rotterdam, Leuvehaven and Oude Haven are being promoted as the city's Maritime District (see e.g. Rotterdam Partners, 2018). The area includes the Maritime Museum (opened in 1986) and the Harbour Museum (in Leuvehaven), an outdoor museum exhibiting historic vessels, cranes and other maritime heritage assets. The two museums were merged in 2014. The Mariniersmuseum (Marines Museum) explores the history of the Dutch Marines corps. The area also includes heritage assets such as Het Witte Huis (The White House, a late 19th-century Art Nouveau building) and a number of cafes and restaurants in Oude Haven, which is being promoted as a leisure waterfront area. This is creating a maritime cultural quarter in Leuvehaven (interview, event team member 2, April 2018; interview, expert 5, April 2018; Figure 7.13), supported by the amenities in the nearby Oude Haven, which is contributing to attracting visitors.

In Genoa, today's Porto Antico is the result of three decades of urban policies using mega events as catalysts for the transformation of the historic harbour into a leisure waterfront. The area includes a number of maritime cultural assets and other facilities, such as the Aquarium, the crane-inspired panoramic lift Bigo and the Galeone Neptune. Some of these facilities were built for the 1992 Specialist Expo. Before 2020, the Aquarium used to attract more than a million visitors each year (Acquario di Genova, 2018). Waterfront activities, including museum and restaurants, and port tours are part of this maritime

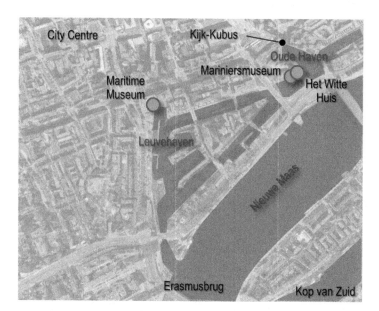

Figure 7.13 Maritime cultural quarter developing in Rotterdam's Oude Haven and Leuvehaven.

Source: Background map: Imagery ©2019 Google. Map data ©2019 Google. Reprinted with modifications from: Tommarchi, E. (2020) Port Cities, Heritage Cities. A comparative perspective on maritime cultural quarters. *PortusPlus*, 9, 1–18. Available at: www.portusplus.org/index.php/pp/issue/view/9.

and waterside cultural offer (interview, policy maker 5, June 2018) and attract a large number of residents and visitors. In the nearby Darsena Comunale, a small-scale maritime cultural quarter has emerged as part of the legacy of the European Capital of Culture 2004. The Galata Open Air Museum includes the Galata Museo del Mare (the only *ex novo* cultural facility directly linked to the event) a submarine and a floating structure used to host ephemeral exhibitions and events (Figure 7.14).

In Valencia, the Museu de la Mar project proposed by the Ayuntamiento and APV aims at addressing the absence of a maritime museum in the Mediterranean city and at rediscovering the city's maritime history and heritage. This idea emerged from both a demand from the local community and the intention to overcome the traditional discourse of disconnection between the city and the sea (interview, policy maker 9, May 2018). The proposed museum would involve the restoration of three maritime heritage assets (Navarro Castelló, 2016; interview, policy maker 9, May 2018): Casa dels Bous, a late 19th-century building in El Cabanyal-El Canyamelar, which was originally used as a shelter for the animals that pulled fishing boats onto the shore; the aforementioned historic shipyard Les Drassanes; the Antiguo Varadero Público, a 1914 dry dock building in the inner harbour. If implemented, the project would connect maritime heritage assets which have been neglected, visually hidden or damaged by urban development and major sporting events and would develop a maritime cultural quarter (Figure 7.15).

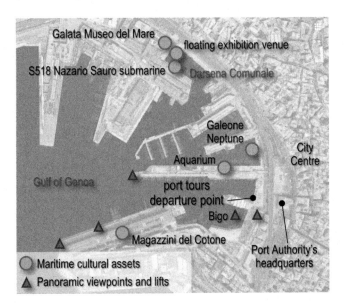

Figure 7.14 Maritime-related cultural assets in Genoa's Porto Antico and maritime cultural quarter in the Darsena Comunale.

Source: Background map: Imagery ©2019 Google. Map data ©2019 Google. Reprinted with modifications from: Tommarchi, E. (2020) Port Cities, Heritage Cities. A comparative perspective on maritime cultural quarters. *PortusPlus*, 9, 1–18. Available at: www.portusplus.org/index.php/pp/issue/view/9.

Figure 7.15 Valencia's Museu de la Mar proposed venues.

Source: Background map: Imagery ©2019 Google. Map data ©2019 Google, Inst. Geogr. Nacional. Reprinted with modifications from: Tommarchi, E. (2020) Port Cities, Heritage Cities. A comparative perspective on maritime cultural quarters. *PortusPlus*, 9, 1–18. Available at: www.portusplus.org/index. php/pp/issue/view/9.

Maritime cultural quarters appear to be a recurrent feature across port cities pursuing culture- or heritage-led regeneration. As discussed by Tommarchi (2020), these environments can be interpreted as 'repeated instances' (Jacobs, 2006, in Robinson, 2016, p. 14) of structural processes such as the gradual touristification of many port cities. However, their novelty in comparison with waterfront redevelopment schemes implemented since the 1980s is that they are not based on the provision of generalist – whether or not maritime-related – cultural facilities. Rather, they openly engage with local maritime heritage and port city cultures. In addition, these schemes do not necessarily imply extensive physical transformation.

These spaces are opportunities to explore, restore and showcase maritime heritage assets, and to present local port city cultures to residents and visitors. The restoration of heritage assets and the associated small-scale regeneration schemes (e.g. public realm improvements) can contribute to improving the permeability of waterfront areas, and to address any remaining issues of permeability after event-led regeneration has taken place. In addition, these schemes may help contrast cultural demaritimisation, by strengthening symbolic port-city relationships.

However, an open question remains as to whether these initiatives develop authentic maritime cultural offers or whether they are examples of cultural remaritimisation driven by economic goals. Threats to local maritime cultures may arise from a number of factors. Distorted maritime narratives may be fostered by emphasising certain, 'sanitised' aspects and by neglecting other, 'undesirable' elements of local maritime history and identity. A related issue is the commodification of local port city cultures to boost cultural tourism, to the detriment of authenticity. This aspect may assume a critical relevance in the case of future cultural events or mega involving the use of maritime cultural quarters, considering the potential of events to foster staged authenticity.

Port cities of culture and events 'on the ground': the role of local values and meanings

Existing symbolic ties between ports and cities, together with the meanings attributed to the port and port city culture, play a growing role in mega events and their legacy. These ties encompass local geography and history, presence and social composition of maritime-related workforce, the attachment of local communities to the port and the city's maritime identity, the interest of the public in modern port activity. Such immaterial and sometimes elusive links are often overlooked in event-led regeneration. This neglect may generate unintended, possibly negative consequences on established symbolic port-city links and may undermine regeneration programmes. This section examines the connection between event-led regeneration and the 'actually existing' symbolic links between ports and cities, and explores the interest of residents and visitors in maritime history and modern ports.

Actually existing symbolic port-city links

Event-led regeneration in port cities operates at a certain moment of time within the evolution of centuries-old port-city relationships, which they can relate to in different ways. These may span from a harmonious integration with traditional relationships to the extreme case of the imposition of new ways for cities to relate to their ports and their marine and maritime nature. As mentioned earlier, Kowalewski (2018, p. 3) underlines that features of the preindustrial past of port cities are now part of an artificial, saleable imaginary of the port. These stereotypes and myths about the port and the sea, whether consciously or not, contribute to framing urban planning strategies (Kokot, 2008, p. 10).

Such processes raise questions as to whether and how new or refashioned port city imaginaries capture, build on or attempt to suppress socio-spatial and cultural relations arising from former or existing maritime industries and maritime working-class populations. The relation between event-led regeneration and existing port-city links encompasses a range of spatial, social, economic, cultural and symbolic outcomes, which ultimately impact on both processes.

While the impacts of culture- and event-led waterfront redevelopment schemes have been discussed in the literature for example with regard to issues of standardisation, the socio-cultural and symbolic impact of these processes in maritime port cities has so far been overlooked.

The case studies provide different perspectives on this matter. There are different views as to whether the maritime nature of Hull has been captured in the UKCoC programme. As already mentioned, the bidding team overlooked the city's fishing history in the UKCoC bid. This choice might understandably have been made in the light of the painful collective memories associated with distant-water trawler fishing, which at the time could be interpreted as 'dissonant heritage' (Tunbridge & Ashworth, 1996). However, as the event was being delivered, a growing emphasis was placed on fishing narratives, to the extent that fishing overshadowed other aspects of the city's maritime history and heritage (interview, expert 1, January 2018; interview, expert 2, January 2018), such as shipbuilding, coal handling or transmigration. This might be explained by considering Hull's established cultural offer – for example the Maritime Museum's collection – and heritage-related activism, which have traditionally focused on trawler history and fishing heritage, despite the fact that this may not necessarily be the most important aspect of the city's maritime heritage (interview, city planner 1, February 2018).

In Rotterdam, the ECoC and other subsequent cultural events raised issues of intercultural dialogue in a multicultural society. Historically, in order to fulfil the needs of the developing port, low-educated workers from abroad had been welcome in Rotterdam. They often departed from the most deprived areas of their own countries (interview, expert 6, April 2018). With the rise of automatisation and containerisation, a vast multicultural working class living in the city's maritime districts was severely hit by unemployment. More recently, the city has been the destination of migrants in particular from Morocco and Turkey. These phenomena have been generating a complex social milieu, where highly funded, mainstream cultural events may encounter opposition. This is also reflected in culture-led regeneration more broadly. An example is the clash in Katendrecht between the original population and the higher-income households who are now attracted by the edgy atmosphere created by the redevelopment of the district (interview, city planner 4, April 2018).

Genoa and Valencia show how similar event-led regeneration schemes in inner harbours can lead to different outcomes where traditional socio-cultural port-city links are substantially dissimilar. In Genoa, event-led regeneration made it possible to 'reopen' Porto Antico for the benefit of the local community. This process restored the traditionally tight connection between the city centre and the harbour, which had been interrupted by the development of the modern industrial port and, subsequently, by its migration and restructuring. As a result, Porto Antico has become a new centrality for both residents and tourists. Valencia is an example of how mega events and event-led regeneration may be used as a means to generate new symbolic port-city links in discontinuity with traditional relationships. This contrast is particularly striking considering the traditional discourse of Valencia's detachment from the sea. As well summarised by Llavador (2010, p. 31):

> Valencia had always been a river city, and the river served as a major link when it came to establishing its relationship with the seaport. However, the city experienced its romance with the sea from a distance, or, to put it another way, it could be said that the romance never found the right climate to form the perfect bond – and this was the case not only from a political perspective but also where urban development was concerned.

If it is true that the city 'used to give its back to sea' (interview, city planner 5, May 2018; interview, port actor 5, May 2018; interview, expert 13, May 2018; interview, event team member 6, June 2018; interview, policy maker 9, May 2018), mega events and event-led regeneration have undoubtedly contributed to building a connection. The conditions for this process to take place were set by the redevelopment of the inner harbour, particularly through the construction of the new port exit channel and the opening of the area as a leisure port (interview, city planner 5, May 2018; interview, policy maker 8, June 2018). However, the way in which the leisure port was designed and the whole process was framed appears hardly connected with either the city's maritime identity or its long-term trajectory of urban development. This suggests that remaritimisation in Valencia has 'imposed' a new, different port city culture. As put by one informant:

> [a]nd somehow what I think [is] that this will to connect the city to the sea was a will . . . to impose to the Valencia that was facing the sea a certain manner to be by the sea. . . . With the tools of orthodox planning and the projects [they] were trying to get the city close to the sea when actually the city was there, or at least part of the city was there.
>
> (interview, event team member 6, June 2018)

Furthermore, it is worth noting that connecting Valencia to the sea had been a key aim of the Conservative local government (1991–2015), which also appeared in the 1997 strategic plan. This was part of the broader political project aiming at repositioning Valencia as an international tourist destination. As mentioned in Chapter 5, the Balcón al Mar project was reframed as Valencia was designated as the host city of the 2007 America's Cup and the inner harbour was redesigned. The resulting pronounced post-industrial, 'anyplace' appearance of the redeveloped leisure port, as well as the fact that it was clearly addressed to middle and higher-income cultural consumers, arguably contributed to strengthening the artificiality of this attempt to connect the city with the sea. These aspects can explain the reasons why the new leisure port has been underused after the America's Cup and why residents have begun 'colonising' the area more than ten years after its completion.

Residents' and visitors' interest in maritime history and modern ports

Both maritime heritage and the presence of working ports are mobilised within symbolic processes of regeneration in maritime port cities. It is worth asking how these aspects are perceived by residents and visitors, who are the final recipients of event-led regeneration schemes. Although it is not the purpose of the book to approach a longitudinal study of residents' and visitors' interest in ports and their perceptions of the maritime dimension within event-led regeneration processes, a few elements can be underlined. Unlike maritime history and heritage, modern ports and port activity are not necessarily an aspect of a port city's identity that is immediately perceived by visitors and, to some extent, residents. Mega events and event-led regeneration may emphasise – certain, possibly distorted – aspects of a city's maritime identity, in some cases displaying shallow thinking by event promoters who may tend to lever on maritime stereotypes. However, such an effort appears to raise awareness of the economic importance of ports and to stimulate interest in maritime history and heritage, rather than changing the way in which the public perceives modern maritime practices.

In Hull, event promoters and local stakeholders reported a certain appetite of the local community for maritime history and heritage and the role of the port. This interest was exposed by the success of maritime-related cultural events under the UKCoC umbrella, such as the exhibition *In-Port Stories*. The UKCoC was perceived to have raised awareness amongst locals, and this was considered as helpful in relation to ABP's goal of taking people, in particular young people, inside and around the port (interview, port actor 2, February 2018). As put by a senior ABP official:

> So, one said to me, perhaps six months ago, that traditionally ABP and the port of Hull generally is a bit like Willy Wonka's chocolate factory: there is a big wall, and behind that wall no one really knows what's going on. We have . . . And I think City of Culture probably has helped with this a little bit . . . We are fairly determined to get people through and let them see what we do.
>
> (interview, port actor 2, February 2018)

Arguably, a key role in this was played by one single event within the UKCoC programme, *Blade*, which spectacularised the production of wind turbines at Hull. The event contributed to raising awareness of the economic role of Hull's port and its future development trajectory focusing on renewable energy (interview, city planner 1, February 2018; interview, city planner 2, January 2018; interview, port actor 1, December 2017). However, the extent to which this stimulated an intertest in current maritime activities should be problematised. A small number of street surveys with residents and visitors by Hull Marina suggested that the awareness of Hull's port was mainly connected with Siemens Gamesa's wind turbine manufacturing facility, which was mentioned in relation to its positive socio-economic effects and the visual impact of *Blade*. No particular interest was reported about the working port or current maritime activities, while the UKCoC 2017 was not perceived to have stimulated a new interest in this. Nonetheless, visitors from other parts of the UK reported that their visit to Hull made them more interested in maritime history and heritage and to the socio-economic impact of port activity on cities.

In the case of Rotterdam, major and mega events have been attempting to celebrate the reconstruction and the city's relationships with the river, while, as mentioned by Richards and Wilson (2004, p. 1938), the use of futuristic architecture has long been a means to market the city internationally. Tourist boat tours set sail from the Erasmusbrug area, giving visitors the opportunity to look at the high-rise architecture at Kop van Zuid as well as to have a glimpse of some of Rotterdam's working port areas. A number of street surveys suggested that visitors coming to Rotterdam for its architecture might not have any interest in the port and might not perceive ports as offering anything to tourists. Nevertheless, visitor embarking on boat tours along the river do display an interest in the modern port. If the port of Rotterdam is attracting tourists, as mentioned earlier in relation to the popularity of the Wereldhavendangen, port tours and the success of FutureLand, these tourists might still constitute a rather specialist audience.

In Genoa, the event-led redevelopment of Porto Antico was undoubtedly successful in terms of attracting residents and visitors to the new leisure port. However, it is debateable whether a certain interest in maritime history is coupled with an interest in the modern working port, in part due to the fact that the local maritime cultural offer is still unstructured (expert 9, May 2018; expert 10, June 2018; port actor 6, June 2018; port actor 7, June 2018). As in the case of Rotterdam, boat tours departing from Porto Antico play a role in showcasing the working port (policy maker 5, June 2018), together with the appeal of cruise ships and liners entering and exiting the harbour:

> [cruise] ships and liners pass close to the dockside, which is open to the public. So, there is this inception of [the element of] the ship into the cityscape, which while in Venice is tragic . . . in Genoa . . . you see these big things passing by and that is an exciting event.
>
> (interview, expert 9, May 2018, author's translation)

Nevertheless, along with Andrade and Costa (2020, p. 194), it is worth noting that processes of touristification fuelled by cruise tourism risk undermining the effort to reconnect the city with its waterfront through mega events and redevelopment schemes: waterfronts and leisure harbours may simply be taken over by cruise tourists. The interest in the working port among Genoa's residents arguably focuses on its economic 'health' and its ability to bring resources and wealth to the city (interview, event team member 9, June 2018), rather than on maritime practices. This means that the waterfront is fundamentally a collection of leisure spaces and activities, while the working port stands in the background (interview, policy maker 5, June 2018). A few surveyed residents in the Magazzini del Cotone area underlined this connection with the port in relation to the city's wealth, suggesting that Genoese residents 'must be interested' in the modern port because of its economic relevance, despite the fact that fewer people work in the port now. Of course, mega events in Genoa played a crucial role in these relationships as they were the opportunity to remove physical barriers at the port-city interface and to unveil Porto Antico to residents and visitors as a new centrality:

> the transformation of the waterfront put local people in contact with the port, at least with this part of the port, with no doubt. Because it was completely separated, I mean, it was a kind of unknown universe. Even I, when I was a child, had no perception of it. You could get here by car, there was this wall, you could go along Via San Lorenzo by bus, which is now a pedestrian zone, so there was a continuous flow of cars. So, Genoa, actually, from the early 1990s until today, has undergone an epoch-making transformation of the city centre, absolutely epoch-making.
>
> (interview, port actor 4, June 2018, author's translation)

The unveiling of Porto Antico was also an opportunity to reconnect residents with local maritime heritage (interview, expert 9, May 2018). A more indirect and long-term legacy of events is the gradual re-appropriation of maritime heritage. For example, the 16th-century Lanterna lighthouse, now managed by the Maritime Museum, is open to visitors for a greater number of days throughout the year. However, it is worth noting that events were not only about promoting Genoa's maritime history and heritage. For example, the ECoC 2004 emphasised other aspects of its identity, including its history as a financial pole in the Renaissance.

The spatial legacy of mega events contributed to increasing civic pride, while the improved image of the city means that external perceptions are no longer limited to its industrial past but now encompass culture, heritage and tourism (Gastaldi, 2012, pp. 33–34). Nevertheless, as regards residents' awareness of the port, officials from the Port Authority call for better communication, underlining the difficulty of communicating port culture (interview, port actor 4, June 2018). As mentioned earlier, the reopening of Genoa Port Center is a step in this direction and it may be a key tool for combining the imaginaries of Genoa as a port city and as a city of culture.

In Valencia, the 2007 America's Cup undoubtedly had an impact in terms of external perceptions about the city. However, the initial enthusiasm among residents quickly faded away when it was clear that the event would have no long-lasting effects (interview, event team member 6, June 2018; Parra Camacho et al., 2016). Despite the fact that the working port is relatively close to the city, and that port cranes are clearly visible from Malvarrosa beach, an intangible port-city separation is observable. A number of street surveys with residents and visitors on Paseo Marítimo and Paseo Neptuno suggested that most people gathering on the waterfront were not interested in the port and, in the case of some tourists and newcomers, were not aware of its existence prior to their arrival. Virtually every visitor taking part in street surveys related their lack of interest in Valencia's working port to the fact that ports are not tourist attractions and offer tourists nothing to see. Interestingly, this appears in contrast with other cases such as Rotterdam and Genoa, where the port itself, even the working port, generates some interest. A possible explanation should be sought in the different kind of tourism and different visitors' expectations across these cities, as tourism in Valencia is more associated with heritage (in the Ciutat Vella) and seaside tourism. In addition, port-city conflicts appear to be a critical aspect generating a sense of detachment from port activities.

The reason why residents and visitors in Valencia appear now more interested in using the leisure port and the waterfront should be sought neither in the appeal of maritime practices nor in the intangible legacy of events themselves. In the immediate short term, international sporting events in the Dársena undoubtedly brought more residents and visitors into the inner harbour and, to some extent, 'introduced' the port to those who had never been around it before (interview, port actor 5, May 2018). However, it is difficult to point at a causal relationship between mega events and the subsequent, gradual appropriation of the leisure port and the adjacent seafront by Valencian residents. Other aspects were arguably more important, such as the seafront promenade. As observed by one informant:

> I think that the local community and visitors [are more interested] . . . because of the attempts of integration of the port and the city – [such as] removing the port wall, and so on – I think the city is closer to the port. And then, with the intervention in Cabanyal and so on, there is sort of a flow of Valencian residents towards the port. . . . What caused this was having built a seafront promenade, in Malvarrosa, which was done by the same government who promoted these events. That meant that people used the seafront. . . . Now that it's better integrated, you have a greater number of residents going to the port. They like being there, having a glass of wine and so on, enjoying the promenade with their children. This is what is gradually emerging, but it was generated neither by the America's Cup nor by Formula [One]. By no means I would say that.
>
> (interview, policy maker 7, May 2018, author's translation)

Although a broad survey exploring residents and visitors' perceptions and attitudes towards modern ports would be necessary, the few elements collected through the research behind the book suggest the possibility of a misalignment between the goals of event-led regeneration strategies and their actual impacts on residents' and visitors' attitude towards ports and port city culture.

Lessons from the (re)generation of symbolic port–city links

The willingness of projecting an attractive image of the city to gain a competitive advantage in interurban competition is behind the exploitation of proximity to water as a powerful selling point. This approach may focus on water itself, as an element shaping the urban environment, rather than on the maritime exceptionalism of port cities. Such a branding strategy poses risks of generation of inauthentic maritime culture and loss of distinctiveness, eventually contributing to demaritimisation or remaritimisation under different conditions. The mobilisation of port city cultures also raises questions about how the port city image that is promoted aligns with local meanings and the significance attributed to ports and maritime activities by residents and visitors. Culture- and event-led regeneration often overlook actually existing symbolic port-city links, such as traditional relationships with the port and the sea or the distinctive social fabric of port cities. For example, the promotion of sanitised port- and maritime-related images and environments might generate strong opposition where local communities are still attached to the presence of an industrial or fishing port. Similarly, the creation of a saleable port city image *ex novo*, where local communities have not developed any particular sense of attachment to the port or their proximity to the sea, is likely to be problematic and contested. A misalignment between event-led regeneration strategies in port cities and the existing local meanings and significance attributed to their maritime identity eventually leads to unintended consequences, such as the underuse of new cultural and leisure spaces and facilities and the disruption of established relations, and possibly to the failure of event-led regeneration processes themselves.

Notes

1 For a discussion of the cultural dimension of processes of demaritimisation and remaritimisation, see also Tommarchi (2021).
2 *Flood – Part Two* was a play performed on a floating platform at Victoria Dock.
3 Before the COVID-19 crisis, large cruise ships used to call at Rotterdam up to once every week. Cruise calls had become a public event, advertised as such on the Port Authority's website (www.portofrotterdam.com/en/events/cruise-calls), while a calendar of cruise calls was available at: www.cruiseportrotterdam.nl/cruise-calls/.
4 For example, *Flood* was a year-round event, including live performances on a floating stage at Victoria Dock, to creatively reflect on Hull and the UK's future as frontliners in climate change and rising sea levels.
5 Sea Trek was a public event held in 2001 which made use of tall ships to recreate migration routes from Northern Europe to America.
6 A folk music festival promoting intangible maritime heritage.
7 An analysis of maritime cultural quarters in the case-study cities of the book appears in Tommarchi (2020).

Bibliography

Acquario di Genova (2018) Acquario di Genova: Una struttura di successo con circa 30 milioni di visitatori. *Acquario di Genova*, 31st August. Available at: www.acquariodigenova. it/wp/wp-content/uploads/2018/07/Acquario-di-Genova-cartella-stampa-luglio-2018. pdf [Accessed 16/08/2019].

Andrade, M. J., & Costa, P. J. (2020) Touristification of European port-cities: Impacts on local populations and cultural heritage. In Carpenter, A., & Lozano, R. (eds.) *European Port Cities in Transition: Moving Towards More Sustainable Sea Transport Hubs*. Cham: Springer, 187–204.

Andres, L. (2011) Marseille 2013 or the final round of a long and complex regeneration strategy? *Town Planning Review*, 82(1), 61–76.

Atkinson, D. (2007) Kitsch geographies and the everyday spaces of social memory. *Environment and Planning A*, 39, 521–540.

Atkinson, D., Cooke, S., & Spooner, D. J. (2002) Tales from the Riverbank: Place-marketing and maritime heritages. *International Journal of Heritage Studies*, 8(1), 25–40.

BBC (2021) Liverpool stripped of Unesco World Heritage status. *BBC*, 21st July. Available at: www.bbc.co.uk/news/uk-england-merseyside-57879475 [Accessed 23/12/2021].

Binns, L. (2005) Capitalising on culture: An evaluation of culture-led urban regeneration policy. In *Futures Academy*. Dublin: Dublin Institute of Technology.

Boykoff, J., & Mascarenhas, G. (2016) The Olympics, sustainability, and greenwashing: The Rio 2016 summer games. *Capitalism Nature Socialism*, 27(2), 1–11.

Broudehoux, A.-M., & Carvalhaes dos Santos Monteiro, J. C. (2017) Reinventing Rio de Janeiro's old port: Territorial stigmatization, symbolic re-signification, and planned repopulation in Porto Maravilha. *Revista Brasileira de Estudos Urbanos e Regionais*, 19(3), 493–512.

Byrne, J. (2015) After the trawl: Memory and afterlife in the wake of Hull's distant-water fishing industry. *The International Journal of Maritime History*, 27(4), 816–822.

Byrne, J. (2016) Hull, fishing and the life and death of trawlertown: Living the spaces of a trawling port-city. In Beaven, B., Bell, K., & James, R. (eds.) *Port Towns and Urban Cultures: International Histories on the Waterfront, c.1700–2000*. Basingstoke: Palgrave Macmillan, 243–263.

Carrasco, J. S., & Pitarch-Garrido, M. D. (2017) Analysis of the impact on tourism of the megaproject-based urban development strategy: The case of the city of Valencia. *Cuadernos de Turismo*, 40, 723–726.

Chang, T. C., & Huang, S. (2011) Reclaiming the city: Waterfront development in Singapore. *Urban Studies*, 48(10), 2085–2100.

Doucet, B., Van Kempen, R., & Van Weesep, J. (2011) Resident perceptions of flagship waterfront regeneration: The case of the Kop Van Zuid in Rotterdam. *Tijdschrift voor Economische en Sociale Geografie*, 102(2), 125–145.

Dovey, K. (2005) *Fluid City: Transforming Melbourne's Urban Waterfront*. Sydney: University of New South Wales Press.

Europa Press (2015) La noria móvil más alta de Europa, en el Puerto de Valencia. *Europa Press*, 3rd June. Available at: www.europapress.es/comunitat-valenciana/noticia-noria-70-metros-panoramica-360-grados-abre-puertas-marina-20150306121329.html [Accessed 12/09/2019].

Evans, G. (2003) Hard-branding the cultural city: From Prado to Prada. *International Journal of Urban and Regional Research*, 27(2), 417–440.

Foster, J. (2018) *Stigma Cities: The Reputation and History of Birmingham, San Francisco, and Las Vegas*. Norman: University of Oklahoma Press.

García, B. (2004) Cultural policy and urban regeneration in Western European Cities: Lessons from experience, prospects for the future. *Local Economy*, 19(4), 312–326.

Gastaldi, F. (2012) Grandi eventi e rigenerazione urbana negli anni della grande trasformazione di Genova: 1992–2004. *Territorio della Ricerca su Insediamenti e Ambiente*, 9, 23–35.

Gourlay, G. (2007) 'It's got a bad name and it sticks . . . ' Approaching stigma as a distinct focus of neighbourhood regeneration initiatives. *EURA Conference 'The Vital City'*, Glasgow, 12–14 September.

Hajer, M. A. (1993) Rotterdam: Re-designing the public domain. In Bianchini, F., & Parkinson, M. (eds.) *Cultural Policy and Urban Regeneration: The Western European Experience.* Manchester: Manchester Press, 48–72.

Hein, C. (2018) Oil spaces: The global petroleumscape in the Rotterdam/The Hague area. *Journal of Urban History*, 44(5), 887–929.

Hobsbawm, E., & Ranger, T. (eds.) (2012) *The Invention of Tradition.* Cambridge: Cambridge University Press.

Horobin, G. W. (1957) Community and occupation in the Hull Fishing Industry. *The British Journal of Sociology*, 8(4), 343–356.

Hull City Council (2019) Hull: Yorkshire's Maritime City. *Hull City Plan.* Available at: https://cityplanhull.co.uk/index.php/hull-yorkshires-maritime-city/ [Accessed 06/11/2019].

Johnsen, B. E. (2009) What a maritime history! The uses of maritime history in summer festivals in southern Norway. *Journal of Tourism History*, 1(2), 113–130.

Kokot, W. (2008) Port cities as areas of transition: Comparative ethnographic research. In Kokot, W., Wildner, K., & Wonneberger, A. (eds.) *Port Cities as Areas of Transition: Ethnographic Perspectives.* Bielefeld: Transcript Verlag, 7–24.

Kowalewski, M. (2018) Images and spaces of port cities in transition. *Space and Culture*, 24(1), 53–65.

Llavador, J. M. T. (2010) Valencia y el mar, un idilio hecho realidad. Valencia and the Sea, a Romance come True. *Portus*, 20, 30–35.

Lorente, J. P. (2002) Urban cultural policy and urban regeneration: The special case of declining port cities – Liverpool, Marseilles, Bilbao. In Crane, D., Kawashima, N., & Kawasaki, K. (eds.) *Global Culture: Media, Arts, Policy and Globalization.* New York: Routledge, 93–104.

Lynch, K. (1960) *The Image of the City.* Boston: Massachusetts Institute of Technology.

MacCannell, D. (1976) *The Tourist: A New Theory of the Leisure Class.* New York: Schocken Books.

Malone, P. (ed.) (1996) *City, Capital and Water.* London: Routledge.

Miles, M. (2005) Interruptions: Testing the rhetoric of culturally led urban development. *Urban Studies*, 42(5–6), 889–911.

Muñoz, F. (2006) Olympic urbanism and Olympic villages: Planning strategies in Olympic host cities, London 1908 to London 2012. *The Sociological Review*, 54(2_suppl), 175–187.

Musso, E., & Bennacchio, M. (2002) Demaritimisation o remaritimisation? L'evoluzione dello scenario economico delle città portuali. In Soriani, S. (ed.) *Porti, città e territorio costiero. Le dinamiche della sostenibilità.* Bologna: Il Mulino, 199–254.

Musso, E., & Ghiara, H. (2009) The economic port landscape: From traffic to remaritimisation. *Portus*, 18, 62–67.

National Lottery Heritage Fund (2019) £13.6 million national lottery boost for Hull's maritime heritage. *National Lottery Heritage Fund*, 10th February. Available at: www.heritagefund.org.uk/news/136million-national-lottery-boost-hulls-maritime-heritage [Accessed 08/11/2019].

Navarro Castelló, C. (2016) El museo marítimo de Valencia tendrá tres sedes y se llamará 'Museu de la Mar'. *El Diario*, 17th September. Available at: www.eldiario.es/cv/maritimo-Valencia-multiespacio-Museu-Mar_0_559594768.html [Accessed 15/05/2020].

Norcliffe, G., Bassett, K., & Hoare, T. (1996) The emergence of postmodernism on the urban waterfront: Geographical perspectives on changing relationships. *Journal of Transport Geography*, 4(2), 123–134.

Parra Camacho, D., Añó Sanz, V., & Calabuig Moreno, F. (2016) Percepción de los residentes sobre el legado de la America's Cup Residents perceptions about the legacy of America's Cup Percepção dos moradores sobre o legado da Copa América. *Cuadernos de Psicología del Deporte*, 16(1), 325–338.

Pijbes, W. (2016) Rotterdam City of Culture and tourist destination: A study. *IABx Rotterdam*. Available at: https://iabrotterdam.com/iab-en/assets/File/Analysis%20by%20Wim%20 Pijbes.pdf [Accessed 22/07/2019].

Porto Antico Spa (2018) Il ritorno della ruota panoramica. *Porto Antico di Genova*, 2nd November. Available at: www.portoantico.it/2018/ritorno-della-ruota-panoramica/ [Accessed 26/05/2020].

Povey, G., & Van Wyk, J.-A. (2010) Culture and the event experience. In Robinson, P., Wale, D., & Dickson, G. (eds.) *Events Management*. Wallingford: CABI, 1–18.

Richards, G. (2007) Culture and authenticity in a traditional event: The views of producers, residents and visitors in Barcelona. *Event Management*, 11, 33–44.

Richards, G., & Wilson, J. (2004) The impact of cultural events on city image: Rotterdam, cultural capital of Europe 2001. *Urban Studies*, 41(10), 1931–1951.

Richards, G., & Wilson, J. (2006) Developing creativity in tourist experiences: A solution to the serial reproduction of culture? *Tourism Management*, 27, 1209–1223.

Robinson, J. (2016) Thinking cities through elsewhere: Comparative tactics for a more global urban studies. *Progress in Human Geography*, 40(1), 3–29.

Rotterdam Partners (2018) Maritiem District. De maritieme oorsprong van Rotterdam. *Rotterdam Tourist Information*. Available at: https://rotterdam.info/gebieden/centrum-gebieden/maritiem-district/ [Accessed 16/08/2019].

Silvestre, G. (2017) Rio de Janeiro 2016. In Gold, J. R., & Gold, M. (eds.) *Olympic Cities: City Agendas, Planning, and the World's Games, 1896–2020*. London and New York: Routledge, 400–423.

Tomlinson, J. (1999) *Globalization and Culture*. Chicago: University of Chicago Press.

Tommarchi, E. (2020) Port cities, heritage cities: A comparative perspective on maritime cultural quarters. *PortusPlus*, 9, 1–18.

Tommarchi, E. (2021) (Re-)generating symbolic port-city links: Urban regeneration and the cultural demaritimisation and remaritimisation of European port cities. *European Journal of Creative Practices in Cities and Landscapes*, 4(1), 59–75.

Tommarchi, E., & Bianchini, F. (2020) Hull UK city of culture 2017. In Ponzini, D., Bianchini, F., Georgi-Tzortzi, J.-N., & Sanetra-Szeliga, J. (eds.) *Mega-Events and Heritage: The Experience of Five European Cities*. Krakow: International Cultural Centre, 184–254. Available at: www.tau-lab.polimi.it [Accessed 09/03/2020].

Tommarchi, E., & Bianchini, F. (2022) A heritage-inspired cultural mega event in a stigmatised city: Hull UK City of Culture 2017. *European Planning Studies*, 30(3), 478–498.

Tunbridge, J. E., & Ashworth, G. J. (1996) *Dissonant Heritage: The Management of the Past as a Resource in Conflict*. Chichester: John Wiley & Sons.

Tzonis, A. (1993) The Kop van Zuid project in Rotterdam. In Bruttomess, R. (ed.) *Waterfronts: A New Frontier for Cities on Water*. Venice: Centro Internazionale Città d'Acqua, 157–157.

Van Hooydonk, E. (2007) *Soft Values of Seaports: A Strategy for the Restoration of Public Support of Seaports*. Antwerp: Garant.

Van Hooydonk, E. (2009) Port City Identity and Urban Planning. *Portus*, 18, 16–23.

Van Tuijl, E., & Van den Berg, L. (2016) Annual city festivals as tools for sustainable competitiveness: The World Port Days Rotterdam. *Economies*, 4(11), 1–13.

Wacquant, L. (2007) Territorial stigmatization in the age of advanced marginality. *Thesis Eleven*, 91(1), 66–77.

Wacquant, L. (2008) *Urban Outcasts: A Comparative Sociology of Advanced Marginality*. Cambridge: Polity Press.

Wacquant, L., Slater, T., & Pereira, V. B. (2014) Territorial stigmatization in action. *Environment and Planning A*, 46, 1270–1280.

Wang, N. (1999) Rethinking authenticity in tourism experience. *Annals of Tourism Research*, 26(2), 349–370.

Ward, S. (2011) Port cities and the global exchange of planning ideas. In Hein, C. (ed.) *Port Cities: Dynamic Landscapes and Global Networks*. London and New York: Routledge, 70–85.

Zukin, S. (2006 [1995]) *The Cultures of Cities*. Cambridge and Oxford: Blackwell.

8   Conclusions

A forward look at port cities of culture and events

The book has explored mega events and related processes of event-led regeneration in the context of port-city relationships, in particular across Europe. A comparative analysis of event-led regeneration in four European port cities – with additional examples from other port cities across the world – has examined the mutual influence between these processes and the spatial, socio-cultural and symbolic relationships between ports and cities. The main rationale for this study has been the recognition that, although a substantial number of culture- and event-led regeneration schemes have been implemented in port cities, little attention has been devoted to understanding how these processes influence – and are influenced by – the maritime character of these cities. This interest stems from the idea that European port cities display cultural exceptionalism (Belchem, 2000; Bianchini & Bloomfield, 2012; Mah, 2014) because of their history as maritime gateways to the outer world. The book has shown that culture- and event-led regeneration schemes are not necessarily different when they are implemented in maritime port cities. As a matter of fact, event-led regeneration in these cities is guided by forms of urban entrepreneurialism, as in any other city. Nevertheless, the way in which these schemes are delivered, and their spatial, socio-economic and symbolic legacy may present particular features which need to be explored considering the exceptionalism of these cities. Although other factors such as maritime trade patterns have far more prominent a role in the evolution of port-city relationships, mega events and event-led regeneration do produce impacts on these relationships, which may emerge in the long term in combination with broader processes of socio-economic restructuring. What distinguishes event-led regeneration in port cities is that, despite being driven by transitory occasions such as mega events, it tends to encourage the permanent presence of people and activity at the port-city interface and in former port areas. In turn, mega events and event-led regeneration are also shaped – whether unintentionally or as a political choice – by the maritime character of these cities and their spatial, functional and symbolic ties with their ports. The main contribution of the book is that it enriches the study of mega events taking into account the exceptionalism of port cities, while at the same time it explores culture- and event-led regeneration as a factor influencing – albeit contingently – the evolution of port-city relationships.

DOI: 10.4324/9781003165811-8

It also considers the 'size' of mega events from a relative perspective, on the basis of the context where these events are held, rather than relying on standard definitions or quantitative thresholds.

In this final chapter, firstly, the key arguments of the book are summarised, looking at the spatial, political and symbolic aspects of event-led regeneration in port cities. Secondly, a heuristic model to interpret event-led regeneration cycles in port cities is introduced. Thirdly, the wider implications of the book are commented upon against broader issues such as the study of the evolution of port-city relationships; the changing nature and meaning of waterfront redevelopment; the politics of economic development; the role of local meanings in event-led regeneration. Fourthly, some reflections on the future trajectories of the core case-study cities are presented. Finally, policy recommendations for European port cities of culture and events are outlined, together with a potential agenda for future research.

The nexus between mega events and port-city relationships: key aspects

Event-led regeneration has been examined in the book in relation to the spatial, political and symbolic dimensions of the ties between ports and cities. The next sections summarise the key takeaways emerging from this study.

The spatiality of event-led regeneration in port cities

Chapter 5 has shown how event-led regeneration may produce rather different outcomes at the port-city interface, ranging from marginal transformation and refurbishments (e.g. Hull and Rotterdam) to the reconversion of large former port areas (e.g. Genoa and Valencia). The extent of event-led transformation in any city is of course a matter of political intention. In the case of the port-city interface, this also depends on whether former port areas have already undergone processes of redevelopment. In other words, the spatiality of event-led regeneration at the port-city interface is directly linked to the position and trajectory of the host city along Hoyle's model of port-city relationships.

Mega events and event-led regeneration do not necessarily impact substantially on the spatial competition between cities and ports. Current port-city conflicts are more likely to emerge at the interface between working port areas and urban fringe areas, where port development and urbanisation are in direct competition for space. This relatively mild tension between cultural and port uses can be explained considering the transitory character of mega events and that many of the functions they introduce are temporary. In addition, permanent cultural and urban uses introduced by mega events and event-led regeneration are located mostly in abandoned former port areas.

However, sources of spatial port-city conflicts in the case of mega events and event-led regeneration do emerge. Firstly, port land ownership is a crucial factor in these processes. One could argue that event-led regeneration may be facilitated by public ownership of port areas and that it may be more difficult to implement large-scale regeneration schemes in privately owned port areas. Nonetheless, state ownership of abandoned port areas may lead to lengthy and complex negotiations, sometimes within unclear institutional frameworks, eventually hampering event-led regeneration altogether. Secondly, the unintended spatial outcomes of mega events and event-led regeneration in the long term may be a source of substantial spatial and political port-city conflict. Thirdly, although waterfront redevelopment in European port cities largely tends to recover the physical connection between these cities and their waterfront – which in many cases was lost due to the development of modern industrial ports and subsequently to their restructuring – a full permeability of waterfront areas is hardly achieved. This is in part due to remnants of port infrastructure and facilities that are neither redeveloped nor perceived as heritage. These remnants may include, for example, port ring roads (whether or not in use), material and immaterial port 'borders' that are retained as a result of failed (or lacking) negotiations with state-run or private port authorities, light maritime functions located in formerly industrial spaces which raise issues of safety and security.

The politics of event-led regeneration in maritime port cities

Chapter 6 has shown how port authorities may engage with mega events, especially where they have traditionally supported arts and culture. The fact that port authorities, regardless of their agendas, are increasingly interested in engaging with the city's cultural life, suggests a reshaping of port-city relationships around different conditions, values and meanings, where culture plays a relevant role. This interest should be read in relation to two aspects. Firstly, the quest of ports for legitimation and public acceptance of maritime activities against their negative socio-economic and environmental externalities. Secondly, the growing awareness that port competitiveness is closely connected with the attractiveness of port cities. In this case, culture is part of promotion strategies linked to public support and port competitiveness, in the context of strong local dependence in which port actors operate. In some cases, this interest might be related to the emergence of forms of enlightened capitalism, where certain port companies recognise their social responsibility and seek to play a greater role in the city's cultural life.

Arguably, one of the elements that distinguish contemporary port-city relationships is the fact that the development and competitiveness of ports are tied to how their cities perform in interurban competition. As a consequence, both port development and culture-led regeneration are addressed in the spatial strategies of many port cities. This leads to the juxtaposition of partially overlapping, yet potentially clashing, imaginaries related to the 'port city' and the 'city of culture', as exemplified by the policy discourses of 'energy port city' and 'world-class visitor destination' within Hull's City Plan 2013. In this context, maritime activities are more economically relevant, while cultural activities are understood as a catalyst for urban regeneration and development, ultimately contributing to the growth and competitiveness of the port.

If it is true that there is evidence of an increasing interest of port actors in culture and the city's cultural life, it is not necessarily the case that urban policy makers are more open to embrace port city culture as the backbone of local identities. Policy makers in European port cities may use event-led regeneration as a means to reframe, minimise or get rid of the maritime image of their cities. A more or less intentional neglect of local maritime identities may be driven by the willingness of policy makers to free their cities from the 'disadvantage' of hosting a port. This perceived 'disadvantage' is linked with the stigmatisation of port cities as deprived, dangerous and polluted places and with the fierce interurban competition resulting from the hegemonic global capitalism. Such willingness of policy makers to transform port cities into ordinary cities is arguably driven by the belief that this would allow them to compete with non-port cities on the same grounds and possibly more effectively than in the past.

As in the case of spatial port-city links, no substantial culture-related tension appears to emerge between port and urban actors in the case-study cities of the book as a direct result of mega events and event-led regeneration processes. The transitory character of the former and the fact that the latter generally focuses on abandoned port areas – through negotiations and agreements between city councils and port authorities – are the main reasons. Despite the myth of the rebellious attitude of port cities, most of the events analysed did not trigger substantial opposition from residents. It is suggested here that this acceptance could in some cases be explained by considering the collapse of the industrial port city model, to which culture- and event-led regeneration were perceived as a response. In addition, this is also related to the fact that contemporary class struggle does not follow conventional class division, for example due to the fragmentation of the maritime working class into a myriad of social groups and sub-cultures.

Nevertheless, Chapter 4 has underlined where political struggle and activism develop. Much of the research on mega events and event-led regeneration deals with their direct, short-term impacts of these processes. However, if one embarks on the task of approaching the indirect outcomes and the legacy of mega events and event-led regeneration against long-term structural processes of spatial and socio-economic restructuring of maritime port cities, socio-political conflict is revealed. It is argued here that mega events and event-led regeneration in European port cities, whereby the negative impacts of deindustrialisation were tackled, may have put down the foundations for, or contributed to, structural processes such as gentrification and touristification. In many port cities, these processes are generating substantial conflicts among residents, port actors and local institutions. For example, a recurring theme in the literature on urban entrepreneurialism is that culture- and event-led regeneration have been deployed as a means to rebrand many declining port cities as tourist destinations. Considering that this rebranding exercise is now commonplace, one could wonder whether certain ports are becoming tourist attractions themselves, as in the case of Rotterdam and Genoa. An increased attractiveness of port cities and of port cityscapes is arguably one of the factors behind the remarkable growth of cruise tourism in cities such as Barcelona, Genoa, Màlaga, Marseille and Rotterdam, and activism against overtourism in some of these cities. These structural processes increase both inward and outward pressures on urban port areas, fuelled by the growth of certain maritime activities and the proliferation of waterfront redevelopment and culture-led regeneration schemes at the port-city interface. Such pressures thus require more complex political negotiations between ports and cities.

The symbolic connections between event-led regeneration and port-city links

The aforementioned tensions are visible in many event led regeneration schemes across European port cities, which are shaped to promote a sanitisation and reframing of local port city cultures in a number of ways. These include the promotion of partial or distorted narratives of local maritime history and heritage, the delivery of cultural events celebrating specific aspects of local maritime identities and promoting certain ways to relate to the waterfront, the homogenisation of urban space at the water's edge and the mobilisation of water – rather than local port city cultures – as a branding device. These phenomena are not dissimilar from the homogenisation of regenerated urban areas and the promotion of inauthentic culture which are driven by processes of capital accumulation and by entrepreneurial governance in non-port cities. However, they generate particular impacts on port cities due to the specificity of these contexts.

In Chapter 7, and building on Tommarchi (2021), the concepts of cultural demaritimisation and cultural remaritimisation have been introduced to discuss these processes. Cultural demaritimisation has been used to describe the loss of aspects of local port city cultures or the loss of maritime heritage assets, suggesting that the maritime character of certain port cities is being sanitised or deprioritised against other aspects of the city's identity (e.g. generalist cultural consumption). Conversely, the concept of cultural remaritimisation has been deployed to comment on the growing attention to and celebration of port city culture locally, through either the restoration of maritime heritage assets and traditional maritime narratives or the construction of a new maritime image of the city. Chapter 7 has shown how the recovery of existing assets and aspects of local port city culture can be attempted through the establishment of maritime cultural quarters, while a newly constructed port city image may rely more on the symbolic connection of water rather than on the city's maritime tradition.

These processes, emerging either as the unintended outcome or the deliberate goal of cultural urban policies, may fail to take into account the 'actually existing' symbolic links between cities and ports. For example, the replication of standardised strategies or supposedly successful templates may raise issues of misalignment with the significance that is attributed to ports and maritime history and heritage. This departure from local meanings implies the neglect of existing port-city links, which, in the case of mega events and event-led regeneration, may generate opposition against these schemes or may lead to their partial or total ineffectiveness where they stand in conflict with strong local port city cultures.

Finally, it is worth interrogating on the role of mega events in raising awareness of port cultures and fuelling the interest of port city dwellers in contemporary maritime practices. In Chapter 7, it has been argued that highly engaging cultural events and mega events can be effective platforms for disseminating port culture and engaging residents and visitors with the (current) activity of the port. However, it has also been shown that the consumption of port culture still relies on rather specialist audiences. Mega events and event-led regeneration appear to be more effective in encouraging residents and visitors to engage with maritime history and heritage and in boosting civic pride.

A heuristic framework to explore trajectories of culture- and event-led regeneration within port-city relationships

Mega events and event-led regeneration have stepped into the macro-phenomenon of port-city relationships, albeit producing a relatively small impact in comparison with other structural processes. This section outlines a heuristic model of culture- and event-led regeneration in port cities. Such a heuristic model is tied to Hoyle's model and allows us to explore aspects of contemporary port-city relationships that are not commonly taken into account in port city studies, such as changing attitudes and meanings attributed to waterfront areas and the pressures on port areas generated by cultural activity (Table 8.1).

It is important to note that this heuristic model only works for European port cities and, at best, for some port cities in other parts of the world. This is due to the fact that port-city relationships display different patterns as a result of rather diverse generative processes behind them (see e.g. Lee et al., 2008). The case-study cities can be mapped on the four stages of the model explained here. Hull is at the end of stage II. Valencia is at the beginning of stage III, after a long and troubled 'post-event' period. It could be argued that Genoa is at stage III, while Rotterdam is arguably facing the issues associated with stage IV.

Port restructuring and the rationale for event-led regeneration (I)

The starting point of this model is Hoyle's (2000) idea of the 'retreat from the waterfront', which portrays how technological advancements and changes in international trade patterns triggered the abandonment of port areas in central city locations. This built the rationale for incorporating these areas into the city, and culture- and event-led regeneration were seen as a means to achieve this repurposing.

Table 8.1 The role of culture- and event-led urban regeneration in port-city relationships.

I. **BUILDING THE RATIONALE FOR CULTURE-/EVENT-LED REGENERATION** *(Corresponding to 'retreat from the waterfront' – Hoyle, 1988, 1989, 2000)*
- Inner harbours/former urban port areas are abandoned and fenced off
- Port-city physical separation; non-permeability of waterfronts
- The decay of these areas builds the rationale for/generates momentum around waterfront redevelopment

II. **KICK-START OF CULTURE-/EVENT-LED REGENERATION – RECONNECTION WITH THE WATERFRONT**
- Big events/spectacles to either launch culture-led regeneration strategies (Genoa 1992, Valencia 2007) or celebrate the redevelopment of inner harbours (Rotterdam 2001, Hull 2017)
- No tension in this phase between cultural/urban uses and port uses – culture-/event-led regeneration involve areas that are no longer interesting for the port

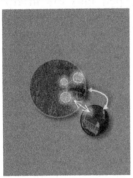

III. **GRADUAL RECONNECTION WITH THE WATERFRONT THROUGH CULTURE-/EVENT-LED REGENERATION**
- Legacy/process of gradual reconnection between the city and its waterfront
- Further smaller-scale culture-/event-led regeneration schemes and supporting strategies of waterfront redevelopment
- More structured maritime cultural strategies (e.g. maritime cultural quarters)
- Spillovers of regeneration; more pressure on waterfront areas
- Possible tension in relation to the growing permanent presence of people at the port-city interface; port-city conflicts are still largely unrelated to culture-/event-led regeneration

IV. **MATURE PORT CITIES OF CULTURE – FURTHER COMPLEXITY ON THE WATERFRONT** *(May overlap with the 'renewal of port-city links' stage – Hoyle, 2000)*
- Cities and ports appear to be increasingly connected – e.g. port regionalisation, greater need for high-skilled workers
- Renewed interest in urban port areas for (light) maritime activities (light port industries, cruise/ferry terminals, managerial functions, maritime services, etc.)
- Culture-/event-led regeneration contribute to fostering gentrification, growth of cruise tourism, touristification, pressure on waterfront areas; further schemes may be implemented in the periphery or along the port-city interface
- Potential conflict between cultural/urban uses and (lighter) port uses

Source: Author's work, inspired by Hoyle (2000). Background maps from Google Maps: Imagery ©2020 Ajuntament de València, Instituto Cartografico Valenciano, CNES/Airbus, Landsat/Copernicus, Maxar Technologies, Map data ©2020 Inst. Geogr. Nacional.

Kick-start of culture-led regeneration and attempts of reconnection with the waterfront (II)

Although some caveats and adaptations must be put in place in those cities where non-culture-led waterfront redevelopment processes started before any of these strategies were implemented, it is possible to distinguish a phase of kick-start of culture- and event-led regeneration. In Europe, in the 1990s and the beginning of the 21st century, mega events and ambitious culture-led regeneration schemes have been implemented in many port cities. In some of these cities, such as Barcelona and Genoa, mega events have triggered long-term processes of urban regeneration. In other cities such as Rotterdam, mega events have played a different role, as they celebrated the outcomes of urban regeneration policies. In either case, an initial event or culture-led regeneration scheme triggered longer-term processes of regeneration or marked the beginning of a different policy approach to the role of culture. The 1992 Specialist Expo kick-started the redevelopment of Genoa's Porto Antico, while the ECoC 2001 in Rotterdam contributed to framing the role of culture as a place-making device.

In this stage, while conflicts continue to take place along the port–city interface, no substantial tension arising from these schemes is visible. This does not mean that such processes are uncontroversial: the little tension associated with them is related to the fact that regeneration processes take place in abandoned port areas, surrendered to city councils under port–city agreements.

Gradual culture-led urban development and reconnection with the waterfront (III)

The experience of the four case-study cities suggests that the processes triggered through mega events and other schemes are usually followed by other, not necessarily related actions which foster a gradual – either physical or symbolic – reconnection with the waterfront. Nevertheless, this phase should not be interpreted as the intrinsic legacy of initial mega events or culture-led schemes. Subsequent policies may take place after an initial 'cliff-edge effect' (Tommarchi et al., 2018, p. 162) in the immediate aftermath of mega events and may be disconnected from or even in opposition with the strategy underpinning initial schemes. For example, a change of local government may lead to the implementation of culture-led regeneration policies which nonetheless act in discontinuity with previous approaches. Similarly, some of the actors involved in the initial process may not take part in future schemes.

The idea of the reconnection with the waterfront, which underpins a gradual takeover of former port areas by urban functions, may continue to be included in culture-led regeneration strategies and policy documents. Policy makers may bid for and deliver other mega events in the attempt of retaining momentum. Smaller-scale schemes may be implemented along the port–city interface and usually consolidate the achievements of the previous phase. More structured policies may be implemented, for example in the case of maritime cultural quarters. These processes may generate spillovers and may cause port-city tension in relation to an increased permanent presence of people and activities in these areas.

Mature port cities of culture (IV)

Some European port cities where these processes have taken place may have stepped into the final stage of the proposed model, which may parallel the last stage of Hoyle's model depicting a renewal of port-city links. In this case, culture- and event-led regeneration processed are consolidated, while more complex interrelations with other aspects of port-city relationships are visible. These interrelations arise from a renewed interest in urban port areas for maritime activities, such as light maritime industries, cruise and ferry terminals, maritime services such as shipping, brokering and insurance, port authorities and companies' headquarters. This can be interpreted as a result of a retightening of port-city relationships under different conditions than those at the basis of the industrial port city. The long-term impacts of culture- and event-led regeneration, influenced by structural processes such as touristification and the gentrification of maritime working-class districts, contribute to port-city tension and conflicts. Smaller-scale events or regeneration schemes may be implemented in the periphery or further along the port-city interface, putting pressure on working port areas.

Implications for port city and mega-event studies

The analysis of event-led regeneration in European maritime port cities undertaken in the previous chapters raises a number of issues for both port city and mega event studies in the 21st century. This is particularly the case for the study of the evolution of port-city relationships, the changing meaning of waterfronts and their redevelopment, the politics of economic development and the growing importance of local values and meanings in the context of mega events. The wider implications of the book are therefore examined against these themes.

Understanding the role of mega events in 21st-century port-city relationships

As pointed out in Chapter 2, mega events and event-led regeneration contribute – either directly or contingently – to the urban takeover of former port areas and the rise of the city – rather than the port – as the driving force of urban development. Direct transformation at the port-city interface is not the only way in which event-led regeneration may contribute to this. Mega events and event-led regeneration also act on the city's attractiveness, contingently fuelling urban pressures at the interface. In the long term, these processes may also encourage or operate in combination with structural processes of socio-economic restructuring, and generate greater pressure on working port areas. This builds a stronger case for taking into account processes of culture- or event-led regeneration in the study of port-city relationships.

However, mega events and event-led regeneration may also help promote a shift from 'port out, city in' logics to more balanced strategies. The former approach, characterising many waterfront redevelopment schemes, entails the complete replacement of maritime-related activities with housing, commercial, retail or leisure functions (i.e. the urban takeover mentioned earlier), which put pressures on the port-city interface. In the case of the latter strategies, some port activities are retained on redeveloped waterfronts as integral parts of these environments rather than remnants of their past. Such an approach promotes a richer blend of functions and portrays what future urban waterfronts could look like. In the case of event-led regeneration, these more balanced redevelopments may be the outcome of the adaptation of mega-event schemes to local values and meanings. In 'mature' port cities of culture, port authorities and companies may be more involved in the city's cultural and political life. This may encourage a broader cooperation with urban actors beyond the domain of cultural policy and thus tighter political port-city relationships. Nevertheless, the clash between imaginaries of the 'cultural city' – fuelled by event-led regeneration – and traditional narratives of the 'port city' may influence port development and urban planning strategies.

Port cities are exceptional cases because of the presence of the port-city interface as a liminal geographical space between the city and the port as socio-spatial and political entities. Such a space epitomises the tension between local forces (local stakes, values and meanings) and global pressures (in this case, coming in particular from maritime world trade) that characterises relational understandings of contemporary urbanism. A wider recognition of the role of the symbolic aspects of urban regeneration – alongside its spatial and political outcomes – is needed in the analysis of port-city socio-spatial tension. Symbolic aspects such as the framing of maritime narratives and imaginaries through event-led regeneration are significant, yet underexplored factors in the evolution of port-city relationships.

Beyond waterfront redevelopment

'Port out, city in' logics have been behind attempts to transform many declining port cities into 'waterfront cities'. Historic port areas have often been spoiled of their maritime character and incorporated into the urban fabric through waterfront redevelopment, which has introduced commercial, housing, cultural and leisure functions in these areas. In some cases, once thriving port city cultures have been reduced to marketing devices for real estate operations. The longer-term perspective of the book has helped build backward and forward connections among mega events, structural processes impacting on the port-city interface (e.g. the touristification of European port cities) and broader planning and policy issues (e.g. the reframing of long-term spatial and economic development strategies), which all contribute to reshaping new spaces of waterfront redevelopment.

Mega events and event-led regeneration contributed to fundamentally changing the very nature and meaning of urban waterfronts. Many of these once maritime or industrial environments have become sites for cultural production (as they attract artists and creative industries) but more importantly consumption, as they are increasingly associated with leisure. This cultural change is visible for example in the way in which the very term 'waterfront' has become synonym for leisure spaces at the water's edge or for sites of exclusive forms of urban living (as an expression the post-modern values mentioned by Norcliffe et al., 1996). Waterfronts shape once again the skylines of European maritime port cities. The redevelopment of these spaces transformed port cityscapes from derelict industrial areas into an element of civic pride. However, this transformation is yet to be complete. Issues of land ownership, unclear distribution of competences among institutions, the partial failure of certain culture- or event-led regeneration schemes and difficult negotiations among multiple actors mean that the full permeability of waterfronts is seldom achieved. As a result, non-regenerated spaces, physical or intangible port-city boundaries may act to the detriment of the public use of these areas. These issues underline the need for mixed methods in the analysis of the port-city interface, combining spatial and governance approaches. The interface should be understood, as suggested by Daamen and Vries (2013, p. 6), as constituted by 'a pluralistic community of actors' and should also be embedded into the relational – yet territorialised – space of urban politics.

Nonetheless, the book has hinted at examples of future waterfronts in the making. Experiences such as Rotterdam's Makers District suggest that future urban waterfronts in port cities may blend urban and cultural functions with light industrial or maritime-related uses. On the one hand, culture- or event-led regeneration can contribute to reinstating or creating a renewed port city culture on these changing waterfronts. On the other hand, a more balanced mix of functions may free future urban waterfronts from the excessive reliance on cultural consumption and leisure that has been marking the last decades. This latter point is of particular relevance considering the negative impacts of consumption-oriented redevelopment strategies (e.g. gentrification and overtourism) and the fact that consumption patterns may be disrupted, as happened with the COVID-19 outbreak.

Governance, urban growth and the politics of local economic development

Mega events and event-led regeneration have been criticised due to their nature of urban spectacle, their 'exceptionality alibi' and their role in promoting entrepreneurial urban agendas and revanchist urbanism. In European port cities, they are often tools to redesign waterfronts or reframe their meaning to target affluent households and cultural consumers, in the attempt to profit from urban growth and real estate development. This often translates into 'revanchist' forms of control and policing of public spaces, which in the case of the port-city interface may be exacerbated by issues of security in and around ports.

Mega events can be interpreted as delivered by coalitions of interest. Coalitions of local actors – including city and regional councils, port authorities and companies, event promoters – emerge around these events in European port cities. Of course, the rationale for these actors to join coalitions of interest around mega events varies. However, the involvement of key local actors may be the result of political pressures and expectations arising from the very nature of mega events, as for certain actors such as port authorities it is not a viable option to avoid engaging with them.

Coalitions of interest around mega events usually take the form of pro-growth coalitions, directly seeking urban growth and profit. In some cases, where these coalitions operate through aggressive strategies and undemocratic or controversial processes, North American conceptualisations of the city as a growth machine (Molotch, 1976) may successfully be applied to the study of certain mega events in European cities. Nonetheless, event-driven coalitions in port cities develop around a range of strategies to pursue economic development. These may include countering the stigma of being a disadvantaged maritime port city (Hull), assisting port competitiveness (Rotterdam), reconverting vast former port areas that would hardly be regenerated otherwise (Barcelona, Genoa and Rio de Janeiro), branding the city – not necessarily in relation to its maritime heritage and culture – as a tourist destination to pursue urban growth (Barcelona, Cape Town, Singapore and Valencia), attracting public funding from central governments (where local policy makers feel they have been 'left behind' by the state, as in Genoa, Valencia and, to some extent, Hull), counteracting 'inferiority complexes' towards other cities (e.g. Rotterdam vs. Amsterdam and Valencia vs. Barcelona), building political consensus locally or nationally (Valencia), pursuing socio-economic regeneration (Hull). Due to recurrent challenges such as the socio-economic impacts of port restructuring, geographical and political isolation or the political struggle with the state, policy makers in port cities are arguably likely to adopt strategies that can be described as urban diplomacy or urban speculation (as defined by Phelps & Miao, 2020). This helps explain the 'pioneering' attitude of port city policy makers towards event-led regeneration (as mentioned in Chapter 1), considering that mega events are ideal platforms to implement entrepreneurial strategies of this kind.

Coalitions of interest empower certain actors and disempower others. For example, mega events create the rationale for establishing post-event or permanent 'culture companies' (e.g. Absolutely Cultured Ltd, Rotterdam Festivals[1]) or leisure harbour management bodies (e.g. Porto Antico Spa and La Marina de València). However, the negative consequences of mega events may affect the credibility of certain actors, as in the case of Valencia's Regional Council. Other actors are disempowered through mega events, such as certain individuals and groups (e.g. local artists and cultural organisations in Hull who felt detached from the UK City of Culture), activist groups (e.g. anti-F1 collectives in Valencia) or those local communities who do not benefit from these events and yet have to cope with their negative externalities (e.g. El Cabanyal-El Canyamelar and Natzaret residents in Valencia).

Mega events provide pro-growth coalitions in port and non-port cities with exceptional circumstances that help them override ordinary or commonly acceptable practices to pursue their goals. Exceptional measures may include *ad hoc* planning tools and fast-tracked procedures displaying ambiguous legal bases. Despite the lack of substantial opposition against mega events in European port cities, which to some extent questions assumptions about the universal rebellious character of these cities, event-led regeneration processes may display very little consultation and participation, especially in the case of residents and local organisations who experience the negative externalities of these events. In some cases, policy makers circumnavigate local democratic politics and planning procedures to secure and deliver mega events, as in the case of Valencia, where promoters worked within the grey areas of local and national regulations to host the America's Cup and Formula 1 and where populist political tactics were deployed to build political consensus around the events.

The quest for urban growth is arguably the primary reason behind the willingness of policy makers to get rid of the port-related image to counteract the negative external perceptions related to deprivation, unemployment or crime that characterise many European port cities. Mega events are platforms for this operation, as they create the conditions for reframing and disseminating – and also building public acceptance around – new maritime narratives and imaginaries of the 21st century, globalised 'waterfront city'.

The role of local meanings in the promotion and consumption of mega events in European port cities

Connecting with local meanings is increasingly important in the context of mega events. On the one hand, as a result of their exceptionality, visibility and magnitude, these events have a significant impact on the daily lives of host communities and the way in which residents and visitors attribute meaning to a place. On the other hand, context-specificities and local meanings strongly influence mega events and their legacy. Arguably, the role of meaning-making processes is gaining relevance as mega events are being questioned. It appears reasonable to suggest that this trend will be fuelled by the socio-economic and cultural impacts of the COVID-19 pandemic, as cultural events and mega events may need to be reimagined in relation to changing public attitudes towards gatherings.

In port cities, the way in which mega events relate to port city cultures and actually existing symbolic port-city links is fundamental. To different extents, mega events and event-led regeneration are place-making devices as they are a means to 'design' or 'manage' the way in which residents and visitors engage with local maritime cultures and waterfronts. However, when the goals and expectations of event-led regeneration are misaligned with local specificities and meanings, unintended consequences may disrupt port-city relationships and contribute to the failure of mega events and their legacy. The 'imposition' of certain values and meanings – for example redeveloped waterfront areas targeting tourists and the middle-class, to the detriment of local cultures, heritage and communities – is likely to generate opposition in the form of protests and activism. Engagement activities – for example volunteering programmes – within the framework of mega events are a recurrent feature across host cities: they can operate either as a means to seek broader participation and improve social cohesion, or as a tool to construct public acceptance around these events and stifle opposition.

The place-making role of mega events and event-led regeneration can deeply influence local port city cultures. These processes are powerful tools for policy makers to convey, reframe or prioritise certain maritime narratives, according to their agenda. Yet, the consumers of mega events – attendees, visitors, local communities – bring their own values and meanings into the process and ultimately contribute to shaping events and their legacy (e.g. in the case of fishing narratives in Hull). In this context, mega events may contribute to the cultural demaritimisation of port cities – where elements of local maritime cultures are eroded or lost – and their remaritimisation, where new, potentially inauthentic elements are introduced. Such processes may contribute to transforming port cities into coastal or riverside cities, depriving them of all aspects of their maritime character but their proximity to water.

The future of four port cities of culture

A brief overview of opportunities and threats related to culture- and event-led regeneration and port-city relationships in the core case-study cities helps set the scene to discuss future research perspectives in the next section. In each of these cities, policy makers are dealing with specific challenges arising from culture- and event-led regeneration, increased attractiveness as places of consumption and the evolution of port cities relationships.

Hull: port, culture, 'political insularity' and climate change

One of the threats to the legacy of the UKCoC 2017 in Hull is arguably related to the current political climate in the city. The local results, discussed in Chapter 4, of the 2016 EU referendum, the 2019 European Elections and the 2019 General Elections, together with the data on electoral turnout, show that Hull is among the areas of the UK where populism and post-politics are hitting the most. If the UKCoC 2017 has contributed to circulating positive narratives of Hull as an outward-looking port city of culture, there is evidence of a rising climate of 'political tribalism' (as defined by Chua, 2018) and isolationism and of the emergence of accounts of Hull as an inward-looking, insular place. As in part happened in Rotterdam, such climate risks undermining the legacy of the event, potentially hampering international partnerships and downscaling the city's role as a cultural capital. As the UK left the EU in early 2020 and trade patterns with the bloc are being reshaped, port development faces both opportunities and threats, arising from the prospect of Hull becoming a 'free port'.

Hull also epitomises the opportunities and threats for port-city relationships and event-led regeneration at the port-city interface in relation to climate change. Since it is located on a flood plain by the Humber Estuary, Hull is particularly at risk due to rising sea levels. Ambitious projects such as Lagoon Hull (which aims to move the urban section of the A63 on a flood defence structure on the Humber, BBC, 2019; Lagoon Hull, n.d.) may redefine port-city relationships and reshape the waterfront. The UKCoC 2017 may have contributed to fuelling a debate on the role of culture in these processes, as well as more generally in policy making in the context of climate change.[2]

Rotterdam: embracing the post-oil transition

As mentioned, Rotterdam may arguably be considered as being in the last stage outlined in the proposed model. As a result of a 20-year event policy and a four-decade experience in waterfront redevelopment, culture is commonly understood as a place-making device. Although the city's event policy may be considered over now, cultural events, including large-scale ones, still play an important role. Undoubtedly, the attractiveness of Rotterdam has been increasing since the 1990s, in part as the result of the Council's policy agenda. In addition, the port of Rotterdam may be slowly becoming a tourist attraction *per se*, despite it being less and less part of the everyday lives of Rotterdammers.

Yet, interviews with local informants suggest that petrochemical activities at the port are at the beginning of their demise. The port may be entering a phase of profound restructuring, as a result of the transition to a post-oil economy. This means that large port facilities such as the Europoort may become obsolete and it is not certain whether these areas would be reincorporated, with new functions, into the working port. In addition, new, lighter maritime-related activities are colonising the city's urban waterfronts, generating innovative urban blends encompassing commercial functions and housing. As in the case of Hull, the emerging non-fossil economy is strongly connected with port activity, although it is no longer framed as port economy but more broadly as 'maritime cluster'. If the awareness among policy makers of the role of culture as a place-making device has increased in the last decades, the question is whether and how culture can coexist with – and contribute to facilitating the blending of – these functions, playing once again the role of catalyst for urban development on the waterfront.

Genoa: port, urban waterfronts and populism

Policy makers, port actors and experts in Genoa believe that the 'mega-event era' in the city has ended. Policy makers appear more interested in smaller-scale cultural events that are perceived to be more in line with local meanings.

However, this does not mean that waterfront redevelopment or culture- and event-led regeneration at the port-city interface are no longer interesting to them. Rather, the Blueprint vision shows the ambition of pursuing further waterfront redevelopment towards the southeast, with the ambitious goal of creating the longest waterfront – again, understood as indissolubly linked with leisure – on the Mediterranean. The implementation of this scheme is intrinsically tied to port development: Genoa is one of the largest and busiest ports on the Mediterranean, while port activities still play a crucial role in the local economy. Cruise tourism is developing and may soon need more space, should pre-2020 trends resume after COVID-19.

All this suggests that Genoa may be experiencing a clash between the spatial imaginaries of the 'port' and the 'cultural' city. Such port-city tension would need political leadership and mediation to be addressed. However, the rise of populism and post-politics was mentioned by many interviewees as a key challenge for the future of port-city relationships. Personal clashes and political tribalism may be behind a lack of leadership and dialogue. Ultimately, and conversely from the political climate behind the transformation of Porto Antico, this hampers the development of shared visions based on mutual trust and dialogue among port actors, local institutions, cultural organisations and risks undermining the legacy of event-led regeneration in terms of reconnection of the city with the sea and its maritime character.

Valencia: rebuilding port-city relationships

The case of Valencia shows how a political project of reframing of port-city links that overlooks local meanings may generate socio-spatial tension at the port-city interface. Undoubtedly, mega events contributed to repositioning Valencia and to boost its tourist economy. Yet, this was achieved at high social costs. After the splendours of the five-year mega-event era, Valencians had to deal with its legacy: the need to manage a hardly recoverable public debt, to make sense of event infrastructure and facilities, to counteract an 'event-induced' port-city separation and to internalise the new connection of the city with the sea. Furthermore, port development has produced social opposition to port activities. And the port is on the verge of another leap in scale.

Some of these issues may be addressed through cultural activity. Since 2015, and with the establishment of La Marina de València as the company responsible for the management of the harbour, the vision for the Dársena shifted towards the issues of productive activation, the role of the harbour as a public space and connection with the city and economic sustainability (Marrades, 2018). The emerging cultural role of La Marina de València may be an opportunity to revitalise the partially redeveloped historic harbour. This could take place through culture-led regeneration processes that are more connected with local history, heritage and meanings, such as the creation of a maritime cultural quarter around the proposed Museu de la Mar. Such activities may reconcile residents with the inner harbour and the waterfront, allowing them to establish their own relationship with these spaces. APV could play a role in this, consolidating its cultural role.

However, the increased attractiveness of Valencia is putting pressure on maritime urban districts and on the port-city interface. Gentrification and touristification, especially in El Cabanyal-El Canyamelar, may produce further negative impacts on socio-spatial and symbolic port-city relationships. Similarly, there is the risk that speculative and aggressive approaches to the redevelopment of mega-event spaces, such as Valencia Street Circuit, hinder the opportunity to achieve greater permeability at the port-city interface.

Where to go next? Policy recommendations and further research perspectives on port cities of culture and events

In a moment of rapidly evolving port-city relationships, profound societal and political change and economic turmoil, the regenerative role of mega events in port cities that emerged as a response to deindustrialisation needs to be reimagined. In other words, what future port cities of culture and events ought to look like? As a conclusion to the book, this final section examines a number of aspects of this nexus to which port city policy makers and scholars could devote their efforts. Firstly, a series of recommendations addressed to port city policy makers wishing to pursue event-led regeneration are outlined. Secondly, building on the limitations of the book, a research agenda for port city scholars is presented.

Recommendations to port cities of culture

The book has explored the crucial role of local policy makers in shaping trajectories of culture- and event-led regeneration in port cities and their long-term impacts on spatial, political and symbolic port-city relationships. This section presents a number of simple prepositions that could steer cultural urban policy that aims at achieving a more balanced and sustainable nexus between port and cultural activity.

Mega events are not a panacea to solve structural challenges in port cities

Policy makers should first interrogate themselves on whether bidding for mega events is appropriate considering the local context and expectations about mega events and event-led regeneration should be realistic.[3] These processes may help counteract stigmatisation and negative perceptions related to port restructuring. However, mega events alone are insufficient to reverse structural declining trends.

Mega events and event-led regeneration should mobilise port city cultures and value port activity

Mega events and event-led regeneration may help port-city relationships in many ways: a more attractive city as a result of these process may help port competitiveness; event-led regeneration may promote a more diversified economy that is not solely dependent on port activity. However, policy makers and mega-event promoters should acknowledge the role of the port as an integral part to the identity of port cities, rather than using these events to transform these cities into 'cultural' or 'waterfront' cities.

Mega-event programmes and event-led regeneration strategies should acknowledge and build on actually existing port-city links

Mega events and event-led regeneration in port cities impact on the symbolic relations between cities and ports. These should be embraced and valued to promote sustainable symbolic ties. If mega events are deployed to affirm new imaginaries and new ways to relate to waterfronts that departs from established meanings and practices, they are likely to be unsuccessful and to damage existing relations.

Event-led regeneration strategies should aim at blending maritime and urban functions in redeveloped waterfronts, pursuing more balanced redevelopment strategies

Event-led regeneration provides the opportunity to redesign waterfronts and reframe their meaning for local communities. Mixed-use schemes including maritime activities (compatible with housing and commercial and cultural uses) could ease port-city spatial competition and promote more balanced relationships.

Mega events and event-led regeneration should incorporate from the outset legacy policies and strategies for the reuse of event spaces at the port-city interface

Mega events may foster regeneration at the interface and greater permeability of waterfronts. Legacy policies should be put in place from the beginning to avoid that these positive impacts fade away after the event and to prevent that abandoned event facilities produce further port-city separation.

A research agenda on port cities of culture and events

The book has a number of limitations. Its spatial focus has been on (part of) the port-city interface, namely redeveloped port areas and waterfronts in central city locations. It examined primarily industrial and commercial ports – and therefore port cities hit by deindustrialisation – without engaging for example with naval ports. Although some examples from outside Europe have been discussed, the book has a marked European focus. No extensive surveys or ethnographic research activities were undertaken involving substantial numbers of port city dwellers or visitors. Finally, the research at the basis of the book was undertaken between 2016 and early 2020, before the COVID-19 outbreak in Europe. In the light of these limitations, it is important to outline pressing issues in port cities of culture and events that further research could address.

One first key aspect that is also underlined by recent scholarship (Jones & Ponzini, 2018; Ponzini et al., 2019; Di Vita & Wilson, 2020) is the apparent shift towards smaller-scale and more sustainable events, which hints at a 'crisis' of the mega-event paradigm. The future of mega-event schemes, in relation to their financial and social costs and their disruptive effects, needs to be further explored in the light of the issues discussed in Chapter 4 and in particular against the economic impact of the COVID-19 pandemic and related restrictions. The impact of the 2020 global economic recession on maritime trade patterns, port development, real estate markets, urban regeneration policies and mega events is far from being fully clear. Many mega and large-scale cultural events scheduled in 2020 were either cancelled or postponed to 2021. Some of them did not take place in 2021 either, while the return to large-scale events and mass gatherings appears destined to be reframed at best. In order to alleviate the negative socio-economic impact of the pandemic, Keynesian-inspired economic stimuluses have been implemented by some national governments, in contrast with the post-2008 austerity discourse. Nonetheless, even if these actions continued to be implemented in the years to come, they might operate in a context of lack of public funding for culture and events, reiterated or unclear travel restrictions, vaccine passport discrimination, changing public attitudes towards travelling and mass gatherings. Arguably, unsettling political and media discourses (e.g. 'we are at war' slogans) may have exacerbated the negative socio-economic impacts of the pandemic by fostering ontological insecurity. All these factors might significantly aggravate the crisis of mega events and pose further challenges for deprived port towns and cities (in combination with other, in part unrelated factors such as the demise of high streets UK), in a context where the fragility of the global capitalist economy has been dramatically exposed. Despite the political propaganda minimising problems and praising undemonstrated success (including the success of capitalism itself) in many countries, the COVID-19 crisis has indeed highlighted the weakness and unreliability of global supply chains, the impacts of deindustrialisation and delocalisation of productive plants and, in general, the societal dangers posed by the 21st-century unbridled capitalism.

Secondly, it can reasonably be assumed that port-city relationships and large-scale culture- and event-led regeneration processes have a broader impact on the port city as a whole. As observed in the early 1990s by Bianchini (1993, p. 201), these processes tend to generate 'centre-periphery' conflicts, which in the case of port cities translate into unprecedented spatial disparities between redeveloped waterfronts or urban port areas and the periphery (Porfyriou & Sepe, 2017, p. 3). Future research could focus on what the culture-led redevelopment of derelict port areas means for the 'rest' of the city. The case of Hull's peripheral housing estates, where it is debatable whether event-led regeneration has produced any positive outcome, and of port-city conflicts along the interface in Genoa and Valencia's peripheral areas are examples.

Thirdly, the book shows that policy makers in many port cities conceive waterfront redevelopment and the regeneration of former port areas as processes that transform unproductive areas into places of consumption. This tendency is epitomised by the way in which the term 'waterfront' is often understood as inherently related to leisure. Such a belief is also coupled with pressures from real estate developers to include potentially lucrative land-use provisions into redevelopment plans. As a consequence, these schemes are at best mixed-use redevelopments including housing, commercial and cultural uses, although such 'cultural uses' are often translated into gentrifying urban amenities. However, as pointed out by some port specialists (Van Hooydonk, 2009; Andrade Marques, 2018) urban regeneration processes should not necessarily imply that maritime functions are banished. Future urban waterfronts could arguably include light maritime industries, renewable energy, research and innovation hubs, alongside energy-efficient housing, thus abandoning the 'port out, city in' approach behind many waterfronts redevelopment schemes in the 20th century. This is particularly relevant as the patterns of cultural consumption on which culture- and event regeneration in port cities largely rely are being questioned due to COVID-19.

Fourthly, the book has occasionally pointed to the tendency of culture- and event-led regeneration processes to exacerbate social inequalities. This is an established critique of these processes (e.g. Harvey, 1989; Evans, 2005), and it is sometimes connected with the emergence of revanchist forms of urbanism (MacLeod, 2002; Tufts, 2004; Paton, 2018). Due to their history as maritime gateways and their social composition, often characterised by a large proportion of social groups described as 'working class', port cities are interesting contexts for the study of these phenomena. An anthropological enquiry could explore more in depth the impacts of event-led regeneration in maritime districts (e.g. Valencia's El Cabanyal-El Canyamelar), peripheries (e.g. Hull's housing estates and Rotterdam's southern bank) or multicultural, run down city centres (as in Genoa) and how these populations react to such processes.

Fifthly, although only contingently related to event-led regeneration, the rapid pre-COVID-19 growth patterns of cruise tourism have regularly emerged as a challenge for port cities. In the book, cruise tourism has been interpreted as a structural, recurrent phenomenon across many port cities, which nonetheless is – albeit contingently – fuelled by the increased attractiveness of the city as a result of the branding power of culture- and event-led regeneration. The growing anti-tourism sentiment and activism in many European cities and the fact that a Code of Good Practice for cruise and ferry activities has been issued (ESPO, 2016) are symptoms of how a recovered global cruise industry – assuming that pre-2020 trends are resumed – may impact on future port-city relationships. The short- and medium-term impact of COVID-19 on cruise tourism may involve a major contraction of passenger flows, changing routes due to different restrictions across the world, financial difficulties for cruise companies and the need of social distancing measures and onboard quarantine protocols.

Sixthly, the book has not explored issues of environmental sustainability. These aspects may be gaining increasing policy relevance, as a result of the growing climate activism, and will be influencing public attitudes towards, and political legitimisation for, many human activities. Anthropogenic climate change, with prospects of runaway global warming, may radically transform port-city relationships and the very meaning of urban development. However, initial debates on the nexus between culture and climate change in port cities, as shown in the case of Hull, hint at the opportunities arising from holistic accounts of port cities of culture and events.

Finally, the transition to a low-carbon, post-oil economy and society might lead to another large-scale restructuring of ports across the world. Such a structural process could produce even vaster derelict port areas than deindustrialisation did in the late 20th century. In the light of the uncertainties that lie ahead, it cannot be assumed that – provided that this was feasible and desirable – these areas would continue to be working port areas, nor that they would be entirely incorporated into the fabric of the city, as it was achieved through event-led regeneration in the case of historic harbours. Assuming that the current pattern of urbanisation – strongly influenced by entrepreneurial governance and often expressed through creative city policy packages – continues, culture- and event-led regeneration – this time possibly based on smaller-scale, more sustainable events – may assume greater relevance. Nonetheless, it is important to underline that both port development and urban regeneration will probably be subjected to stronger pleas for economic viability, environmental sustainability and social justice. The redevelopment of some port areas into hubs for the development of renewable energies, as in the case of Green Port Hull, is an example of a circular economy approach applied to port development (Karimpour et al., 2020), which could break the traditional linear life cycle of port areas within 'port out, city in' strategies.

Notes

1 A growing awareness of the role of cultural events in urban development was amongst the reasons to establish Rotterdam Festivals in 1993 (interview, event team member 3, May 2018).
2 The 2013 City Plan clearly set the development of renewable energies and cultural tourism among its pillars, albeit these two policy areas do not extensively interrelate. The Final Evaluation Report of Hull UK City of Culture 2017 makes reference to the rising global climate and environmental activism (Culture, Place and Policy Institute, 2019, p. 80). In addition, during the conference 'Cultural Transformations: What's Next?', Hull, 19–21 November 2019, Andrew Jonas suggested that Hull has found its 'cultural fix' and should now search for its 'sustainability fix' (White et al., 2004), stimulating conversations about the nexus between culture and climate change in the city (see e.g. Young, 2019).
3 As mentioned in relation to heritage in the *Charter for Mega-events in Heritage-rich cities* (HOMEE, 2021).

Bibliography

Andrade Marques, M. J. (2018) The port-city in the post-crisis context: Identity and humanisation in the process of touristification. *25th APDR Congress 'Circular Economy: Urban Metabolism and Regional Development'*, Lisbon, 5–8 July.

BBC (2019) Hull unveils lagoon plans to protect against flooding. *BBC*, 25th October. Available at: www.bbc.co.uk/news/uk-england-humber-50172317?intlink_from_url=&link_location=live-reporting-story [Accessed 30/01/2020].

Belchem, J. (2000) *Merseypride: Essays in Liverpool Exceptionalism*. Liverpool: Liverpool University Press.

Bianchini, F. (1993) Culture, conflict and cities: Issues and prospects for the 1990s. In Bianchini, F., & Parkinson, M. (eds.) *Cultural Policy and Urban Regeneration: The West European Experience*. Manchester: Manchester Press, 199–213.

Bianchini, F., & Bloomfield, J. (2012) Porous cities: On four European cities. *Eurozine*, 3rd July. Available at: www.eurozine.com/porous-cities/ [Accessed 22/11/2018].

Chua, A. (2018) *Political Tribes: Group Instinct and the Fate of Nations*. London: Penguin Books.

Culture, Place and Policy Institute (2019) *Cultural Transformations: The Impacts of Hull UK City of Culture 2017. Main Evaluation Findings and Reflections*. November. Hull: University of Hull.

Daamen, T. A., & Vries, I. (2013) Governing the European port-city interface: Institutional impacts on spatial projects between city and port. *Journal of Transport Geography*, 27, 4–13.

Di Vita, S., & Wilson, M. (eds.) (2020) *Planning and Managing Smaller Events: Downsizing the Urban Spectacle*. London and New York: Routledge.

ESPO (2016) *ESPO Code of Good Practice for Cruise and Ferry Ports*. Brussels: European Sea Ports Organisation (ESPO). Available at: www.espo.be/media/espopublications/ESPO%20Code%20of%20Good%20Practices%20for%20Cruise%20and%20Ferry.pdf [Accessed 31/10/2019].

Evans, G. (2005) Measure for measure: Evaluating the evidence of culture's contribution to regeneration. *Urban Studies*, 42(5–6), 959–983.

Harvey, D. (1989) From managerialism to entrepreneurialism: The transformation in urban governance in late capitalism. *Geografiska Annaler*, 70(1), 3–17.

HOMEE (2021) *Charter for Mega-Events in Heritage-Rich Cities*. Available at: https://mck.krakow.pl/homee-charter [Accessed 10/08/2021].

Hoyle, B. S. (1988) Development dynamics at the port-city interface. In Hoyle, B. S., Pinder, D. A., & Husain, M. S. (eds.) *Revitalising the Waterfront: International Dimensions of Dockland Redevelopment*. London: Belhaven Press, 3–19.

Hoyle, B. S. (1989) The port—city interface: Trends, problems and examples. *Geoforum*, 20(4), 429–435.

Hoyle, B. S. (2000) Global and local change on the port-city waterfront. *The Geographical Review*, 90(3), 395–417.

Jones, Z. M., & Ponzini, D. (2018) Mega-events and the preservation of urban heritage: Literature gaps, potential overlaps, and a call for further research. *Journal of Planning Literature*, 33(4), 433–450.

Karimpour, R., Ballini, F., & Ölcer, A. I. (2020) Port-city redevelopment and the circular economy agenda in Europe. In Carpenter, A., & Lozano, R. (eds.) *European Port Cities in Transition: Moving Towards More Sustainable Sea Transport Hubs*. Cham: Springer, 53–71.

Lagoon Hull (n.d.) *Lagoon Hull*. Available at: www.lagoonhull.co.uk/ [Accessed 03/02/2020].

Lee, S. W., Song, D.-W., & Ducruet, C. (2008) A tale of Asia's world ports: The spatial evolution in global hub port cities. *Geoforum*, 39, 372–385.

MacLeod, G. (2002) From urban entrepreneurialism to a 'revanchist city'? On the spatial injustices of Glasgow's renaissance. *Antipode*, 34(3), 602–624.

Mah, A. (2014) *Port Cities and Global Legacies. Urban Identity, Waterfront Work, and Radicalism*. Basingstoke: Palgrave MacMillan.

Marrades, R. (2018) La Marina de València: La apropiación ciudadana y la activación productiva del frente marítimo de la ciudad. In Baron, N., & Romero, J. (eds.) *Cultura territorial e innovación social. ¿Hacia un nuevo modelo metropolitano en Europa del sur?* Valencia: Universitat de València, 193–204.

Molotch, H. (1976) The city as a growth machine: Towards a political economy of place. *American Journal of Sociology*, 82(2), 309–332.

Norcliffe, G., Bassett, K., & Hoare, T. (1996) The emergence of postmodernism on the urban waterfront: Geographical perspectives on changing relationships. *Journal of Transport Geography*, 4(2), 123–134.

Paton, K. (2018) Beyond legacy: Backstage stigmatisation and 'trickle-up' politics of urban regeneration. *The Sociological Review*, 66(4), 919–934.

Phelps, N. A., & Miao, J. T. (2020) Varieties of urban entrepreneurialism. *Dialogues in Human Geography*, 10(3), 304–321.

Ponzini, D., Jones, Z. M., Bianchini, F., Tommarchi, E., Tzortzi, N., Dova, E., Sivitanidou, A., Purchla, J., Sanetra-Szeliga, J., Knaś, P., Dabrowski, A., & Koziol, A. (2019) *HOMEE Literature Review of Mega-Events Addressing Cultural Heritage Issues.* Available at: www. tau-lab.polimi.it/homee-literature-review-regarding-mega-events-cultural-heritage/ [Accessed 07/01/2020].

Porfyriou, H., & Sepe, M. (2017) Introduction. Port Cities and Waterfront Developments: From the Re-actualization of History to a New City Image. In Porfyriou, H., & Sepe, M. (eds.) *Waterfront Revisited: European Ports in a Historic and Global Perspective.* New York and London: Routledge, 1–16.

Tommarchi, E. (2021) (Re-)generating symbolic port-city links: Urban regeneration and the cultural demaritimisation and remaritimisation of European port cities. *European Journal of Creative Practices in Cities and Landscapes*, 4(1), 59–75.

Tommarchi, E., Hansen, L. E., & Bianchini, F. (2018) Problematising the question of participation in Capitals of Culture. *Participations*, 15(2), 154–169.

Tufts, S. (2004) Building the 'competitive city': Labour and Toronto's bid to host the Olympic games. *Geoforum*, 35, 47–58.

Van Hooydonk, E. (2009) Port city identity and urban planning. *Portus*, 18, 16–23.

White, A., Jonas, A. E. G., & Gibbs, D. (2004) The environment and the entrepreneurial city: Searching for the urban 'sustainability fix' in Manchester and Leeds. *International Journal of Urban and Regional Research*, 28(3), 549–569.

Young, A. (2019) Can culture be fused with climate change to give Hull a new identity for the 21st century? *Hull Daily Mail* [Online], 22nd November. Available at: www. hulldailymail.co.uk/news/hull-east-yorkshire-news/culture-climate-change-university-hull-3559528 [Accessed 26/11/2019].

Index

Note: Page numbers in *italics* indicate a figure and page numbers in **bold** indicate a table on the corresponding page.

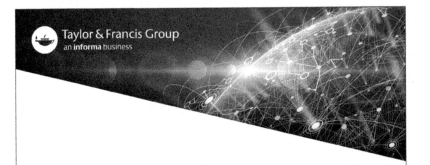

Printed in the United States
by Baker & Taylor Publisher Services